Women of the Klan

Women
of the Klan

Racism and Gender in the 1920s

Kathleen M. Blee

UNIVERSITY OF CALIFORNIA PRESS
Berkeley · *Los Angeles* · *Oxford*

University of California Press
Berkeley and Los Angeles, California

University of California Press, Ltd.
Oxford, England

© 1991 by
The Regents of the University of California

Library of Congress Cataloging-in-Publication Data

Blee, Kathleen M.
    Women of the Klan : racism and gender in the 1920s / Kathleen M.
Blee.

        p.   cm.
    Includes bibliographical references (p.   ) and index.
    ISBN 0-520-07263-4 (cloth)
    ISBN 0-520-07876-4 (ppb.)
    1. Ku Klux Klan (1915–   )—History. 2. Women of the Ku Klux Klan—
Indiana—History. I. Title.
    HS2330.K63B44   1991
    322.4′2′082—dc20   90-11287
                                                                   CIP

Printed in the United States of America

    2   3   4   5   6   7   8   9

The paper used in this publication meets the minimum requirements of
American National Standard for Information Sciences—Permanence of Paper
for Printed Library Materials, ANSI Z39.48-1984. ♾

Contents

Acknowledgments

Numerous people helped with this research. Over the six years I worked on the project, Dwight Billings and Ann Tickamyer prodded me, read parts of the manuscript, and gave advice at crucial stages. Nancy Schrom Dye first suggested the idea of a case study of the Indiana women's Klan and offered valuable insights into women's history. Ronald Aminzade introduced me to the joys of historical sociology. Paula Baker made careful, detailed suggestions and criticisms of the entire manuscript. I received support and assistance also from Michael Baer, Kate Black, Janice Carter, Sally Ward Maggard, Julie Smoak, Cecil Tickamyer, John Watkins, Eileen Van Schaik, Grace Zilverberg, and the women of the Feminar.

Dwight Hoover of Ball State University generously shared his time as well as his research on the Klan in Muncie, Indiana. On the women's Klan in Virginia, John T. Kneebone provided valuable information and documents, as Allen Safianow of Indiana University at Kokomo did on the Klan in Kokomo, Indiana; Bill Lutholtz on D. C. Stephenson; the Sisters of Providence of Saint Mary-of-the-Woods, Indiana, on the Klan's anti-Catholic campaigns; and Cecil Beeson and William E. Ervin on the Klan in Hartford City, Indiana.

My unorthodox interest in the history of their home state of Indiana did not deter my parents, Phyllis Blee and Thomas Blee, from encouraging my research and helping to locate invaluable primary source materials in the archives of *Our Sunday Visitor*, the newspaper of the

Fort Wayne–South Bend Roman Catholic diocese, that the diocese generously shared with me. On my trips in search of Klan materials, Peter Caulkins, Cynthia Costello, Charles Geisler, Ben Goldman, Dorothy Goldman, Betsy Hutchings, Mark Lancelle, and Neil Weinberg welcomed and assisted me.

I presented earlier research on this topic at the 1987 Berkshire Conference on the History of Women and the 1985 Eastern Sociological Society annual meeting; it appeared in *Sociological Spectrum* (1987) and *Feminist Studies* (1991). Grants from the Kentucky Foundation on Women, the Southern Regional Education Board, and the University of Kentucky Research Foundation and a summer stipend (FT-28250-86) and travel award (RY-20332-84) from the National Endowment for the Humanities funded the project. A sabbatical leave and faculty grant from the University of Kentucky allowed me to complete the writing of this manuscript.

Florence Estes and Anneen Boyd expertly transcribed the interview tapes. I benefited from research assistance by Melissa Latimer, Gloria Lester, Norma Mansfield, and Becky Rau and from secretarial assistance by Melissa Forsyth, Marlene Pettit, and Linda Wheeler. For their unfailing help and courtesy I thank the interlibrary loan department staffs at the University of Kentucky and Cornell University and librarians at the Indiana Historical Society, the Indiana State Library, Cornell University Library, the Indiana Commission on Public Records, the New York Public Library, Library of Congress, Anti-Defamation League of New York, State Historical Society of Wisconsin, the National Archives–Philadelphia Branch, and the Ball State University Library. Staff at dozens of libraries and county historical societies throughout Indiana waded through boxes and files to locate Klan-related materials, often with only fragmentary descriptions of the source. I thank also Sheila Levine, Amy Klatzkin, and Edith Gladstone of the University of California Press for editorial suggestions.

Pam Goldman's help on the manuscript was invaluable. She read, criticized, and reread every chapter, endured countless discussions about the Klan, encouraged me when the task seemed endless, instructed me on interviewing techniques, and fixed a myriad of highly traumatic word-processing quirks. My son Eli's love of tractor-feed paper and experiments with floppy disks did little to advance this project but much to keep me sane and happy. This book is dedicated to Pam and Eli.

Introduction

An elderly white Protestant woman from rural northern Indiana described her time in the Ku Klux Klan movement of the 1920s with remarkable nonchalance, as "just a celebration . . . a way of growing up." The Klan fit easily into her daily life, as it did for many white Protestants in Indiana. At most, it was an exceptional chapter in an otherwise ordinary life. Even in hindsight, she showed little remorse over the devastation left in the wake of the Klan's crusade against Catholics, Jews, immigrants, and blacks. What she remembered—with pride, not regret—was the social and cultural life of the Klan; the Klan as "a way to get together and enjoy."[1]

For thousands of native-born white Protestant women like this informant, the women's Klan of the 1920s was not only a way to promote racist, intolerant, and xenophobic policies but also a social setting in which to enjoy their own racial and religious privileges. These women recall their membership in one of U.S. history's most vicious campaigns of prejudice and hatred primarily as a time of friendship and solidarity among like-minded women.

But the Klan's appeal to this Indiana woman was not based purely on racism and nativism. In an effort to recruit members among women newly enfranchised in the 1920s, the Klan also insisted that it was the best guarantor of white Protestant women's rights. The political efforts of a women's order, the Klan claimed, could safeguard women's suffrage and expand women's other legal rights while working to preserve white Protestant supremacy.

Decades later, former Klanswomen barely remember the victims of
the Klan's malicious racist, anti-Catholic, and anti-Semitic campaign.
Many insist that there were no victims, that to suggest otherwise is to
fall prey to lies spread by enemies of the Klan. Most deny that hatred
of racial and religious "outsiders" fueled the Klan in the 1920s. The
woman in northern Indiana, though, still spoke in the dichotomies favored by the Klan, with rigid divisions between "us" (good white
Protestant Klan sympathizers) and "them" (evil foreigners, minorities,
and other Klan opponents). "All the better people," she assured me,
were in the Klan. Bristling at comparisons between the Klan of the
1980s and "her" Klan, she insisted that hers was "different." Women
were forced to join to defend themselves, their families, and their communities against corruption and immorality:

> Store owners, teachers, farmers . . . the good people all belonged to the
> Klan. . . . They were going to clean up the government, and they were go-
> ing to improve the school books [that] were loaded with Catholicism. The
> pope was dictating what was being taught to the children, and therefore
> they were being impressed with the wrong things.

Many white Protestant women in the 1920s—perhaps half a million or more—joined the Women of the Ku Klux Klan (WKKK).
Women constituted nearly half of the Klan membership in some states
and were a significant minority of Klan members in many others. And
women were major actors in the Klan, responsible for some of its most
vicious, destructive results.

Nevertheless, women's involvement in one of the largest and most
politically powerful racist right-wing political movements in U.S. history has been virtually overlooked in the voluminous writings on the
Ku Klux Klan (KKK).[2] Most historians of the Klan dismiss the activities of Klanswomen as incidental to the movement or as mere cultural
screens behind which men carried out the real politics of the KKK.[3]
Both popular and scholarly accounts portray the terror of the Klan
through images of bigoted, hate-filled white men, not women.

Yet the story of the immense and politically powerful Klan of the
1920s is incomplete without serious attention to the role of Klanswomen. Not only were women a significant portion of the Klan's
membership, but their activities and ideologies differed sufficiently
from those of Klansmen that an examination of the women's Klan
changes our interpretation of the Klan as a whole. For example, when
we look only at highly visible actions of Klansmen like electoral cor-

ruption, night riding, and gang terrorism, we might conclude that in many places the Klan's attack on Catholics, Jews, blacks, and other minorities was relatively ineffectual. When we include the less public actions of Klanswomen—the "poison squads" that spread rumor and slander or organized consumer boycotts—the picture changes. Klanswomen acted in different ways that complemented those of Klansmen, making the Klan's influence both more extensive and more deadly than the actions of Klansmen alone would suggest.[4]

An examination of the role of Klanswomen also reveals the Klan's pervasiveness and subtle influence in the 1920s. Women of the Klan drew on familial and community ties—traditions of church suppers, kin reunions, and social celebrations—to circulate the Klan's message of racial, religious, and national bigotry. They spread hatred through neighborhoods, family networks, and illusive webs of private relationships. The Klan's power was devastating precisely because it was so well integrated into the normal everyday life of white Protestants.

The story of 1920s Klanswomen exemplifies the complex ways in which attitudes on race, religion, and gender interact. Klanswomen asserted a political agenda that mixed support for white Protestant women's rights with racist, anti-Semitic, and anti-Catholic politics. In this, they do not fit the traditional categories that characterize political movements, such as right wing and left wing.[5] Like their male counterparts, Klanswomen held reactionary political views on race, nationality, and religion. But their views of gender roles were neither uniformly reactionary nor progressive.

Extremist right-wing and reactionary women are nearly absent from studies on women in political movements, which have focused on progressive and women's rights movements or, to a lesser degree, on antifeminist movements. We have no clear evidence whether this paucity of research comes from the unimportance or numerical insignificance of women in extreme right-wing organizations or whether women are assumed to be pacifist, social-welfare-oriented, and apolitical. It is likely, however, that the omission of women from studies of extremist right-wing movements limits, and perhaps minimizes, scholars' assessment of the consequences of reactionary politics. Traditional (and male-centered) definitions of politics that focus on workplaces, electoral contests, courts, and organized voluntary associations ignore the political effects of actions and organizing in neighborhoods or through kin and informal networks.

Without attention to the often-complicated ideologies and agendas of extremist political women, researchers might conclude that right-wing movements have uniformly reactionary ideologies. This assumption obscures important ways that such movements appeal to majority populations and conceals the reactionary elements within the political discourse of racial and religious majorities. To understand why people embrace political movements based on hatred and fear, we must examine the multiple, even contradictory, levels on which reactionary movements seek to attract ordinary people into extremist politics.[6]

METHODOLOGY OF THE RESEARCH

The Klan movement of the 1920s carefully guarded its membership lists (even when individual members felt free to flaunt their identities in public) and shrouded in secrecy the author, audience, and intent of most Klan documents. This policy created a number of methodological challenges.

A first challenge involved the two levels of reality in the extralegal Klan movement: the Klan's publicly disseminated image and its internal, secret reality. The public face of the Klan was often what attracted members. Many left the organization after a short time, dismayed at the disparity between the image and the reality of Klan life. Although former Klansmembers' testimonies to ignorance of the Klan's political agenda when they enlisted were often self-serving, the large number of such reports suggests that many members did see the Klan differently from without and within. This book examines both realities of the women's Klan: the moralistic public image for women's equality that brought many women into the secret order and its internal declarations of racial, nationalistic, and religious hatred and violence that were the private face of the WKKK.

A second challenge was to identify Klanswomen. Without access to membership lists, I could not use standard techniques to analyze Klan membership and recruitment. Only scattered rosters of the immense Indiana Klan, on which I focus, exist in public archives or in private collections, and none list more than a few women members. I identified Klanswomen in three ways. First, I used historical documents to trace Klanswomen who publicly revealed their membership, who were identified as WKKK members by anti-Klan organizations, or who were listed on Klan documents. Second, I used newspaper obituaries to identify women who were given WKKK funeral rituals by sister Klanswomen. Third, I interviewed living former Klanswomen, together with WKKK contemporaries and victims.

To locate interview informants, I mailed a notice about my research to every local newspaper, advertising supplement, Catholic church bulletin, historical society, and public library in the forty-two counties of Indiana in which the WKKK was most active. Twenty-eight people responded. Of these, six sent written recollections, three agreed to an interview, if unrecorded, and fifteen agreed to a recorded interview. In addition, I received many letters from local librarians, local and county amateur historians, newspaper editors, and descendants of Klansmembers who contributed material from private and small public collections.

Interviewing was difficult. Problems of memory distortion, selective recall, and self-censoring that plague all interview situations were compounded by the age of the informants and the topic of the interview. Almost all the informants were elderly—most of them over eighty years old—and some had difficulty recalling the exact sequence of events. Some informants felt uneasy about discussing a political past that subsequent generations had condemned for its violence and hatred.

Several aspects of the interviewing process, though, were surprisingly easy and productive. Many informants had little remorse about their time in the Klan. Some were proud of their Klan membership and anxious to clarify what they saw as historical misunderstandings of the order. For all, participation in the 1920s Klan was one of the most significant aspects of their lives. Many informants had remarkable recall for details of events over sixty years before, memories that I confirmed with newspaper and documentary sources.

In my notice soliciting informants, and in the interview itself, I gave no indication of my own judgment of the Klan. Few informants were satisfied with this; nearly all tried to elicit my evaluations of the Klan. Many interviews included polite sparring, with informants making laudatory comments about the Klan and seeking a positive response in return. Once informants decided that I was unlikely to denounce their Klan membership during the interview, though, they were forthcoming with opinions, prejudices, and memories. The ease with which we established such rapport is itself revealing. My own background in Indiana (where I lived from primary school through college) and white skin led informants to assume—lacking spoken evidence to the contrary—that I shared their worldview.

Other aspects of the interviewing process were difficult. When I pressed informants to talk about *why* they felt or acted a certain way, puzzlement or bemused forebearing often greeted me, as if they were carefully and patiently explaining the obvious to a child. Life in the Klan, to most of my informants, simply needed no explanation. What needed to be explained was the reputation that the 1920s Klan later acquired, the peculiarly negative way in which it was recorded in history.

I was prepared to hate and fear my informants. My own commitment to progressive politics prepared me to find these people strange, even repellent. I expected no rapport, no shared assumptions, no commonality of thought or experience. What I found was more disturbing. Many of the people I interviewed were interesting, intelligent, and well informed. Despite my prediction that we would experience each other as completely foreign, in fact I shared the assumptions and opinions of my informants on a number of topics (excluding, of course, race, religion, and most political topics).

Some of the women I interviewed who participated fully and enthusiastically in the Klan, expressing few regrets, were active in progressive politics, favoring peace and women's equality in the decades after the Klan collapsed. They saw their fight in the Klan as a campaign against the reactionary forces of Catholicism, Judaism, and rural Southern black culture—one they viewed as fully in accord with struggles to extend Social Security benefits or promote equal pay for men and women. These former Klansmembers were not the "other," with strange, incomprehensible ways of understanding the world, as I had earlier assumed. On some level, many were sympathetic persons. Even more disturbing, some Klanswomen had a facile ability to fold bitter racial and religious bigotry into progressive politics. One former Klanswoman, for example, insisted that she saw no inconsistency between participation in the 1920s Klan and her support of economic redistribution and feminism.

To conclude that Klanswomen were not the uniformly hate-filled stock characters in popular images of the Klan movement is not to diminish the destructive power of the women's Klan. The 1920s Klan shattered countless lives. It further eroded public tolerance of racial, ethnic, and religious difference and heightened discrimination against blacks, immigrants, and Jews. The outburst of majority hatred against minority populations left scars on individuals, communities, and American public life that remain to the present time.

But the popular stereotype of Klan members—as ignorant, simplistic, brutal, and naive—is historically and politically misleading. The true story of the 1920s Klan movement, and the political lesson of Klan history for those working toward a more just and egalitarian society, is the ease with which racism and intolerance appealed to ordinary people in ordinary places. The Klan perhaps exaggerated, but certainly did not create, ambitions of white Protestants for social and political supremacy. These citizens, comfortable in daily lives in which racial, ethnic, and religious privilege were so omnipresent as to be invisible to their possessors, found in the Klan a collective means to perpetuate their advantages.

White Protestant women and men with considered opinions, who loved their families and could be generous to neighbors and friends, were the backbone of the 1920s Klan. Generations of privilege blinded them to the lives of those who did not share that privilege. Those "others"—blacks, Catholics, Jews, immigrants, Mormons, labor radicals, bootleggers, moonshiners, theater owners, dance hall operators, radical feminists, and conservative oppressors of women—were targets precisely because their lives were so distant from the privileged majority. As incomprehensible others, they could be victimized by ordinary upright and God-fearing women and men. The mainstay of the 1920s Klan was not the pathological individual; rather, Klan promoters effectively tapped a pathological vein of racism, intolerance, and bigotry deep within white Protestant communities. In this sense, the history of the 1920s Klan, although distant in time, is frighteningly close in spirit to the pervasive strands of racism and unacknowledged privilege that exist among dominant groups in the United States today.

ORGANIZATION OF THE BOOK

The first part of this book examines the political symbols of gender in the 1920s Klan movement. Chapter one analyzes the use of "masculinity" and "womanhood" as motivating symbols in the first Klan and in the men's KKK of the 1920s; their significance changed when financial opportunism and power battles among KKK leaders prompted the creation of a women's Klan. Chapter two discusses conflicts that resulted as women entered the male bastion of the Klan. Although Klansmen and Klanswomen shared a political agenda on many issues, they differed on questions of women's place within society, the family, and the Klan. Chapter three analyzes the Klan's use of symbols of morality and sexuality, focusing on the large women's and men's Klans in Indiana.

The second part of the book examines the activities of the women's Klan of Indiana and the backgrounds of women who joined the WKKK. Chapters four and five present the political backgrounds of leaders and rank-and-file Indiana Klanswomen and explore the development and activities of women's Klans within the state. Chapter six examines the use of family and social ties by the women's Klan to create a political culture of "klannishness." The brief epilogue gives the history of the Ku Klux Klan after the collapse of the second Klan movement.

PART I

The Klan
and Womanhood

CHAPTER I

Organizing 100% American Women

Gender and sexuality were compelling symbols in the two largest waves of the Ku Klux Klan, those of the 1860s and the 1920s. Although the post–Civil War Klan's agenda of racial terrorism differed considerably from the racist, nativist politics of the Klan in the early twentieth century, at times both groups used a similar rhetoric of gender and sexuality. Each Klan summoned white men to protect threatened white womanhood and white female purity. Both dissolved a myriad of social, economic, and racial issues into powerful symbols of womanhood and sexual virtue.

Political symbols like those of the KKK are complex. A single symbol can compress a multitude of meanings. Some layers of meaning are clear, others ambiguous. One meaning may contradict another, either intentionally or inadvertently. As a form of communication, political symbols exist in the relation between sender and receiver. The audience's own assumptions and attitudes shape its reception of symbolic messages, so different receivers understand the same symbol differently. Some audiences receive the message intended by the sender, others do not. The representation of political symbols is also unstable over time. Symbols convey meanings that are embedded within a historical context; they may convey very different meanings at different periods. To understand political symbols, it is important to examine these three aspects: the underlying as well as the explicit message, the received as well as the intended message, and the historical contexts in which symbols are created and in which they are received.

These aspects of symbolic communication help us understand the apparent historical continuity in political symbolism between the first and second Klans. The message conveyed by symbols of white womanhood to the all-male Reconstruction-era Klan came through quite differently to a second Klan organized during the campaign for women's suffrage. The first Klan used symbols of imperiled womanhood to represent assault on Southern white men's racial privileges and regional autonomy. The second Klan, too, tried at first to use white womanhood to symbolize threatened religious, national, and racial supremacy. But newly won female enfranchisement and women's political experience complicated this strategy.

From the rallying cry of Southern white female vulnerability in the postbellum first KKK to the ambivalent call for women's rights in the second one, symbols of gender and sexuality blurred conflicts over race, religion, nationality, and region. Masculinity and femininity were not simply abstractions of individual persons; rather, they summarized and masked a complex system of privilege and subordination of which gender relations were only one aspect. Understanding the contradictory role of women in the second Klan movement requires an examination of both gender politics and symbolism in the Reconstruction-era Klan and the conditions under which women were invited to join the Klan in the 1920s.

THE FIRST KU KLUX KLAN

From the beginning, the rituals and organized terrorism of the first KKK were based on symbols of violent white masculinity and vulnerable white femininity. When the KKK was organized in Tennessee immediately after the Civil War, it summoned defeated sons of the Confederacy to defend the principles of white supremacy against interference by Northerners and retaliation by freed black slaves. As it grew from a prankish club of dejected soldiers to a loosely knit and highly secret vigilante terrorist network in the defeated Southern states, the Klan continued to merge ideas of sexual menace with those of racial and political danger.[1]

During the late 1860s the Klan spread its reign of terror throughout Southern and border states. Gangs of Klansmen threatened, flogged, and murdered countless black and white women and men. But the Klan's violence was not arbitrary. It applied terror to bolster the crumbling foundations of Southern supremacy against political inroads by blacks, Republicans, and Northern whites. Schoolteachers, revenue collectors, election officials, and Republican officeholders—those most involved with dismantling parts of the racial state—as well as all black persons, were the most common targets of Klan terror.[2] The KKK was particularly expert in the use of sexual violence and brutality. Klan mobs humiliated white Southern Republicans ("scalawags") by sexually abusing them. Klansmen routinely raped and sexually tortured women, especially black women, during "kluxing" raids on their households. Widely reported acts of lynching, torture, and sexual mutilation intimidated Klan opponents and terrorized its enemies.[3]

The secrecy and juvenile rituals of the early KKK borrowed heavily from the long tradition of male fraternal societies. Men bound themselves to one another through allegiances of race, gender, and a shared desire to preserve the racial state of the South in the face of military defeat. Even the Klan's name, derived from the Greek *kuklos* (circle), reinforced its quest for white male commonality across divisions of social class and local status.[4] Although the Klan's politics would become fervently anti-Catholic over time, the first Klan created a culture whose costumes and secret ritual mimicked the symbolism and ritual of the male-based hierarchy of the Roman Catholic church. It barred white women (and all nonwhites) from membership, just as the Southern polity did. If the abuse and exclusion of blacks reinforced an ethos of racial power, strength, and invulnerability among the fraternity of white Klansmen so, too, the exclusion of white women served to celebrate and solidify the masculinity of racial politics.[5]

Although women did not participate openly in the actions of the first KKK, the idea of "white womanhood" was a crucial rallying point for postbellum Klan violence. Klansmen insisted that white women benefited from the Southern racial state, even as strict gender hierarchies within white society ensured that women would not be consulted on this matter. In an appearance in 1871 before the U.S. Senate, Nathan Bedford Forrest, the first Grand Wizard, argued that the Klan was needed because Southern whites faced great insecurity. He pointed dramatically at a situation in which "ladies were ravished by some of these negroes, who were tried and put in the penitentiary, but were turned out in a few days afterward."[6]

This theme of imperiled Southern white womanhood echoed throughout writings by the first KKK and its apologists. White women, especially widows living alone on isolated plantations, were highly visible symbols through which the Klan could rouse public fears that blacks' retaliation against their former white masters would be exacted upon white daughters, wives, and mothers. Without the Klan, white men were powerless to assist white women who faced frightful sexual violations by newly freed black men:

> We note the smile of helpless masculinity give but feebly assuring answer to its mate's frown of distressful inquiry, as the sullen roll of the drum and the beastly roar of the savage rasp the chords of racial instinct. As we watch the noble countenance of modest, innocent Southern maidenhood pale into death-defying scorn, as she contemplates the hellish design of the black brute in human form.[7]

Women were symbols for the first KKK in another way. The feared assault on white women not only threatened white men's sexual prerogatives but symbolized the rape of the Southern racial state in the Reconstruction era as well. In *Hooded Americanism*, David Chalmers notes the double meaning of white womanhood for white men in the antebellum and immediate postbellum South:

> [White womanhood] not only stood at the core of his sense of property and chivalry, she represented the heart of his culture. By the fact that she was not accessible to the Negro, she marked the ultimate line of difference between white and black . . . it was impossible to assault either the Southern woman or the South without having implicitly levied carnal attacks on the other.[8]

The complexity of gender and sexual symbolism in the first Klan shows also in the propaganda circulated among and by Klansmen. Klansmen saw the abolition of slavery both as the loss of sexual access to black women and as the potential loss of exclusive sexual access to white women. An enfranchised black man, the Klan insisted, "considered freedom synonymous with equality and his greatest ambition was to marry a white wife." Klan propaganda steadfastly portrayed women as passive sexual acquisitions of men and insisted that black men used physical coercion to wrest sexual favors (and even marriage vows) from white female victims. Underlying this message, however, was the concern that, given free choice among male sexual partners, at least some white women might choose black men. As a threat to the racial and sexual privileges of white men in the postbellum South, black husbands nearly equaled black rapists of white women.[9]

All histories of the first Klan emphasize that the success of the Klan depended on images of rape and miscegenation between white women and black men. Accounts that lack a feminist-informed analysis, however, miss some of the political significance of references to actual and symbolic rape and miscegenation. In *The Fiery Cross,* for example, Wyn Craig Wade argues that slavery corrupted sexual relations between white men and white women. Placed on a pedestal in antebellum Southern society, white women became "like statues in bed," as Wade remarks, sexually inaccessible to white men. In response white men turned to powerless black female slaves, to "release the passion they were unable to experience with their wives." As the Confederacy crumbled, white men feared that black men would retaliate in like manner by sexually assaulting now vulnerable white mothers, daughters, sisters, and wives.[10]

The interpretation of rape and miscegenation given in *The Fiery Cross*—one shared by most histories of the Klan—presents images of interracial sexuality in the postbellum South as a battle among groups of men divided along racial, class, and regional lines. As men struggled to preserve or challenge a racial caste system, all women were reduced to a common function as political symbols—symbols of racial privilege or subordination, regional self-determination or subjugation. This interpretation superposes hierarchies of gender on the greater cleavages of race and class in Southern society.

A feminist analysis differently interprets the images of rape, gender, and sexuality in the first Klan. Modern feminist scholarship considers rape to be foremost an issue of power, not sexual desire. The Klan's call to defend white women against rape by black men signified a relation of power between men and women as well as between white and black men. On one level, the Klan's emphasis on the rape threat that white women faced was a message about the sexual violation of women by men. Underlying this level, however, was a deeper threat to white men's sexual privileges. As Catherine MacKinnon argues, "the definitive element of rape centers around male-defined loss, not coincidentally also upon the way men define loss of exclusive access."[11]

Rape was a volatile issue in both antebellum and postbellum Southern society divided by race and gender. The racial state of the slave South, like the racialist state that followed the Civil War, was built on a foundation that dictated a hierarchical division of male and female, as well as white and black. It kept white women within a role that was exalted in prose but sharply divided from and inferior to the privileged social role of white men. White men monopolized rights to property and the franchise and dictated the rules by which their wives, children, slaves, servants, and hired labor would live. Social privileges were formed along overlapping hierarchies of race, gender, and social class. Political, economic, and social power were reserved for white men, especially propertied white men.[12]

Within this context of hierarchies in Southern society we must imagine the mobilizing power of interracial sexual issues for the Ku Klux Klan. The Klan avowed horror of miscegenation but practiced it, as did antebellum white plantation masters, as a tactic of terror. Too, the Klan characterized rape equally as a metaphor for Southern white male disempowerment and as an atrocity committed against women. We cannot reduce this complex symbolic layering of race, sexuality, and gender in the language and the political practice of the Ku Klux Klan to a collective manifestation of psychosexual frustration, repression, and fear by white Southern men. Rather, we must analyze the massive social movement of the first KKK in the context of long-standing cleavages underlying Southern society.[13]

In these hierarchies of Reconstruction-era Southern states, black men were a threat to white men's sexual access to women (both black and white). Sexual torture and emasculation of black men by mobs of Klansmen validated the claim that masculinity ("real manhood") was the exclusive prerogative of white men. The rape of black women by white Klansmen represented the Klan's symbolic emasculation of black men through violating "their" women while affirming the use of male sexuality as a weapon of power against women.[14] Southern women, white and black, occupied a symbolic terrain on which white men defended their racial privileges. The symbols of white female vulnerability and white masculine potency took power equally from beliefs in masculine and in white supremacy.

The first Klan movement collapsed quickly. Despite an elaborate hierarchy, the Klan lacked direction and political focus. By the late 1860s many local Klan units became chaotic unorganized gangs of terrorists; the federal government intensified its military and political control of the Southern states. In 1870 the Grand Wizard ordered the organization dissolved, insisting that atrocities blamed on the Klan were in fact committed by opportunistic nonmembers. The remaining local remnants of the first Ku Klux Klan disintegrated during the mid-1870s.[15]

REBIRTH OF THE KLAN

After lying dormant for several decades, the Ku Klux Klan reemerged in 1915. By the mid-1920s approximately four million women and men had enlisted in its racist, nativist crusade. What accounts for the spectacular growth of this second Klan? It is tempting to search for exceptional events to explain the Klan's dramatic appeal. And in part the Klan's strength did result from conditions that made the early twentieth century ripe for a political movement championing nationalism and white Protestant supremacy. In many rural areas declining agricultural prices caused widespread hardship among farmers and agricultural laborers, making them susceptible to Klan propaganda about "Jewish bankers" and "foreign interests" in the U.S. economy. Rapid technological and social changes, high rates of immigration and internal migration, postwar nationalism, rapid urbanization, and the migration of large numbers of Southern blacks to the North also heightened the appeal of the Klan's open racism and nativism to Northern and urban white Protestants.[16]

Although these factors were important in the Klan's success, they do not explain the Klan's appeal. Racist, nativist, and antiradical sentiments long predated—and would long outlive—the second Klan. If some communities in which the Klan flourished were economically depressed, others were prosperous. If some Klansmembers enlisted in reaction to sweeping changes in their lives, many lived in relatively stable communities. The Klan took deep root among populations whose supremacy was rarely challenged and in areas with little racial and religious diversity. For some, Klan membership celebrated and affirmed long-held privileges.[17]

It is more helpful to understand the second Klan by considering it within—rather than as an aberration from—the ideas and values that shaped white Protestant life in the early twentieth century, fueling religious fundamentalism and prohibitionism as well as the Klan. Seen in this light, the racist appeal and whites-only membership policy of the second Klan movement were remarkable mainly for their explicit call to violence in defense of white supremacy. The Klan's underlying ideas of racial separation and white Protestant supremacy, however, echoed throughout white society in the 1920s, as racial and religious hatreds determined the political dialogue in many communities. Few white-controlled institutions or organizations in the United States either practiced or espoused racial integration or equality, allowing the Klan to proudly proclaim its continuity with established sentiment among whites. A 1924 defense of the Klan's racial exclusivity, for example, noted—correctly—that many fraternal lodges practiced racial prejudice by restricting membership to white males.[18]

Vitriolic public statements of racism and nativism were pervasive in the early twentieth century. D. W. Griffith's immensely popular feature film, *Birth of a Nation,* glorified the racial terrorism of the first Ku Klux Klan. The trial of Leo Frank, a Jewish businessman accused of assaulting a young girl in his employ, was a cause célèbre to anti-Semites. In 1921, the U.S. Congress passed an emergency act to restrict immigration; pressure by racial hate groups resulted in an openly racist system of national quotas by 1924. Ironically, many anti-Klan activists opposed the Klan solely on political or religious grounds but supported white privilege as strongly as Klansmembers did.[19]

What, then, accounts for the resurgence of the Klan in the 1920s? Although widespread acceptance of white supremacist and anti-Catholic, anti-Semitic ideas made the Klan possible in the 1920s, both the immediate impetus to its rebirth and the factors underlying its recruiting success lay in part outside the realms of ideology and politics. It was financial opportunism that shaped the Klan's rebirth and a sophisticated marketing system that fueled its phenomenal growth.

The second Klan began in 1915 through the efforts of William J. Simmons, a circuit-riding minister, unsuccessful itinerant salesman, and fraternal society organizer. Simmons claimed that a mystical vision instructed him to unite native-born white Protestant men in battle against the forces of "aliens," "commodity madness," political corruption, excessive taxation, and religious infidelity that were destroying the nation. Like Klan leaders after him, Simmons began on the "hell and brimstone" revival circuit, preaching on such topics as "red heads, dead heads and no heads," "women, weddings and wives," and "kinship of kourtship and kissing." His popular lectures defended traditional sexual morality against the forces of "ungodly modernism," a position that his new Klan quickly embraced. Although Simmons often used womanhood as a symbol of the white Protestant values in need of protection against imminent destruction, the notions of gender that characterized Simmons's Klan were somewhat different from those of its Reconstruction-era predecessor.[20]

This difference can be seen in Simmons's bizarre and rambling writings. Like his Klan forefathers, Simmons insisted on the one hand that the Klan was a fraternity exclusively for "real American manhood," men of mental toughness and dedication. "No man," he declared, "is wanted in this Order who hasn't manhood enough to assume a real OATH with serious purpose to keep the same inviolate." Simmons also mimicked a successful tactic of the first Klan, invoking fears of black rapists and miscegenation to encourage white men to enlist.[21]

On the other hand, Simmons often compared himself to Jesus Christ, a prophet and victim living among devils and infidels. In this theocratic vision based largely on images of Victorian family life, Simmons pictured Klansmembers as children with himself, the Christ figure, as mother, not father. Symbols of womanhood and motherhood represented strength and constancy as well as racial vulnerability in Simmons's writing. A description of the Klan's birth, composed to defend Simmons's supremacy in the organization, is illustrative:

> I was [the KKK's] sole parent, author and founder; it was MY creation—
> MY CHILD, if you please, MY first born. I, ALONE, am responsible for
> ITS borning and being. . . . No devoted mother ever endured for her babe
> more mental anguish and gave more constant attention, through many
> sleepless nights and troubled days. . . . Every dime I earned was earned to
> preserve its life and promote its development.[22]

The meaning of manhood in the second Klan also shifted from the explicitly violent masculinity of the first Klan to fraternal brotherhood. Simmons admonished Klansmen to live by a higher ethical code than that of the "alien" (non-Klan) world. Klansmen were to respect fellow Klansmen, reject the lure of sexual debauchery, and refrain from carnal conduct with nonwhite women. Of course, Simmons's code was image, not reality. Probably few Klansmen adhered to it. Nonetheless, the meaning of masculinity as a political symbol had changed.[23]

Simmons imposed a strict mandate of secrecy on his Klan followers. Together with Simmons's disdain for publicity, it prevented the fledgling Klan from reaching many potential recruits. Moreover, Simmons was an incompetent political leader. Disaffected Klansmen characterized him as an immoral and waffling ruler, "a man of weakness and vice [whose thoughts] run to women and liquor." Simmons's grandiose plans—for five Klan universities, a company to publish Klan-written history texts, a banking and trust institution to aid ailing farmers, free homes for all newly married Klan couples, a national full employment policy, a program to support Klan orphans, several medical research centers, and a chain of hospitals—went unfulfilled.[24]

In 1920 the Klan's fortunes improved immeasurably with the arrival of Elizabeth Tyler and Edward Clarke and their Southern Publicity Association. Tyler, the first major female leader of the 1920s Klan, began her public career as a volunteer hygiene worker visiting tenements to advise new mothers as part of the "better babies" movement of the 1910s. At an Atlanta harvest festival in which she sponsored a better babies parade, Tyler met Clarke, the festival organizer. Clarke's early career as an itinerant promoter was marred by a number of unsuccessful money-making schemes, but by the time of the Atlanta festival his fortunes had changed. Billing himself as a "doctor of sick towns," Clarke had launched a lucrative scheme arranging festivals and publicity for communities around the South.[25]

Tyler and Clarke jointly organized the Southern Publicity Association to market their talents in promotion and publicity to groups like the Anti-Saloon League, Salvation Army, and Red Cross. When Tyler's son-in-law joined the KKK, the Southern Publicity Association found its perfect client. Under Simmons, membership in the Klan was virtually stagnant and its financial future bleak. Moreover, Tyler and Clarke had experience with fraternal organizations after which the new Klan was modeled. Clarke had worked with the Woodmen of the World. Tyler was a member of the Daughters of America, an auxiliary of the Junior Order of United American Mechanics.[26]

Clarke and Tyler contracted with Simmons to create a Propagation Department to publicize and recruit for the Klan in exchange for a percentage of the Klan's $10 initiation fee. They reworked Simmons's image into that of a sincere and important civic leader. Although Simmons hired Tyler and Clarke to work only as publicity agents, their success in promoting the Klan soon gave them additional authority in the Klan and made Simmons increasingly peripheral. During the first six months of Clarke and Tyler's association with the KKK, an additional 85,000 members (representing $850,000 in dues) joined. By 1922 Simmons claimed in a *New York Times* interview that the Klan was accepting 3,500 new members a day and had a total of five million members in all forty-eight states plus Alaska and the Canal Zone. No doubt Simmons was exaggerating, but the Klan had undergone a dramatic reversal of fortune.[27]

A key to Tyler and Clarke's success was their expanded notion of the Klan's enemies. No longer were blacks the sole objects of Klan hatred. Now Catholics, Jews, nonwhites, Bolsheviks, and immigrants became targets, a shift that greatly increased the Klan's recruitment potential in Northern states. A particularly successful strategy was the focus on local minorities. Kleagles (paid organizers) were encouraged to study their territories, identify the sources of concern among native-born Protestant whites, and offer the Klan as a solution. Tyler published a weekly newsletter in which she instructed kleagles on building chapters by scapegoating local "enemies": Mormons in Utah, union radicals in the Northwest, and Asian Americans on the Pacific Coast.[28]

Using skills honed in organizing festivals and parades, Tyler and Clarke built the Klan with the modern marketing and advertising techniques of twentieth-century capitalist consumerism. They sent kleagles around the country to recruit members by soliciting their friends, and their friends' friends, as potential recruits and following all contacts with application blanks, Klan propaganda material, and a solicitation for dues. Often, kleagles first approached local Protestant ministers, seeking to enlist them openly or covertly in the Klan cause. The national offices of the Klan assisted kleagles' efforts, sending lecturers (often ministers) throughout the country to speak on the need for the Klan's crusade of militant Protestantism.[29]

In addition to the publicity generated by Tyler and Clarke's promotional machine, the *New York World* inadvertently fueled interest in the Klan with an exposé that greatly overstated its membership and strength. The *World*'s coverage in 1921 also began Tyler and Clarke's downfall. It charged them with financial misdeeds and with sexual impropriety based on their 1919 arrest for disorderly conduct in a house owned by Tyler in a "morally suspect" district of Atlanta. The arrest had been instigated by Clarke's wife, May Clarke, who had earlier sued him for divorce on the grounds of desertion. Clarke and Tyler denied the charge but did little to hide their continuing liaison.[30]

Tensions within the Klan also surfaced in testimony that same year before the U.S. House Committee on Rules. Here the issue was the role of Elizabeth Tyler in the revived Klan. Insurgent Klansmen charged that Tyler was the actual head of the Klan and that Simmons—and even Clarke—were figureheads. Despite denials from Klan officials, the allegation caused widespread discontent among Klansmen who were recruited believing that the Klan would be a male fraternal preserve.[31] Conflict intensified after the congressional investigation concluded that Tyler was indeed the true power behind the Klan. This characterization—an ostensibly all-male Klan organized and dominated by a woman—echoed in other forums:

> In this woman beats the real heart of the Ku Klux Klan today. . . . If there are fools in the K.K.K. Mrs. Tyler is not one of them. She knew better than any one else what Ku Kluxism was leading to. . . . She has a positive genius for executive direction. Her courage is a thing to admire.[32]

A more negative characterization of Tyler's role in building the second Klan was expressed by Edgar I. Fuller, a former secretary to Edward Clarke. Like many of his contemporaries, Fuller attributed Tyler's power and success to her power over men. Tyler, he argued, had amassed great influence within the KKK in part through her knowledge of the South but foremost through her intimate knowledge of men: "Her experience in catering to [men's] appetites and vices had given her an insight into their frailties. She knew how to handle them all."[33]

Those who feared a breach in the all-male domain of the Klan grew alarmed when Simmons, to recapture his authority in the Klan, appointed Tyler to oversee plans for a women's organization. Tyler quickly announced plans to induct into the Klan a class of five hundred prominent women from every section of the country. In fact, Tyler claimed, women were already joining the Klan in large numbers, attracted by the Klan's opposition to Jews, Catholics, Negroes, socialists, and radicals. To dispel any confusion in the minds of Klansmen, Tyler announced that the new women's organization would not be a "dependent auxiliary of the Knights of the Ku Klux Klan" but would be on a par with the men's organization.[34]

Tyler's chance at Klan power through a women's organization went unrealized, however, the victim of internal Klan problems. As charges of immorality and mismanagement continued to mount and four regional Klan leaders filed suit against them, Tyler and Clarke conspired to topple Simmons from power. They persuaded Simmons to embark on an extended vacation and then restructured the Klan hierarchy, giving Simmons the exalted title of lifetime imperial emperor but ending his control of the organization. Actual power in the Klan came into the hands of a Texas dentist, Hiram Evans.

Evans quickly moved to consolidate his power in the Klan, with Tyler and Clarke as allies. He arranged to have his leadership ratified at the November 1922 KKK Klonvokation in Atlanta, a gathering that also lavished praise on Tyler as "a model of American womanhood."

But Evans proved disloyal to Tyler. As soon as he was appointed Imperial Wizard, Evans insisted that Clarke turn over Tyler's share of the proceeds generated by the Propagation Department contract. Clarke refused and Evans dismissed both publicists from the Klan. On his return from vacation Simmons tried to have them reinstated, but it was too late. Clarke, facing charges of mishandling church funds, misuse of the mails, and transportation of liquor, and under indictment by a federal grand jury for violation of the Mann Act's prohibition against "white slavery," fled the country. Tyler left the Klan and died in 1924.[35]

The departure of Tyler and Clarke and the conflict between Evans and Simmons left the Klan in disarray. Klan leaders responded with an expanded call to "real men" to stand firm with the Klan. Officials declared that the current challenges faced by the Klan simply underlined its need for strong, masculine men. Only "true manhood" could meet the crises of the Klan with vigor and courage. One Grand Dragon challenged men of the Klan to see the order's problems as fresh possibilities: "Never before in the history of our great movement have the hearts and souls of manly men been thrilled with such emotion for our righteous cause. . . . The spirit of Klankraft is bringing untold thousands of big, manly men into the fellowship."[36]

The Klan's challenge to masculine loyalty was effective, and under Evans's direction membership swelled. Evans was a master at disguising racist, nativist views in the neutral terms of science. Under his guidance, the Klan's oldest and most effective symbols were reframed. The Klan's opposition to miscegenation, Evans insisted, was based not in moral outrage over the degeneracy of interracial sex (as Simmons and the first Klan argued) but in science, because the offspring of "race-mixing" had been shown to be genetically unstable. Similarly, Evans presented his call for an end to unlimited immigration and his anti-Semitism and anti-Catholicism as important to the development of a biologically and genetically "good stock of Americans."[37]

ORGANIZING KLANSWOMEN

The Klan's protracted leadership struggle created an avenue for women to enter the organization. As Simmons and Evans fought for power between themselves and against increasingly powerful regional Klan leaders, each embraced the idea of a female Klan to bolster their respective positions within the order. Despite the controversy gener-

ated by Tyler's role in the Klan, Evans and Simmons believed that
Klansmen were now ready to accept women as members, even if
grudgingly.[38] Moreover, the recent passage of the women's suffrage
amendment, and women's extensive involvement in the temperance
and suffrage movements, convinced Klan leaders that large numbers of
women might be interested in joining the order.

As early as 1922 the *Fiery Cross*, a Klan newspaper, published letters to the editor from women protesting their exclusion from the
Klan.[39] Although there is no way to validate the authenticity of these
letters (which may in fact have been written by Klansmen), they indicate how Klan leaders envisioned women's place in the "Invisible Empire." The letters compared—unfavorably—women's new right to
vote with their continuing exclusion from the Klan. In pioneer days,
one author wrote, men justly excluded women from many endeavors
in order to protect them from physical harm. In these "new days of
freedom," however, such reasons no longer applied. Now women
wanted to "stand alongside our men and help with the protecting"
rather than be "patted on the head and told not to worry." In another
letter, signed the "unhappy wife," a woman complained about her
marriage to a Klansman. Her husband left her at home with the children, without just cause, while he attended meetings. Why should
white native-born Protestant women be excluded from the Klan, she
protested, along with such inferior groups as the "Knights of Columbus, Jews or negroes"?[40]

Women also challenged the effects of the Klan's oath of secrecy on
their marriages. Fraternal secrecy, they argued, violated the essence of
"new marriages" in which women were equal partners with their husbands.[41] One letter charged that the drain on the family pocketbook
posed by a husband's Klan dues was serious, and not only because of
its financial consequences. More important, it blocked women from
their rightful role in family budgetary decisions:

> I help earn that money. I have a right to know where it goes. Yet my hus-
> band says he dares not tell me. We have always been pals ever working to-
> gether to keep things going smoothly. All at once he drops me out of his
> confidence [although] I have brains and know how to use them.[42]

Other types of appeals for women's inclusion in the Klan appeared
in the *Fellowship Forum*, a weekly newspaper published in Washington, D.C., that became a Klan mouthpiece in the 1920s. One woman
wrote to demand an organization to champion women's equality

along with patriotic virtues. Another reader called for Protestant women to join together both to protect America against the Catholic menace and to safeguard their interests as women.[43]

Before women were admitted officially to the Klan, informal Klan auxiliaries and women's patriotic societies provided an opportunity for many women to participate in Klan work. Tyler herself was a member of the Ladies of the Invisible Eye, a women's secret organization with close ties to the KKK. Some women's patriotic societies and auxiliaries had a public presence and broad memberships, but many adopted the secrecy and exclusionary practices of the Klan itself. The Dixie Protestant Women's Political League, one such group, paraded openly through downtown Atlanta while members guarded their identities by wearing hoods, masks, and costumes similar to those of the Klan.[44]

One of the most prominent right-wing women's societies of the early 1920s was the Grand League of Protestant Women, headquartered in Houston, Texas. The Grand League, a secret society organized in 1922, attracted many members in Southern and western states. In its propaganda the Grand League foreshadowed the Women of the Ku Klux Klan with a call for "white supremacy, protection of womanhood, defense of the flag" and with its social service work. The Houston chapter, for example, ran a "Protestant boarding home and training school" for young women who moved to Houston from rural areas in search of work. Recognizing the low wages available to unskilled women, the League sought to attract to its home—and its influence—any "whose first wage will probably not permit her to pay more than a nominal sum for board."[45]

A similar organization was the White American Protestants (WAP), whose study clubs were started by E. F. Keith, a wealthy oil promoter and a reputed Klansman. The WAP clubs claimed to have twelve thousand women members in the mid-South. The members of this secret society swore never to vote for, or to place as teacher, governess, or instructor of children, any non-American-born, nonwhites, or non-Protestants.[46]

The immediate predecessor to a national women's Klan was the Ladies of the Invisible Empire (LOTIE), known in many locations as the "Loties." Many LOTIE chapters attracted very large memberships. The chapter in Portland, Oregon, for example, initiated more than one thousand women into the order in a single month in 1922. Typical of LOTIE initiations was that of the Baltimore chapter, which required candidates for membership to detail their background in religion, family, and politics and to swear allegiance to the tenets of the Christian religion and the principles of "pure Americanism."[47]

A rare surviving document details the goals of Shreveport and Vivian, Louisiana, LOTIE chapters organized in January 1923 with 150 charter members. Unlike the later women's Klan, the LOTIEs gave little indication that their political agenda would include efforts to improve the status of women, preferring to see themselves as "chosen messengers of men." The LOTIEs' efforts included assisting Protestant women in learning the art of politics, but they directed most of their work toward returning the Bible to public schools, advocating stringent immigration restrictions, opposing racial equality and interracial marriage, and working to "cleanse and purify the civil, political and ecclesiastical atmosphere" of the nation.[48]

Fearing that these competing organizations would undermine the opportunity to build a women's Klan, the KKK turned its attention to the idea of a women's auxiliary. At the 1922 Imperial Klonvokation in Atlanta, Klansmen debated whether they should meet with women's secret organizations; a committee was appointed to make recommendations to the Imperial Wizard and the Imperial Kloncilium (council). The committee quickly concluded that a women's Klan was necessary. Evans concurred and asked the Exalted Cyclops (heads of Klan realms) to meet and elect two delegates to a convention; they, along with the Grand Dragons and Great Titans of organized realms and the King Kleagles of unorganized states and two representatives of growing Klans, would constitute a meeting to decide KKK policy regarding the women's organization. The Klan then summoned representatives of all the major women's patriotic groups and informal Klan auxiliaries to a conference in Washington, D.C., in June 1923.[49]

Conflict within the leadership of the Knights of the KKK slowed the rush to organize a women's Klan. In March 1923, three months before the Klonvokation was scheduled to meet and organize a women's Klan, Simmons announced that he was setting up a competing group, the Kamelia, a move intended to enhance his position vis-à-vis Evans. Simmons declared that the Kamelia would be "a great women's organization adhering to the same principles" as the Klan. Like the LOTIE, Kamelia had a conservative view of women's role in politics, seeking mainly "to educate women in the science of government and history of the United States and to contribute funds to orphanages and similar deserving institutions."[50]

During Evans's absence from Klan headquarters, Simmons called the Imperial Kloncilium into session and received its support for his women's auxiliary. Instantly Evans reacted, claiming that Simmons had signed a secret contract with the owners of the WAP clubs to absorb these into the Kamelia for his own financial gain. Evans prohibited his men from assisting Kamelia but Simmons continued to build his organization. By June there were Kamelia chapters in twenty states and the organization was sponsoring public parades of white-robed women. Simmons staked his future in the Klan on recognition of his women's organization, saying that the Kamelia was "as much my child" as the Klan was.[51]

A second women's group, the Queens of the Golden Mask (QGM), existed primarily in the Midwest. QGM was organized by D. C. Stephenson, a powerful regional Klan leader based in Indiana who also controlled the influential Klan paper, *Fiery Cross*. To head the QGM, Stephenson chose Daisy Douglas Barr, a well-known evangelist. The QGM attracted mainly the wives, mothers, and daughters of Klansmen and recruited women "in the interest of cleaner local politics and for a more moral community." Ultimately the QGM was absorbed into the Women of the Ku Klux Klan and Barr allied herself with Hiram Evans against Stephenson.[52]

In June 1923 Evans counterattacked. Under his control the Imperial Kloncilium established the Women of the Ku Klux Klan (WKKK) to compete with Simmons's Kamelia and Stephenson's QGM. Instantly a propaganda battle began. Stephenson and Evans each spread titillating stories about the other's impropriety with women, resulting in a "ceaseless wagging of tongues" in the Klan. While the forces of Evans and Stephenson traded gossip, Evans and Simmons clashed in the courtroom. Evans first petitioned the Fulton County (Georgia) Superior Court to dissolve all competing women's organizations and appoint a commission to take administrative control of the entire Klan organization. The court approved Evans's petition. Simmons then countersued for an injunction against the WKKK or any other women's association under the name of the Klan, but he was unsuccessful. In February 1924 the court ordered Simmons to resign his rights, title, and interest in the Kamelia and Ku Klux Klan. In exchange he received a $145,000 cash settlement to replace his $1000 per month annuity from the Klan. Shortly thereafter, Simmons resigned from the order.[53]

Judge R. M. Mann of the second division circuit court in Little

Rock, Arkansas, officially chartered the Women of the Ku Klux Klan on June 10, 1923. Its national headquarters were set up in a three-room office in the Ancient Order of United Workmen hall in Little Rock, Arkansas, at some distance from the male Klan's Atlanta headquarters to symbolize the purported independence of the new women's order from its male counterpart.[54]

Membership in the WKKK was open to white Gentile female native-born citizens over eighteen years of age who owed no allegiance to any foreign government or sect, that is, who were not Catholic, Socialist, Communist, or so forth. Applicants were required to have been resident in a Klan jurisdiction for at least six months and to be endorsed by at least two Klanswomen or a WKKK kleagle or Imperial Commander. Klanswomen swore to investigate "carefully and personally" the qualifications and background of every candidate they proposed for office. Dues of ten dollars included one robe and helmet but did not apply to wives of men who were members of the original Klan or a similar organization during Reconstruction. The national offices of the WKKK were supported (in lavish style) by a portion of all dues; an Imperial Tax (a per capita assessment); profits from the sale of regalia, uniforms, stationery, jewelry, and costumes; and by interest and profits from investments.[55]

To set itself apart from Simmons's Kamelia, the WKKK declared itself an organization "by women, for women, and of women [that] no man is exploiting for his individual gain." The structure of the new women's Klan, worked out in a meeting of WKKK leaders in Asheville, North Carolina, would focus on specific functions and each would have a corresponding task department. The major areas of work for the WKKK's initial efforts were Americanism, education, public amusements, legislation, child welfare and delinquency, citizenship, civics, law enforcement, disarmament, peace, and politics.[56]

Women from Texas, Oregon, Arkansas, Indiana, Iowa, and Wyoming were appointed as the officers of the new WKKK. Lulu Markwell of Arkansas, described by the Klan as "well-known in Protestant American women's organization work," became its first Imperial Commander. The WKKK absorbed many women's secret societies and nativistic leagues, including the LOTIEs, League of Protestant Women, Ladies of the Cu Clux Clan, Ladies of the Golden Mask, Order of American Women, Ladies of the Golden Den, Hooded Ladies of the Mystic Den, and Puritan Daughters of America.[57]

Lulu Markwell (born Boyers) was fifty-seven years old when she was appointed to head the national women's Klan. A native of Indiana, Markwell lived in Little Rock in the 1920s. After graduating from business college she worked in Little Rock as an official court stenographer and as a teacher. She married a local physician. Prior to assuming office in the WKKK, Markwell was very active in fraternal, church, women's, and civic affairs. She was both president and a lecturer for the Arkansas state chapter of the Women's Christian Temperance Union (WCTU) for twenty years and was president of the Educational Aid Society, the Woodmen Circle, and the city's Censor Board; she was a member of the Co-operative Club. She was appointed by the governor of Arkansas as a delegate to the Southern Sociological Congress in Nashville and traveled extensively in the United States and to Cuba. A member of the Democratic party and the Presbyterian church, she was also an active advocate of women's suffrage.[58]

The charter membership of the new WKKK numbered 125,000 women. Most lived in the Midwest, Northwest, and Ozarks region, strongholds of the KKK. Not satisfied with a membership drawn from among the wives, sisters, sweethearts, and mothers of Klansmen, Markwell immediately embarked on a recruiting trip throughout the West and Northwest, increasing the WKKK's overall membership and giving the new organization visibility in other regions. Markwell also hired female field agents and kleagles who worked with KKK kleagles to bring the message of the women's Klan to all areas of the country. WKKK kleagles, initially often the wives and sisters of KKK officers, worked on a commission basis, retaining a percentage of the initiation dues collected from each new Klanswoman. Organizers used techniques proven effective in the men's Klan: they recruited through personal, family, and work contacts and held highly publicized open meetings to reach politically inactive women and women not from Klan families. In addition, WKKK kleagles worked to recruit women through existing organizations. Female nativist and patriotic societies, in particular, were courted by WKKK organizers who sought to persuade them to merge into the new national women's Klan organization.[59]

Organizers for the women's Klan were effective. Within four months, the WKKK claimed that its membership had doubled to 250,000. By November 1923 thirty-six states had chapters of the Women of the Ku Klux Klan. Throughout 1924 the WKKK continued to grow, accepting girls over sixteen years old and chartering fifty locals a week in 1924. The following year an influential anti-Klan commentator declared that at least three million women had been initiated into the women's Klan. His estimate was no doubt inflated, perhaps by projecting from the recruitment successes of the strong Ohio and Indiana WKKK realms; indeed, modern scholars judge the entire 1920s Klan to have enrolled no more than three to five million members. It is clear, however, that the WKKK attracted a great many women within a short time.[60]

It is impossible to determine the exact number or location of WKKK chapters across the country in the absence of organizational records, but we can estimate the expansion of the women's Klan by examining the pages of Klan periodicals. During the mid-1920s the *Fellowship Forum* published news about WKKK chapters, women's rights organizations, and women's clubs—mingled with recipes and fashion tips. The September 1925 issue carried news from local WKKK chapters in eleven states: New York, Connecticut, Pennsylvania, Michigan, Ohio, Virginia, West Virginia, Kansas, Oklahoma, Texas, and Colorado. Most chapters were located in small towns; the exceptions were those of Oklahoma City and Norfolk. The following September, in 1926, the *Fellowship Forum* included news from WKKK chapters in sixteen states: New York, Pennsylvania, Maryland, Virginia, Georgia, Florida, Illinois, Indiana, Ohio, Iowa, Minnesota, Wisconsin, Michigan, Nebraska, California, Washington, and in the District of Columbia as well. Again, most chapters were located outside major metropolitan areas although most members of the WKKK, as of the male Ku Klux Klan, probably resided in large or middle-sized cities. Other issues of the *Fellowship Forum* show a similar geographical dispersion of the women's Klan. Many chapters clustered in Pennsylvania, Ohio, Indiana, Michigan, and New York—states where the KKK was also strong—but chapters existed in the West, on the Atlantic Coast, and along the North-South border.[61]

The business of the national WKKK was conducted in Imperial Klonvokations (legislatures), which enacted laws and assigned penalties to violators. The Klonvokation consisted of all imperial officers and realm (state) commanders and one delegate from each realm and each province. Each realm received one vote per hundred members and Excellent Commanders had one vote each. The Imperial Kloncilium (judicial board), composed of all imperial officers, acted as the supreme advisory board and met once a year to decide policy.[62]

National WKKK klonvokations were held irregularly. The first meeting was in 1923 in Asheville. In 1926 one thousand women delegates from the WKKK met in Washington, D.C., at the same time, but separately from, the men's organization. The following year five hundred Klanswomen delegates, representing every state plus the Canal Zone and Alaska, met in St. Louis for a two-day klonvokation to discuss uniform marriage laws, Prohibition, and threats to the sanctity of the home. A second WKKK klonvokation in that year was held in Indianapolis where sixteen hundred candidates received the second-degree obligation of the order and speeches attacked Al Smith for his support of liquor. In October 1928 a greatly diminished WKKK assembled in Dallas.[63]

In chartering its new women's organization, the Klan emphasized the role of women as helpmates to Klansmen. Women's cooperation and assistance were needed, Klansmen insisted, to ensure that the political agenda of the men's Klan could be implemented. The KKK press talked often of the WKKK as its "women's auxiliary" and argued that the men's Klan had created the WKKK with the same ideals and principles as its father organization.[64]

Klansmen were unsure, however, about what Klan membership would mean for women. Women might be convenient symbols for mobilizing men into the Klan, but women's actual political participation was another matter. An early advertisement written by the KKK to solicit members for an organization of Klanswomen illustrates the men's ambivalence. Although it was a recruitment pitch for the WKKK, the advertisement also pointed to a fearful potential in political involvement to masculinize women. Many worry, the ad suggested, that "giving [women] the ballot would foster masculine boldness and restless independence, which might detract from the modesty and virtue of womanhood." To this dilemma, the KKK posed as a solution the creation of a separate organization for Klanswomen. The WKKK would allow women to be politically active without "sacrifice of that womanly dignity and modesty we all admire." The key to the delicate balancing act between a "masculine" and a "feminine" political involvement, according to the KKK, was acquiescence of Klanswomen in the political agenda of Klansmen. By adopting as a whole the Klan's agenda of support for white Protestantism, the English language, public schools, the Bible, and immigration restrictions, women could exercise their newly granted enfranchisement without relying on "masculine" traits of political judgment and strategizing.[65]

A related tactic of recruitment for the women's organization stressed women's political *potential*. Although ostensibly supporting women's involvement in politics, this approach emphasized women's ignorance and limited abilities in the political arena. Excluded from the world of political debate, white Protestant women had developed only a "moral influence" in politics. Their special roles in the family and home gave women good political instincts, the Klan argued, but not mature political judgment. Women now needed to be taught (by men) those principles and attitudes that the world of politics required: clear thinking, intelligence, and collective and individual responsibility for maintaining the principles of Anglo-Saxon Protestantism. Women might have gained the ballot by law, but the ability to use it intelligently required further education—an education the Klan was prepared to provide through its women's organization.

> It has long been cenceded [*sic*] that the Protestant women of America have wielded the greatest influence in this country for greater morality, political purity, the development of a better citizenship and the maintenance of the high standards of the home. The decadence which has come, the increase of vice, the laxity of law enforcement, and the lowered moral standards are largely the result of the unorganized condition of American women who, as individuals, could not cope successfully with those agencies that have sowed the seed of unrighteousness.[66]

From the beginning, there were indications that leaders of the fledgling women's Klan saw the role of Klanswomen in a different light than did their would-be mentors in the men's Klan. A recruiting notice for Klanswomen noted that men no longer have "exclusive dominion" in society. Whether working in the home as a housewife or working in the business world, the ad suggested, a woman should put her efforts behind a movement for 100 percent American womanhood by joining the WKKK.[67] Markwell herself saw great possibilities for the Klan to further the interests of women as women, in addition to their racial and political interests. She noted that women's interest in politics, once latent, had been piqued by the Nineteenth Amendment granting women the vote. Women now saw it as their duty to work "in the maintenance of that amendment."[68]

Propaganda from WKKK headquarters chastised women for their political quiescence in light of women's expanded political rights. Threats to national security or to the superior rights of white Protestants within the nation required women's increased vigilance and readiness to act. Working in the women's Klan, officers insisted, gave women both the knowledge and the collective strength to stand up against the dangers posed by increasing numbers of nonwhites and non-Protestants in the nation. Victoria Rogers, the Major Kleagle for the WKKK Realm of Illinois, likened white Protestant women who had not as yet joined the WKKK to female Rip Van Winkles who will "awake with a jolt to find themselves wholly unprepared to meet the facts and the menaces hiding behind those facts to which they have lent a deaf ear and a blinded eye."[69]

The WKKK advertised its ability to champion the goals of white womanhood as a standard recruiting tool for new members. Its Washington chapter, for example, argued that white Protestant native-born women had common political interests and would be more effective in pursuing those interests if they were politically organized. Their recruitment advertisement posed a number of questions for women to consider:

> Are you interested in the welfare of our Nation?
> As an enfranchised woman are you interested in Better Government?
> Do you not wish for the protection of Pure Womanhood?
> Shall we uphold the sanctity of the American Home?
> Should we not interest ourselves in Better Education for our children?
> Do we not want American teachers in our American schools?

"Patriotic women," those who answered these questions in the affirmative, were needed in the women's Klan. Protestant white women, the WKKK insisted, shared a concern for their children's education and the welfare of the country. It is the "duty of the American Mother" to stamp out vice and immorality in the nation. Joining the Klan was an effective avenue for the political work that white Protestant women needed to do.[70]

THE WOMEN'S KLAN

To understand the nature of the new women's Klan, we need to examine the beliefs, organizations, rituals, and activities of the WKKK in comparison with those of the men's order. But we must use caution in our comparison. When Klanswomen swore to uphold the "sanctity of the home and chastity of womanhood" they echoed the words, but not necessarily the sentiments, of their male Klan counterparts. Although a simple listing of WKKK and KKK principles and rituals would suggest that there was little difference between the two organizations, we must understand how these were interpreted and justified by each organization.

BELIEFS

On one level, many principles of the new women's Klan appear identical to the racist and xenophobic politics of the first and second men's Klans. The WKKK supported militant patriotism, national quotas for immigration, racial segregation, and antimiscegenation laws. Klanswomen cited the need to safeguard the "eternal supremacy" of the white race against a "rising tide of color" and decried Catholic and Jewish influence in politics, the schools, the media, and the business world. Markwell herself saw the mission of the women's Klan as "fighting for the same principles as the Knights of the Ku Klux Klan," although she reserved for the WKKK a special interest in "work peculiar to women's organization, such as social welfare work [and] the prevention of juvenile delinquency."[71]

Like the men's Klan, the WKKK often used politically palatable symbols to present its agenda of nativism and racial hatred to the public. It called for separation of church from state when crusading against Roman Catholic political influence, for free public schools when seeking to destroy parochial schools, and for the purity of race when seeking racial segregation and restricted immigration. In private, the racial bigotry of the WKKK was fully as vicious as that of the KKK, as in Klanswomen's condemnation of "mulatto leaders forced to remain members of the negro group [who] aspire to white association because of their white blood [thus] boldly preaching racial equality."[72]

But if many of the WKKK's basic principles followed existing doctrines of the men's Klan, women and men did not always have a common perception of the problems that required Klan action. Klansmen of the 1920s denounced interracial marriage for its destructive genetic outcomes; their Klan forefathers fought interracial sexuality to maintain white men's sexual access to white and black women. Klanswomen, however, saw a different danger in miscegenation: the destruction of white marriages by untrustworthy white men who "betray their own kind."

In many cases, women and men in the Klan took different messages from common symbols. Klansmen praised womanhood to underscore the correctness of male supremacy; Klanswomen used the symbol to point out the inequities that women faced in society and politics.

Klansmen sought political inspiration in the "great achievements" of white American Protestantism, but Klanswomen read history differently. Rather than mimicking the men's empty gestures of praise for "true American women" in the past, the WKKK complained that women had been excluded from public politics throughout most of this glorious history, even though "our mothers have ever been Klanswomen at heart, sharing with our fathers the progress and development of our country." Klanswomen embraced the KKK's racist, anti-Catholic, and anti-Semitic agenda and symbols of American womanhood but they used these to argue as well for equality for white Protestant women.[73]

ORGANIZATION

For the most part the WKKK adopted the militaristic hierarchical style of the KKK. An Excellent Commander served as president, with a four-year term of office and responsibility for issuing, suspending, and revoking the charters of locals and realms (state organizations). Next in the chain of command was the klaliff (vice-president), who acted as presiding officer of the Imperial Klonvokation; the klokard (lecturer), responsible for disseminating Klankraft; and the kludd (chaplain), who presided over Klan ritual. Other major officers included the kligrapp (secretary), bonded for $25,000 to handle minor Klan funds; the Klabee (treasurer), bonded for $50,000 to handle major Klan funds; and the officers of Klan ritual and ceremony, including the kladd (conductor), klagoro (inner guard), klexter (outer guard), night hawk (in charge of candidates), klokan (investigator and auditor), and kourier (messenger).

Each realm or group of realms of the WKKK was organized by a Major Kleagle with subjurisdictions organized by minor kleagles and supervised by a series of Realm Commanders and Imperial Commanders. Upon retirement from office, Excellent Commanders became Klan Regents, Realm Commanders became Grand Regents, and Imperial Commanders became Imperial Regents. In keeping with the military arrangement of the WKKK, nearly all offices were subdivided into further levels of authority. The rank of kourier, for example, was subdivided into that of kourier private, corporal, sergeant, lieutenant, captain, major, and colonel. Ranks carried more than symbolic authority, as failure to obey the command of an officer was defined as insubordination and could bring harsh punishment.[74]

The similarity between the organization of the male and female

Klans is significant. Consistently, the WKKK denied that it was like the auxiliary of a fraternal association, "merely a social order for social purposes." Instead, Klanswomen embraced the mixture of individualism and deference to authority that characterized the male Klan. Like Klansmen, Klanswomen had at least ostensible opportunities to rise within the organization through individual effort and talent; both organizations used a strict command hierarchy. In this, the WKKK claimed to stand apart from the outside world that discouraged women from individual efforts and achievements. By valuing both obedience and individual effort, the WKKK would "inculcate patriotism, upbuild character, and develop true clannishness among women."[75]

Other features of the WKKK show the contrasting aspects of obedience and commonality that characterized the KKK. Like their male counterparts, Klanswomen typically wore white robes with masks and helmets, although some chapters used red robes. Masks were clearly intended to disguise the identity of Klanswomen in public, but the WKKK insisted that masks had only a symbolic purpose. Through masking Klanswomen hid their individuality as well as identity, exemplifying the Klan motto "not for self, but for others." Similar claims were made about Klan robes (see photograph 2). Although in fact officers' robes had more colors and accoutrements, Klanswomen asserted that their robes symbolized the equality of all women within Klankraft. Robes set Klanswomen apart from the invidious world of social class distinctions in fashion, leveling the divisions of wealth so pervasive in alien society. "As we look upon a body of women robed in white we realize that we are on a common level of sisterhood and fraternal union."[76]

The detailed laws and regulations of the WKKK ensured obedience to authority. Women, no less than men, were expected to conduct themselves according to klannish principles. The WKKK treated as major offenses those of treason to the Klan, violating the oath of allegiance, disrespect of virtuous womanhood, violation of the U.S. Constitution, the "pollution" of Caucasian blood through miscegenation, and other acts unworthy of a Klanswoman. Minor offenses included profane language or vulgarity during a klonklave, acts against the best interest of the Klan or a Klanswoman, and refusal or failure to obey the Excellent Commander. The Excellent Commander assessed penalties for minor offenses; a tribunal handled major offenses. Violators faced reprimand, suspension, banishment forever, or complete ostracism.

RITUAL

At least as central as laws and hierarchy to both women's and men's Klans was an elaborate and intricate web of ceremonials, rites, and protocols designed to increase members' commitment to the order and to sharpen the distinctions between insiders and outsiders ("aliens"). Like the men's Klan, the WKKK used threatening, frightening, and challenging rituals to ensure loyalty and instill fear in its members. Both the WKKK and the KKK referred to themselves as "invisible empires," conveying the Klan's aspirations to universal jurisdiction. Secret klannish words gave members an immediate way to recognize sister and brother Klan members. In Klan ceremonies, days of the week were not Sunday, Monday, and so forth as in the alien world but were desperate, dreadful, desolate, doleful, dismal, deadly, and dark. Weeks of the month became weird, wonderful, wailing, weeping, and woeful. January through December were labeled appalling, frightful, sorrowful, mournful, horrible, terrible, alarming, furious, fearful, hideous, gloomy, and bloody.

The Klan changed historical time as well, setting it to the ascendancy of white Gentile Americans. The reign of Incarnation included all time up to the American Revolution. A first reign of Reincarnation lasted from the beginning of the revolutionary war until the organization of the first Ku Klux Klan in 1866. A second reign of Reincarnation extended from 1866 to 1872, the collapse of the first KKK. The third reign of Reincarnation began in 1915, the reorganization of the KKK, and extended from the present into the future.[77]

The naturalization klonklave was typical of women's Klan rituals (see photograph 4). An altar was placed in the center of a room or in an open-air gathering place surrounded by stations with water, a Bible, a flag, and a sword. WKKK officers entered the klonklave, kissed the flag, proceeded to the altar, and saluted the Excellent Commander or other presiding officer, raising their masks to reveal their identities to this official. When all officers were assembled, the kladd certified that everyone present was a valid member of the WKKK. The entrance to the building or park was secured by the klexter and klagoro and then all masks were removed.

Once assembled, officers were questioned about the seven sacred symbols of Klankraft in a ritualized catechism oddly patterned after the catechism ritual of the Roman Catholic church. Each officer repeated a litany of symbols: the Bible (God), fiery cross (sacrifice and service), flag (U.S. Constitution), sword (law enforcement and national defense), water (purity of life and unity of purpose), mask (secrecy, unselfishness, and banishment of individuality), and robe (purity and equality). Between each restatement of Klan doctrine, the audience and officers sang a Christian hymn.

During the naturalization ceremony, a klokard led the class of candidates through the oath of admission. Candidates swore that they were serious, qualified for admission, believers in klannishness, and willing to practice klannishness toward other Klanswomen and work for the eternal maintenance of white supremacy. Candidates then were greeted by officers and members and congratulated for their "womanly decision to forsake the world of selfishness and fraternal alienation and emigrate to the delectable bounds of the Invisible Empire and become its loyal citizens." At this point, the Excellent Commander conferred the obligation and oath of admission on the assembled candidates and baptized the new members by pouring water and saying:

> With this transparent, life-giving, powerful God-given fluid, more precious and far more significant than all the sacred oils of the ancients, I set you apart from the women of your daily association to the great and honorable task you have voluntarily allotted yourselves as citizens of the Invisible Empire, Women of the Ku Klux Klan. As Klanswomen, may your character be as transparent, your life purpose as powerful, your motive in all things as magnanimous and as pure, and your Klannishness as real and as faithful as the manifold drops herein.

As a quartet of Klanswomen sang and the assembly prayed, the klannish initiates responded with their own ritual. They dipped fingers in water and touched their shoulders, saying "In body," and their foreheads, saying "In mind," then waved their hands in the air, saying "In spirit," and made a circle above their heads, saying "In life." The klokard then imparted the secret signs and words of the Klan. The ceremony closed with an opportunity to raise issues from the floor (probably an infrequent occurrence), followed by a restatement of the need for secrecy in the presence of aliens. The night hawk extinguished the fiery cross, the kludd performed a benediction, and the klonklave was declared closed.[78]

Ceremonies for higher levels in the WKKK followed a similar pattern, although more was required of the candidates. Acceptance into the second-degree obligation, the highest rank below officer level, required candidates to make pledges against slandering other Klanswomen or Klansmen, against materialism, and against selfishness and similar temptations. Candidates for advanced degrees also made greater pledges of duty, swearing that "when pleasure interferes with my duty as a Klanswoman . . . I will set aside pleasure"; they affirmed their loyalty, vowing not to recommend "faithless, contemptuous, careless, or indifferent" women for advancement in the order.[79]

ACTIVITIES

It is difficult to compare the political practices of the women's and men's Klans, as both varied considerably across the nation and over time but the national agendas of each organization give some indication of the differences. The political agenda of the men's Klan ranged from infiltration into legislative and judicial politics on the state, municipal, and county level to acts of violence and terroristic intimidation against Jews, Catholics, and blacks. Many Klansmen, though, used the KKK as primarily a male fraternity, a social club of like-minded white Protestants.[80]

The women's Klan similarly showed a range of activities and purposes. On a national level, the women's Klan worked to legitimate the violence and terrorism of the men's order. It published and distributed a detailed guide to the proper display of the American flag and a pocket-sized version of the U.S. Constitution and circulated a card reminding Protestants to attend church faithfully (see photograph 5); each item prominently displayed the WKKK logo. The WKKK involved itself in national legislative politics, although without much success. It actively supported the creation of a federal Department of Education to bolster public schools and undermine parochial education and opposed U.S. membership in the World Court. Although it claimed to be interested in safeguarding white Protestant children and the home, the WKKK opposed a 1924 bill outlawing child labor on the grounds that it was "a Communistic, Bolshevistic scheme." That same year Klanswomen were active in blocking an attempt by anti-Klan forces to introduce a plank in the national Democratic party platform condemning the Ku Klux Klan.[81]

At times the women's Klan sought to portray itself as an organization of social work and social welfare. One national WKKK speaker announced that she left social work for the "broader field of Klankraft" because of the Klan's effectiveness in promoting morality and public welfare. Many chapters claimed to collect food and money for the needy, although these donations typically went to Klan families, often to families of Klan members arrested for rioting and vigilante activities. A powerful Florida WKKK chapter operated a free day nursery, charging that Catholic teachers had ruined the local public schools.[82]

Some WKKK chapters ran homes for wayward girls. These homes served two purposes: to protect the virtue of Protestant women who were tempted by a life of vice and to underscore the danger faced by delinquent girls placed in Catholic-controlled reform schools. The Shreveport, Louisiana, WKKK chapter, for example, based its fundraising for a Protestant girls' home on the story of a woman whose unhappy fate it was to be sent to a Catholic reform home after being convicted of selling whiskey and prostituting her teenaged daughters.[83]

Another activity of many WKKK locals was the crusade against liquor and vice. WKKK chapters worked to "clean up" a motion picture industry in which they claimed Jewish owners spewed a steady diet of immoral sex onto the screen. Other chapters fought against liquor, as evidenced by the case of Myrtle Cook, a Klanswoman and president of the Vinton, Iowa, WCTU, who was assassinated for documenting the names of suspected bootleggers. In death, Cook was eulogized by Klanswomen and WCTU members alike; all business in Vinton was suspended for the two hours of the funeral.[84]

WKKK chapters in many states were active also in campaigns to prohibit prenuptial religious agreements about future children, bar interracial marriage, outlaw the Knights of Columbus (a Catholic fraternal society), remove Catholic encyclopedias from public schools, bar the use of Catholic contractors by public agencies, and exclude urban (i.e., Jewish and Catholic) vacationers in majority-Protestant suburban resorts.[85]

Some WKKK locals, though, functioned largely for the personal and financial success of their members. F. C. Dunn of Lansing, Michigan, made a fortune after introducing her invention, a new antiseptic powder, at a local WKKK meeting.[86]

Klanswomen tended not to be involved in physical violence and rioting, but there were exceptions. In the aftermath of a 1924 Klan riot in Wilkinsburg, Pennsylvania, Mamie H. Bittner, a thirty-nine-year-old mother of three children and member of the Homestead, Pennsylvania, WKKK testified that she, along with thousands of other Klanswomen paraded through town, carrying heavy maple riot clubs. Morover, Bittner claimed that the WKKK was teaching its members to murder and kill in the interest of the Klan.[87]

The activities of the women's Klan were shaped largely by the existing political agenda of the men's Klan. It is not accurate, however, to portray the WKKK as a dependent auxiliary of the men's order. Klanswomen created a distinctive ideology and political agenda that infused the Klan's racist and nativist goals with ideas of equality between white Protestant women and men. The ideology and politics of Klanswomen and Klansmen were not identical, though at many points they were compatible. But women and men of the Klan movement sometimes found themselves in contention as women changed from symbols to actors in the Klan.

The difference between the women's and men's Klan grew from an underlying message in the symbol of white womanhood. By using gender and female sexual virtue as prime political symbols, the Klan shaped its identity through intensely masculinist themes, as an organization of real men. Clearly, this was an effective recruitment strategy for the first Klan. But in the 1920s, as both financial and political expediency and significant changes in women's political roles prompted the Klan to accept female members, an identity based on symbols of masculine exclusivity and supremacy became problematic. In addition, if Klansmen understood that defending white womanhood meant safeguarding white Protestant supremacy and male supremacy, many women heard the message differently. The WKKK embraced ideas of racial and religious privilege but rejected the messages of white female vulnerability. In its place Klanswomen substituted support for women's rights and a challenge to white men's political and economic domination. The next chapter further examines these contradictions.

CHAPTER II

Womanhood and the Klan Fraternity

Women's entry into the male bastion of the Klan presented the men who led the Invisible Empire with perplexing problems. An organization based on principles of fraternalism, protection of white womanhood, and defeat of alien forces—principles that it steadfastly proclaimed as masculine—now admitted women. Clearly, financial opportunism and intra-Klan conflict, not concern for women's rights, prompted male Klan leaders to create a women's Klan. Klansmen expected their female counterparts to act as klannish subordinates, a position that some women no doubt found acceptable. But in an age in which women's political rights were expanding, other women did not see their place in the Klan in such a limited fashion.

In the mid-1920s women and men of the Klan often differed over the idea and meaning of "Klanswoman." Klanswomen sought to integrate a women's rights agenda with the Klan's nativist and racist politics; Klansmen were averse, even hostile, to the attempt. Male Klan leaders assumed that the women's order would function as a subsidiary auxiliary of the KKK, while at least some WKKK klaverns (chapters) sought autonomy from the male Klan. Ironically, even anti-Klan activists seized on the term of Klanswoman, using it to ridicule Klansmen as effeminate and morally degenerate.

To describe the complex gender ideas and politics within the second Klan and among its opponents, traditional classifications of political movements are inadequate. History is replete with examples in which issues of gender cut across these political categories of progressive or reactionary, conservative or liberal, right-wing or left-wing. At times, political movements that appear similar have had entirely different gender politics; distinct political movements have sometimes had a common agenda on women's rights.

Gender ideology and gender politics are not infinitely adaptable, however. Other ideological positions and agendas greatly limit the range of gender issues and gender politics that a political movement can accommodate. Further, a stance toward gender issues that finds acceptance in the early stages of a political movement may become problematic. Progressive and left-wing movements, for example, often have difficulty sustaining committed supporters without paying at least some attention to issues of gender equality. Similarly, to support a women's rights agenda a right-wing movement like the Klan needed to modify its organization or its ideological commitments. This chapter explores how the second Klan coped with such contradictions over the course of the 1920s.

MASCULINITY AND FEMININITY IN THE KLAN

In its early years, the second Klan's images of masculinity, femininity, and appropriate gender roles largely were inherited from its predecessor Klan. To both Klans, masculinity and membership were virtually synonymous. "True men," "real men," "100 percent men" were Klansmen. Indeed, since the Klan claimed to admit only men whose masculinity was unquestionable, the very act of joining the Klan conferred manhood.

The idea of Klan femininity was much less clear. In the world of the early 1920s KKK, women were invisible. White men alone were political actors, operating in a world of political choice and options they closed to all others. White women (like children) were possessions or symbols on whose behalf men acted and for whom men fought one another. This view allowed women no place as Klansmembers. Indeed, the virtues Klansmembers coveted were identical to those society defined as inherently masculine: assertiveness, bravery, and toughness. Such virtues were the antithesis of the Klan's image of gentle, accommodating femininity.

MASCULINITY

Klan propaganda constantly expounded the manly nature of its fraternal union. The KKK stood for the precise principles that Klansmen thought any intelligent, concerned white Protestant man should espouse: defense of his possessions (including wife and children) from outside intrusion and principled behavior toward like-minded white Protestant men. An often-reprinted poetic plea for real men to join the Klan made this clear:

> God Give Us Men! The Invisible Empire demands strong
> Minds, great hearts, true faith and ready hands,
> Men whom lust of office does not kill;
> Men whom the spoils of office cannot buy.[1]

At first glance, the Klan's call to a masculinity rooted in individualism, courage, self-possession, and protectiveness seems curiously antiquated. The second Klan mimicked its predecessor's use of masculinity to symbolize and affirm the righteousness of white male supremacy, but in a social context that challenged this supremacy. The klannish image of manhood exalted individual exercise of physical violence long after the middle and working classes from which the Klan drew the bulk of its membership had embraced tempered aggression and self-control. Its romantic images of autonomy, absolute male privilege, and fraternal camaraderie harked back to norms of patriarchal and artisanal society long since eroded by industrial capitalist production and the imposition of market values on human relations.

Too, the image of klannish masculinity was contradictory. These "100 percent American" Klansmen were bombarded with lavish emotional appeals entreating them to defend home and nation against imminent peril. Passionate commitment in place of studied rationality was the hallmark of true Klansmen—even as the "passionate natures" of Jewish, black, and immigrant men justified Klansmen's despising them as non-men. Moreover, if the individualism and self-possession that made for klannish manhood were unavailable to most men in the workplace or the family, they were equally implausible goals within the militaristic hierarchical Klan.[2]

The appeal of klannish masculinity stems from multiple layers of meaning within this complex, confusing symbol. Behind the national and racial propaganda of the Klan was one such message. When the second Klan evoked the masculinity of the Reconstruction-era Klan, it highlighted the extent to which white male privileges had deteriorated over half a century. When the Klan called for a restoration of "real" American values, male recruits understood the other message: "real" masculine values needed restoration as well.

Despite the moralistic tenor of Klan propaganda, life in the KKK also promised a heady combination of violent vigilantism and male camaraderie. Clearly, these images were compelling to many "proper, God-fearing" men whom the Klan targeted as recruits. Independence and self-determination, which growing numbers of men found impossible in the world of work, lingered as attributes of masculinity in the early twentieth century. The extralegal violence of the Klan encouraged men to action unfettered by middle-class norms. As important as the male Klan's promise of release from the world of social restraints and obligations was its assurance that autonomy and self-determination would not be bought at the cost of isolation. The KKK heralded the solidarity of "true men" with like-minded individuals. Klannish masculinity was based in tough-minded exercise of personal judgments, but it obligated Klansmen to a common cause and to one another. In this sense, the seeming contradiction between self-determination and the Klan's hierarchy dissolved. Effective self-possession and independence required cooperation, coordination, and obedience to freely chosen authority.

A third source of the appeal of klannish manhood was to give a masculine cast to Protestant religion. By wielding religion as a weapon of terror and political power, the KKK sought to alter the softer countenance of twentieth-century religion and become, in the words of an Illinois pastor, "the masculine part of Protestantism." And while KKK membership validated masculinity, it ridiculed Klan opponents—including alien preachers—as effeminate. Here the Klan drew on a discourse common among fundamentalist Protestant ministers such as Billy Sunday, who used a falsetto voice to mimic the oratory of "modernist" ministers. Catholic priests and Jewish rabbis, the Klan insisted, were the better targets of such characterization: "Why burlesque the Protestant minister and hold him up as a weak sister, an effeminate fellow, a proper subject for ridicule, and let the priest and the rabbi go 'scot free'? I tell you, the Ku Klux Klan is opposed, to the death, to such partiality and favoritism."[3]

FEMININITY

The male Klan, especially in its early years, held two contrasting images of femininity and womanhood. In the abstract, white Protestant women (femininity applied only to these) were innocent, virtuous beings who existed to sustain and serve men. The role of actual wives, mothers, and sweethearts was more ambiguous.

As symbols, white Protestant women were the subjects of voluminous propaganda pledging Klansmen's respect and adoration for white womanhood. The *Klansman's Manual* declared womanhood to be "all that is best, and noblest, and highest in life" and insisted that "no race, or society, or country, can rise higher than its womanhood." The Klan's very existence lay in the "sacred duty" to protect womanhood. Echoing the Reconstruction-era Klan, the second Klan contended that the "degradation of woman is a violation of the sacredness of human personality, a sin against the race, a crime against society, a menace to our country, and a prostitution." In the words of an Illinois Klan minister-lecturer, "After God created man and saw him so desolate he created woman, the most beautiful, the most perfect, and the greatest creation God ever made, for man to cherish and protect."[4]

For the Klan, the embodiment of white women's virtues was motherhood. James Comer set the tone in his address to the first meeting of Grand Dragons by affirming that good mothers were essential to men's accomplishments. Officers and kleagles throughout the KKK hierarchy emphasized the critical role of motherhood in sustaining a white Protestant male-directed nation. A directive from the Indiana KKK Department of Propaganda and Education to all state exalted cyclops and kligrapps on the occasion of Mother's Day 1925, for example, instructed Klansmen to honor their "glorious mothers as the only reliable source of counsel, sympathy, and courage in a man's life."[5]

The Klan's glorification of motherhood was tied to another idealized symbol: the home. Inscribed among the objects and purposes of the KKK was the conviction that "the American home is fundamental to all that is best in life, in society, in church, and in the nation." The *Klansman's Manual* bound members to protect the home by "promoting whatever would make for its stability, its betterment, its safety, and its inviolability." Simmons elaborated this, proclaiming the American home as the "veritable rockbottom of our national well-being" and insisting that if homes were to fail "all our wealth and material achievement is naught but poverty and trash." In propaganda, songs, poems, and rituals the KKK lavished unceasing praise on "the home":

> Home, home, country and home,
> Klansmen we'll all live and die
> For our country and our home.[6]

For Klansmen the home symbolized many things. Fundamentally, the home represented Americanism and the protection of American values from alien influence. The Grand Dragon of the Realm of Colorado directed Klansmen to be zealous in guarding the home, arguing that "all the forces of evil which attack the American home strike at the life of the nation, for when the home is broken, all pretext of government vanishes." Homes gave "real Americans" a stake in the country's future and a stability that separated them from the shifting mass of immigrants.[7]

Klansmen also insisted that the home represented women's dreams and identity. In guarding the home the KKK was protecting the interests of white womanhood. Moreover, white Protestant homes symbolized the future of the Klan and the nation since a proper klannish home life was critical to developing patriotic and klannish values in the next generation. Thus, when the Roman Catholic church insisted that marriage contracts contain the promise to raise children as Catholics, it attacked the very basis of the home and, through the home, the foundation of American Protestant nationhood.[8]

Even as the KKK glorified symbols of home, mothers, and white womanhood, the place it gave to actual white Protestant women was less clear. That of women as wives was particularly unstable. In rallies and meetings Klansmen traded songs and tales about the perils of marriage to demanding, bossy women. One such ditty decried the abuse that wives heap on hapless husbands:

> Oh, Barney Google he belongs to the Ku Klux Klan
> Barney's wife was big and fat,
> She knocked him out from under his hat,
> Because poor Barney he joined the Ku Klux Klan.[9]

To the KKK, women as wives (or sweethearts) had nearly limitless influence over men. Since men were easily influenced by attractive women, the women had responsibility for maintaining men's moral character, a responsibility that placed fearsome power in the hands of females.

> A many a night have I went away from home
> And left my dear wife a weeping
> I'd get drunk and fight and stay out all night
> When I ought to be down home sleeping
> Now those days have past and I quit at last,
> And better days now I am keeping.
> Most any time about the hour of nine
> You can find me right down home sleeping.[10]

The Klan's ambivalence toward wives extended also to women as mothers. Actual mothers (as opposed to the glorious image of motherhood) exercised tremendous influence over men. Unchecked, their monopolization of child rearing would undermine the "building of manly character" essential for Klansmen. The presence and ultimate authority of fathers was critical to the development of Klan children, especially Klan boys.

Although virtually every piece of Klan propaganda from the early 1920s enjoined Klansmen to protect the virtue of white womanhood, the Klan's ambivalence toward flesh-and-blood women was apparent here, also. When Klansmen swore to defend American womanhood, they wanted to be sure that the womanhood they guarded was sexually monogamous and premaritally chaste. At every occasion the KKK reminded women of their obligations, noting "the purity and moral integrity demanded of woman have proven of priceless value to the race." According to a prominent Klan minister, chaste women (but apparently not chaste men) were essential to the preservation of marriage, the home, and the government. The Reconstruction-era Klan used symbols of women's purity and chastity to mobilize white men's fears of the sexual powers of black men. The second Klan sought to protect pure womanhood not only against these alien forces but against unladylike conduct by women themselves.[11]

By romanticizing the idea of home life while pointing to women's untrustworthiness, the KKK strengthened the appeal of the Klan fraternity as a substitute family for Klansmen. The KKK constituted an official family, with God the father and all Klansmen as brothers. (Where women belonged in this spiritual household was unclear.) The Oath of Allegiance swore members to fraternal "klannishness," which prohibited defaming, defrauding, cheating, or deluding other Klansmen or their families. Moreover, all local KKK klaverns functioned to some extent as men's clubs, sponsoring speakers, social hours, group prayers, and a feeling of solidarity in a setting that often excluded women and children.[12]

WOMEN IN THE KLAN FRATERNITY

When contending KKK leaders resolved to enlist women in the Invisible Empire, their decision threatened the male fraternity of the Klan. Although the decision was pragmatic, not ideological, the reality of female members contradicted the Klan's image of itself as an organization of and for masculine white Protestant men. Often in the Klan press and in their speeches Klan leaders wrestled with this problem. How could the Klan define a political role for women that was both subordinate and activist? How could it maintain the Klan's male fraternity and masculine image in the face of this feminine onslaught?

The decision to create the WKKK as a distinct organization for women was part of the answer. In the WKKK women could be enlisted in the Klan's efforts without directly confronting men in the organization. A national Klan minister-lecturer expressed the sentiments of many Klansmen when he demanded separate groups for men and women, with the women's order clearly subordinate: "It isn't because women can't keep a secret. We know they can. It was Adam, not Eve, who did the talking. We will never admit women because they can not do some of the work we have to do." [13]

Resolving the question of women's place in the Klan also required ideological change. Klansmen argued that white Protestant women functioned best in politics as the helpmates of men. Good Klanswomen, the *Fiery Cross* proclaimed, were "the ally of good men." The *Fellowship Forum* argued that unlike men, women were not self-interested and would therefore act for the common good, presumably following the political lead of 100 percent American men. Like other KKK leaders, Evans portrayed the WKKK as an adjunct to the real (male) Klan: "Our women are aiding us . . . let your hearts beat in the women's order also." [14]

At the same time the KKK defined women's political role as separate and subordinate to that of men, it supported women's legal and political rights, issues that would increase its female membership. The *Fiery Cross* reported favorably on the launching of the National Women's party campaign for women in the U.S. Congress, calling it a search for justice for women; it cheered a movement for women's equal representation in legislative bodies of the Presbyterian church. The *Fellowship Forum* applauded the actions of a woman who obtained a passport in her own, rather than her husband's, name and regularly featured "The American Women," a page that mixed reports on women's rights' drives with recipes and fashion news. [15]

The KKK's views on white womanhood reflected these conflicting concerns and the tension between image and political reality. The Ku Klux Klan Katechism asked Klansmen: "What is the attitude of the Klan toward women?" To which they were to reply: "The Klan believes in the purity of womanhood and in the fullest measure of freedom compatible with the highest type of womanhood including the suffrage." The KKK insisted that it advocated the political rights of white Protestant women, but it clung to white womanhood as a central symbol of white supremacy. In the words of the "Bright Fiery Cross," a popular Klan hymn of the 1920s sung at rallies and parades to the tune "Marching to Georgia," these concerns merged:

> Yes, and there were women folks
> who lined up with them, too,
> For they felt there was some work
> that they would need to do;
> Since they have the right to vote,
> they'd help to put it through
> And we go marching to Victory.[16]

As the temperance and moral reform movements of the early twentieth century did, the Klan saw women's inherently moral natures as key to campaigns for clean government and control of vice since women would vote for candidates promising to rid the country of liquor, prostitution, and gambling. Without question, the KKK assured its members, bringing white Protestant women into the electoral arena would result in less corrupt politics: "A woman has conviction and ideals and she is willing to sacrifice party and her own political aspirations for the common good of the country and American ideals."[17]

Its endorsement of women's suffrage and the expansion of women's legal rights, however, threatened to undermine other aspects of the Klan's agenda. A particular difficulty arose from the Klan's emphasis on Christianity as the vehicle for women's equality. In Klan doctrine the spread of Christianity, especially Protestantism, elevated the status of women throughout the world. But the Klan also argued that in the United States—a nation founded on Protestant beliefs—women had only recently begun to assume the place in the world that was rightfully theirs.[18]

One way the Klan handled the apparent lag in gender equality in a Christian nation was to reinterpret U.S. history to emphasize women's hidden power. As the *Imperial Night-Hawk* explained in an editorial, "the American woman has had as much to do with the shaping of the destiny of America as the American man." Women operated through indirect channels, using their control over the home to exercise power in the outside world. As mothers and wives, women had a role in the world that was at least as influential as men's, even if their formal rights were limited.[19]

Another approach was to argue that *both* paid employment and Christianity were necessary for women to achieve full equality. "Women's economic freedom," according to the Klan press, "which has slumbered for ages, awakes." With women in the work force came a struggle "to balance and readjust sex . . . an entirely new conception of the meaning of sex and of the relation of men and women to each other is being born out of this struggle." Christianity was unable to liberate women while they languished in economic bondage to men. Only when women gained a measure of economic independence could the Christian message of gender equality be heard.[20]

Not everyone in the second Klan, of course, had such a positive opinion of women's paid employment. A woman wrote the *Kourier Magazine* to complain that since women had entered the ranks of wage earners, they no longer gave proper attention to the rearing of children. The proper place for women with children, she insisted, was in the home, not in the workplace. Others in the Klan, however, scoffed at this, arguing that such ideas were the legacy of an earlier, less enlightened time: "No longer will man say that in the hand of woman rests the necessity of rocking a cradle only. She has within her hand the power to rule the world."[21]

Klanswomen approached the question of women's status differently than their male counterparts did. While always asserting the centrality of home life to women and to the nation, the WKKK dissented from the idealized view of home and family that was such a powerful symbol in the men's Klan. Instead, Klanswomen described the home as a place of labor for women, the site of "monotonous and grinding toil and sacrifice." The life of a homemaker, the WKKK insisted, was held in "low esteem" by the larger society and women received too little credit for their efforts. It also pictured marriage as a double-edged sword for women—at once women's crowning glory and the burden they bore. As one Klanswoman commented, marriage had always presented problems to American women: "Pilgrim mothers not only endured the hardships of the Pilgrim fathers, but what was a greater burden they had to endure the Pilgrim fathers."[22]

Even motherhood—whether the mothering of children or the nurturance of a nation—the WKKK described as women's *work*. While men portrayed child rearing as women's "glorious mission," Klanswomen called it women's "burden." A massive WKKK celebration of Mother's Day addressed the issue of motherhood:

> Throwing off her hood to reveal a modish bob, and employing a brogue, . . . the leader of the feminine hosts in the realm of New Jersey

cried "I'm glad to be here to speak today with all these girls present, because the girls of today are the mothers of tomorrow! . . . When you see
a lady that acts a little peculiar don't ridicule her. Just remember she's
somebody's mother, and she's working 24 hours a day while you're working 8."[23]

Some women's Klan leaders proposed actions that Klanswomen
could take to change their predicament. One kleagle encouraged
Klanswomen mothers to campaign collectively for an eight-hour day
for the job of mothering. Currently, she argued, women were forced to
shoulder a twenty-four-hour responsibility while men were required to
work only one-third as much time. The ultimate solution for Klanswomen lay in political action. By safeguarding the privileges of all
white Protestants, the WKKK insisted, white Protestant women would
gain better working conditions in the home and more recognition of
their contributions as wives and mothers. Like most Klan propaganda,
the argument provided no further details.[24]

Klanswomen also framed their support of white Protestant wom-
en's political and legal rights in different terms than Klansmen did.
The men's position was instrumental, intended to augment the political muscle of white Protestant men with a cadre of enfranchised
female followers. The WKKK, however, insisted that women needed
the vote for two reasons: to maintain a moral white Protestant nation
and to ensure women's rights. Even while shouldering onerous family
responsibilities, women kept the "spiritual fire of the nation burning"
and acted as the "conscience-keeper of the race." Women's efforts in-
spired "every moral law, every law regarding sanitation, prison reform, child labor, and control of liquor." Klanswomen worried that
men's support for women's rights would wane over time and urged
women to "hold fast" to the franchise and push for additional guaran-
tees of equal treatment with men.[25]

The speeches of WKKK Imperial Commander Robbie Gill show the
development of the WKKK's position on gender equality. Soon after
taking office in 1924, Gill addressed a KKK Klonvokation on "American Women," an address frequently reprinted in the Klan press. Gill
appropriated the Christian emphasis of the Klan and used it to support an agenda of women's rights. "It has never been the purpose of
God," she declared, "that woman should be the slave of man."
Women's subordination was the legacy of "primitive" theologies; in a
Protestant nation women (i.e., white Protestant women) were entitled
to "education, refinement, and honor."

Gill's analysis of women in politics differed significantly from Klansmen's use of images of helpless white Protestant women to incite racial and nationalistic hatred. Until women gained the vote, Gill argued, they were forced to exercise power by influencing men: "The greatest strength of woman's power lies in the way in which men depend upon her and are for the most part absolutely, or nearly so, helpless without her."[26]

In the twentieth century the situation changed. Women's enfranchisement gave them power that was direct and independent of men. Moreover, women's numerical majority in the population meant that women held the balance of electoral power. To Gill, it was not implausible that white Protestant women might be persuaded to vote as a bloc since women's vulnerability to the excesses of men gave them interests in common: "She knows who will suffer most if her husband or son or brother or sweetheart becomes a drunkard or a drug addict . . . if gambling grips the life of her loved one . . . if some silly, irresponsible 'affinity' breaks up her home."

The right to vote would not make individual women less vulnerable to irresponsible or dissolute husbands, Gill conceded, but a unified effort by women could eliminate the vices that led men astray. Gill dismissed the concern raised by antisuffragists (and some Klansmen) that female suffrage would create dissension if husbands and wives held different political views. It was important, she argued, that men recognize women as their political comrades, not their followers. Gill set the terms of a new gender bargain: women would maintain the home as a sanctuary for men, raise men's children, and assist them in business but in turn expected political rights and respect.[27]

Two years later the heady optimism of Gill's first address was gone. Women's suffrage was six years old, but the expected political transformation had not come about. Many women did not vote at all; those who did often voted as their husbands did. More disturbing to Gill Comer (now married), the WKKK had not been able to organize women into a voting bloc. Women did not necessarily cast their political weight behind Klan candidates or even behind candidates supporting temperance or opposing vice. Cleavages of social class, race, and region split women's electoral strength as it did men's.[28]

For Gill Comer, the challenge in 1926 was to justify the need for a women's Klan and the importance of the Klan's attention to women's issues in light of the disappointing record of the female electorate. As she often did, Gill Comer turned to history for explanation and prediction. Through a woman's eyes, Gill Comer argued, all world history was characterized by cycles of advance and retreat on women's rights; advance coinciding with Protestantism and retreat with alien and savage doctrines.

Early prehistory, what Gill Comer called the period of "savagery," was a time when women "sat back outside the circle of their masculine superiors and took the lesser pieces." A woman's responsibility in savage times was great (as keeper of the fire), but she could expect only cruel revenge if she failed and no acknowledgment if she succeeded. When the time of savagery gave way to one of barbarism, women's work (although not their status) changed. A woman was responsible for hewing wood and drawing water but remained to men nothing but "a slave, a chattel, a beast of burden." A third historical stage in Western civilization—that of chivalry—brought a slight elevation of women's status to a "pedestal of reverence and respect" but women continued to be subordinate to men.

In Gill Comer's chronology the turning point for women came with the Christian settlement of America. Early in the Christian history of the new nation, women still lacked legal and political rights—a legacy of chivalry, which exalted women but kept them from learning the "serious responsibilities" necessary for ruling the country:

> How could we be expected to know the intricacies of politics when we had never been trained to understand them? If . . . women do not stand together where they should . . . does not the explanation lie somewhat in the fact that until yesterday she was allowed to have no interests save petty ones?[29]

By the twentieth century, however, white Protestant women had attained political rights and were on their way to gaining economic and social rights as well. Men in the Klan, Gill Comer counseled, should not be discouraged that women lacked political savvy to recognize and act on the interests of white Protestant Americans. Women needed additional time and training to complete their political education. The Klan movement would eventually benefit if it continued to cultivate its female constituency.

Gill Comer's next printed address, in 1928, noted that women had enjoyed equality of opportunity for only a century and the franchise for less than a decade. Again she defended women against the charge of political ineptitude: "Some men speak sneeringly of the fact that we have not yet learned how to use it any BETTER than they, when the remarkable thing is that we are using it as WELL."[30]

In previous speeches, Gill Comer credited enlightened men with giving women the opportunity to advance. By 1928, however, Gill Comer shifted credit for increases in women's status from men's largess to the impersonal advance of technology and economic development. Time-saving inventions for the household, she argued, released women from the slavery of many kinds of household drudgery, and the automobile lessened the isolation of many women, especially those in rural areas. Women were now freed to pursue the social, political, and intellectual concerns that men's lives had always allowed. Women had the time and the means to meet other women, exchange information, and ponder mutual concerns. Moreover, increasing employment opportunities for women meant that they were no longer dependent on the economic beneficence of men. Casting in positive terms an outcome deeply feared by men, Gill Comer declared: "Woman does not now have to accept the first man who asks her hand in marriage. . . . She may choose her time for marriage, or, if she wishes, she may choose not to marry at all and endure no reproach from the world."

Gill Comer spoke of the need for women to have equal power with men in marriage, to be free to stay unmarried, and to be treated as equals in political and economic life. Drawing on her personal experiences, Gill Comer even spoke of tensions in her role as head of the women's Klan:

> Man, by habit, speaks his mind freely on great questions. Woman often hesitates to do so. . . . I feel my limitations, I believe, far more than could any man of equivalent position and experience. I hesitate to say the things that are in my heart lest I may not be taken seriously, lest I may be misunderstood by men and women alike. . . . It is my heritage as a woman.

Gill Comer's support for women's rights did not preclude supporting gender inequality when it would benefit women. Like leaders of women's labor unions and consumer leagues at the time, Gill Comer argued that women needed to hold fast to existing doctrines that granted special protection to women, even if these were based on antiquated notions of gender inequality. Taking pains to separate herself and the women's Klan from feminist "extremists," Gill Comer insisted that women should have special safeguards in industry to compensate for their physical limitations and allow them to compete economically with men and that they should be excused from the military.[31]

Although she supported white Protestant women's rights, Gill Comer maintained a strict view of women's and men's separate responsibilities for the home and family. Her analysis of the causes of society's moral decay is a case in point. Men contributed to moral decline with their drinking, gambling, and sexual exploits, actions that lined the pockets of the purveyors of vice and set a bad example for future generations of men: "What boy may be reproved for intemperance when he steals his whiskey or gin from his own father's illegal pocket flask?"

Women were assessed blame for a different kind of action. Women contributed to moral decline when their paid employment made them unavailable to monitor their delinquent children. Men erred by actions of vice. Women erred by departure from their traditional roles: "What daughter may be reproved for remaining with wild companions into the late hours away from home, when it is a home to which her mother only returns during the day to change her clothes and late at night to sleep?"

In 1929 the Klan's imminent collapse did not preclude a positive note in Gill Comer's address. Answering male critics of women's suffrage, she noted that her faith in women had been vindicated by the decisive influence of women's organizations in the defeat of Catholic anti-Prohibition presidential candidate Al Smith. Smith's mistake was to underestimate the clout of organized women: "Smith ought to have remembered that cradles have gone out of style, and that the hands which once rocked them are now free to cast ballots for decent candidates."[32] The WKKK, Gill Comer boasted, swayed women against voting for Smith whether or not they were members of the Klan. The women's Klan had "awakened the conscience" of women and educated them about their responsibilities to ensure the strength of Protestantism and Americanism, resulting in a large turnout of women at the polls to vote against Smith.

Robbie Gill Comer gave a final klonvokation speech in 1930 when both the women's and the men's Klans were disintegrating. In this address she reflected on the history of her women's order and summed up its accomplishments and weaknesses. The WKKK, she argued, had succeeded in its mission to provide political education to white Protestant American women. The troubles of the Klan movement need not interfere with the political momentum that white Protestant women had achieved. Yet much of the political agenda of the women's Klan remained undone. Women should continue to fight for their rights—as whites, as native-born Americans, as Protestant Christians, and, especially, as women. Gill Comer concluded with a poetic admonition to her female followers.

Be strong!
We are not here to play, to dream, to drift;
We have hard work to do, and loads to lift;
Shun not the struggle—face it; 'tis God's gift.

Be strong!
Say not, "The days are evil. Who's to blame?"
And fold the hands and acquiesce—oh shame!
Stand up, speak out, and bravely, in God's name.

Be strong!
It matters not how deep entrenched the wrong;
How hard the battle goes, the day how long;
Faint not—fight on! Tomorrow comes the sun.[33]

The contradictions and ambiguities of gender ideology were never resolved within the WKKK, just as they remained unresolved within the men's Klan. Gill Comer and her Klanswomen, many attracted to the women's Klan because it supported women's rights along with white and Protestant supremacy, continued to press for women's equality in society—if not within the Invisible Empire itself—even when support for women's rights fit uneasily with traditional Klan beliefs in Christian progress and female helplessness. Yet they were not willing to endorse any political agenda that seemed to link them with feminist "extremists." The Klan principles of white Protestant family life and the creation of the women's Klan by and within the earlier men's Klan tempered Klanswomen's full endorsement of women's equality. Klanswomen sought *rights* in politics, the economy, marriage, and the law. But they stopped far short of supporting full *equality* between white Protestant women and men.

RELATIONS BETWEEN THE WKKK AND KKK

Speeches and publications cannot fully convey how gender issues fared in the 1920s Klan. Although Klan propaganda frequently affirmed support for women's suffrage and increased legal and economic rights for women, within the order itself women were not equal to men. Repeatedly, the Klan grappled with the issue of whether the WKKK should be an autonomous organization or an auxiliary of the KKK, leading on numerous occasions to tension between the two organizations.

Although few documents describe the precise relations between local WKKK and KKK klaverns, records on the Klan in Indiana suggest that they varied among locals of the two organizations over time. At the beginning of the WKKK in Indiana, the "statement of responsibility" for Indiana Klansmen stated emphatically that the WKKK was not to be treated as an auxiliary of the KKK. No Klansmen were permitted to visit official meetings of the women's organization or to know the WKKK membership. Klanswomen were banned from KKK meetings and forbidden access to KKK membership rolls. Joint meetings of the KKK and WKKK were prohibited except between commanders or secret committees needed to ensure "a similarity of purpose."[34]

Two years later, in 1925, Indiana Klansmen reversed this policy to create an official "women's organization committee" within the men's Klan. In defense of this apparent breach of autonomy, KKK leaders argued that they would interfere with the women's order "when advice is solicited by the WKKK only" and function chiefly to promote women's Klan membership and to provide guards and transportation for WKKK klonklaves when requested. By 1927, though, the connections—as well as the tensions—between the Indiana KKK and the WKKK were more clear. Indiana's KKK Grand Dragon exhorted his fellow Klansmen to work with the women's Klan in organizing their national convention, an oddly explicit directive for Klans that prided themselves on mutual support: "The women of this Realm have always cooperated with us in a very splendid way and certainly we want to manifest a spirit of appreciation."[35]

Other evidence also hints at friction between the men's and women's Klans, especially when Klansmen perceived their female counterparts to be overstepping their bounds. When a Spencer, Indiana, KKK kleagle demanded that state officers intervene to stem a flood of anti-Klan propaganda in his area, for example, he blamed the situation on the WKKK kleagle who rebuffed his leadership and advice:

> I was informed by an organizer that first started the ladies organization in Owen County, that she was to counsel with me relative [to] matters of the Order. Things have gone from bad to worse and there is no apparent effort being made to clear the conditions. Anti propaganda is put out and the members do not know what is right or wrong relative to the organization. . . . I have advised the local representative and nothing is done by her to correct the thing, I think it is time that one of us take some decided steps to remedy the matter.[36]

Klansmen spoke more approvingly of WKKK leaders who mixed Klan work with deference to men. The commander of the Ohio Grand

Dragon's Guard noted the harmony between male and female Klans in Ohio and cited a "ties vs. aprons" event in which each Klansman bought a necktie and then escorted to dinner the Klanswoman whose apron matched his tie. He also recalled the kindly nature of Mary Weygandt, then a kleagle in the Ohio WKKK, who recognized the leadership of the male Klan in her address to an Ohio klorero (officials' meeting): "Mrs. Weygandt sketched briefly the situation of the women's organization and asked for the support of the Klansmen of Ohio. She was warmly received and injected a spirit of hope and courage into the meeting at the outset."[37]

Mixed-sex Klan cultural events mirrored the sexual division of labor of the alien world. Klanswomen cooked, transported, and served food at Klan rallies. Klansmen directed traffic, guarded the rally site, and drank near-beer. The women's Klan might advocate women's rights, but they usually performed traditional roles at Klan events. Even high-level officials of the WKKK were not exempt from tending to the needs of Klansmen. One of the most prominent national WKKK lecturers found herself pressed into service as "sort of a secretary" for a visiting male Klan speaker in northern Indiana.[38]

The women's Klan steadfastly maintained that it was not governed by the KKK or by individual Klansmen. Despite denials by WKKK officials, it is clear that links between the KKK and the WKKK were maintained through personal, as well as ideological, ties. These connections among female and male Klan leaders—and the problems they generated—provide another vantage point from which to judge the extent of autonomy of the women's Klan.

For the most part, conflicts among WKKK and KKK organizations revolved around money. Gender ideologies and the place of women in the Klan movement—the ostensible causes of intra-Klan battles—were in fact secondary concerns to Klan leaders scrabbling for larger shares of the Klan's financial empire. To rank-and-file members of the Klan, especially to Klanswomen, however, issues of gender were important. Klanswomen defended their organizational turf against inroads by Klansmen in the name of women's political autonomy as their leaders battled for monetary gain.

Most internal Klan disputes and conflicts left no visible traces from which to construct a historical account. However, legal wrangling in three states—Arkansas, Oregon, and Pennsylvania—brought the normally secret inner workings of the WKKK and the KKK to the public eye. These disputes let us assess the connections between the male and female Klans and officials of these orders on both local and national levels.

The influence of Judge James Comer of Little Rock in the affairs of the Arkansas WKKK became visible in a prolonged series of court actions. A member of the Imperial Kloncilium of the KKK, Comer had ties to the women's Klan that dated to its charter in 1923 in Little Rock. He worked to persuade the Klonvokation to ratify the organization of the WKKK and personally loaned the group $8,000 to get started. In return the WKKK retained Comer as Imperial Klonsel (attorney), a position that made him a visible presence and a frequent public spokesperson for the organization.

Controversy over Judge Comer's role in the women's order began almost immediately. A year after the creation of the WKKK, Imperial Commander Markwell was toppled from her position and replaced— not by Alice Cloud, her organizational heir apparent, but by Robbie Gill, a close associate (who soon became the wife) of Judge Comer. The coup within the women's Klan immediately sparked rumors that a small group of Klansmen led by Judge Comer controlled the affairs of the allegedly autonomous WKKK.[39]

The widely publicized court action that stemmed from Gill Comer's ascendancy to power in the WKKK gives an unusually detailed and valuable look at the internal workings of the women's Klan and its connection to KKK officials. In August 1925 Cloud and two other Klanswomen from Dallas, D. B. George (the Chief Imperial Klokan) and Flora Alexander, filed suit against Gill Comer and Comer in Little Rock's chancery court for mishandling WKKK funds. They charged the Comers with waste, extravagance, and fraudulent misappropriation of the WKKK treasury for their private enrichment. Further, the plaintiffs demanded that Cloud be designated Imperial Commander until a new election could be held, citing their fear that the Comers might retaliate by banishing them from the WKKK.[40]

The fears of the dissident Klanswomen proved justified. Gill Comer removed Cloud and George from their WKKK offices, which increased their anger. They immediately filed a second suit against Gill Comer, charging her with contempt of court for illegally suspending them and for misappropriating $34,666 from the WKKK. Although Hiram

Evans, the head of the KKK, sent a telegram pledging his support to Gill Comer, the plaintiffs filed yet another suit, seeking to recover $17,850 in salary and benefits that included two automobiles and a $750 crown that Gill Comer had gained during her time in office. They also charged that Judge Comer's law firm received $18,000 in legal fees from his wife's organization.[41]

Although the presiding legal officer of the court, a failed anti-Klan candidate for governor, claimed that he lacked jurisdiction to decide the matter, he gave the dissenting Klanswomen permission to examine the WKKK's books. For 1925, these accounts showed that the WKKK took in an impressive $321,809.03 in income from dues and sales and spent all but $18,000. Much of that money, according to the plaintiffs, went to the Comers, who amassed a fortune through the sale of WKKK robes, helmets, regalia, and supplies. Further, Judge Comer sold a factory that manufactured WKKK robes, valued at $23,000, to the WKKK for $72,000—a profit of $49,000. Each Comer earned $1,000 a month from the WKKK and received almost $20,000 in additional payments and more than $20,000 in travel expenses. The plaintiffs documented how in seven months the Comers squandered $70,000 of WKKK funds, equipping WKKK headquarters with goldfish, songbirds, police dogs, flowers, and a piano and purchasing for their personal use a $5,000 luxury sedan. Ultimately, the plaintiffs' suit was dismissed when they failed to submit $250 for court costs and Cloud dropped her claim for Gill Comer's salary. But the attempted suit had long-lasting repercussions for the Comers.[42]

PENNSYLVANIA

In 1927, competing factions of the men's Klan filed suit in the U.S. District Court for the Western District of Pennsylvania, each charging the other and leaders of the WKKK with financial mismanagement and illegal practices. The scores of affidavits, depositions, and other court documents from this case provide an unusually detailed look at the workings of the Klan and the complicated relations between the KKK and the WKKK.[43]

From the beginning, Pennsylvania Klansmembers suspected Hiram Evans of having undue influence over the women's order.[44] William Likins, a Prohibitionist and the author of an anti-Klan tract, charged that all leaders of the national WKKK owed their positions to Evans and claimed to have seen a facsimile of a contract giving ownership of the women's order to Evans as his personal property. Leaders of the women's Klan denied the allegations.[45]

Two incidents drew attention to the relation of the KKK to the Pennsylvania WKKK. One problem revolved around money, a frequent cause of controversy within the Klan. When the Pennsylvania WKKK was organized, it arranged with the state men's Klan to rebate one dollar for every woman who joined the WKKK through the KKK office, thus encouraging Klansmen to enlist their female relatives and friends in the women's order. Mary Goodwin, the WKKK Pennsylvania kleagle, also agreed to reward cooperative Klansmen by selecting their wives as kleagles to work on commission.

This mutually beneficial alliance between the Pennsylvania WKKK and KKK organizations soured when Klan Haven, a WKKK-sponsored Klan orphanage housing forty children, was destroyed by fire. As the WKKK scrambled to raise money to rebuild the building, the men's order, backed by the national offices of the WKKK, moved to establish joint control of the orphanage. Goodwin resisted. James Comer tried to have her removed from office, claiming that she had personally profited from her WKKK office and had delayed chartering WKKK locals. Claudia Goodrich, a sister of Hiram Evans, was then dispatched to Pennsylvania to challenge Goodwin. Goodwin resigned and was succeeded by Martha Turnley, who approved a plan for joint control over Klan Haven. Accusations that the men's Klan and Judge Comer were benefiting financially from the Klan orphanage continued.[46]

A second clash occurred during the 1924 presidential campaign when Likins, then campaign manager for the American party, arranged with Goodwin to have a candidate speak at the WKKK state convention. Five days before the convention Evans sent Goodwin a telegram that threatened to halt the state WKKK convention if it allowed the candidate, Gilbert Nations, to speak and that asserted Evans's authority over both the men's and the women's Klans. Likins felt that Evans opposed Nations because Evans wanted to sell the Klan's political support to a better-funded and more visible political party.[47]

Mary King, a kleagle in the Chester, Pennsylvania, WKKK, argued that the problem was not only Judge Comer and Hiram Evans, but also Robbie Gill Comer herself. "We women," King asserted, "entered the Klan for the highest of ideals, working for the betterment of the nation [but] the actual working out of the ideals has not been so good."[48] In an exchange between King and Mary Weygandt of the WKKK national office, Weygandt admitted that Gill Comer's crown cost $30,000 but said that the uproar among Klanswomen had made the crown "thorns to her since she has it." Further, Weygandt claimed that members of a "militant organization" like the WKKK had no right to question an officer. After her confrontation with Weygandt, King was arrested for larceny of WKKK funds (a tactic that the Philadelphia WKKK also used against a dissident). Although acquitted by a jury, King was officially banished from the WKKK. The Pennsylvania WKKK klaverns of Philadelphia and Chester voted to secede from the national organization until it provided "clean Klankraft."[49]

Other Pennsylvania WKKK chapters experienced similar problems. The Canwin WKKK local—the state's largest, with a membership of fourteen hundred—was headed by Pearl Cantey, the wife of a Klan official. As Canwin Klanswomen discovered, this tie did not prevent the KKK from cheating them out of their fair share of proceeds from joint WKKK-KKK events. In Philadelphia, their Klan comrades charged two Klanswomen and one Klansman with immoral relations. The Klanswomen were promptly suspended from the WKKK local while the Klansman was made treasurer of his KKK local.[50]

OREGON

According to the account by Lem Dever, KKK publicity director, problems between the Oregon WKKK and KKK arose because the women's order was created to replace the state LOTIE as a secret money-making scheme for Oregon's premier Klan family, the Giffords. Mae E. Gifford was the Imperial Kligrapp of the national WKKK, her husband, Fred Gifford, the Oregon KKK Grand Dragon.

R. H. Sawyer, a Portland minister of the Christian church, initially headed the Oregon LOTIEs. When he left the Klan, control over the women's order passed to "Judge" Rush N. Davis, a KKK officer from Shreveport, Louisiana, and husband of Lillian Grigg Davis, a later WKKK Imperial Kladd. Davis proclaimed himself ruler, emperor, pontiff, and boss of the women's organization. In cahoots with Grand Dragon Gifford, Davis merged the Portland LOTIEs into the newly created WKKK, over the opposition of the woman who headed the Portland LOTIE, whom Dever referred to as "Mother Counselor."[51]

The struggle between Davis and Mother Counselor for control over the Portland women's order assumed legendary status. In May 1923 Davis broke into a meeting of the LOTIE in Portland's Redmen's Hall and rushed toward the enthroned and guarded Mother Counselor, demanding that she turn over the group's charter so he could deliver it to the Klan. Dever records the frustrations of male Klan leaders faced by recalcitrant female "followers":

> In an impudent, loud, and threatening manner Davis demanded that the Charter of the organization be surrendered instantly to him. The Ladies calmly regarded him as an obstreperous and insolent intruder, or as a rare and interesting bug. Highly excited, Davis clamored in dictatorial language. The Mother Counselor smilingly held the Charter in her hand. Her attitude was one of serene command and contempt.[52]

Davis physically attacked Mother Counselor in an attempt to seize the charter. Immediately women from the LOTIE Honor Guard "swarmed upon him, pummeling, pounding and hammering" Davis as he cried for help. When a passing policeman finally rescued Davis, "lifted him clear of the Ladies and carried him out of the hall, holding him by an ear," the Mother Counselor led the victorious ladies in a triumphant chorus of the "Star-Spangled Banner." Despite this incident, the Davis and Gifford Klan families prevailed and the Portland LOTIE chapter disbanded. A more compliant WKKK klavern replaced it.[53]

Dissatisfaction was not confined to the women's Klans of Pennsylvania and Oregon. The women's Klan of Little Rock, Arkansas (WKKK's national headquarters chapter), also seceded from the national organization to protest Judge Comer's influence in the WKKK. In its statement of defection, the Little Rock WKKK charged that "we are forced to believe that the women's organization is dominated by men, which is contrary to our principles of women, by women and for women."

WKKK klaverns in various parts of the country experienced similar tensions with Klansmen. The Ohio women's Klans of Massillion and Columbus won legal injunctions to prevent Gill Comer or Comer from interfering with their actions or banishing members. Other dissenting Ohio Klanswomen threatened to organize state chapters independent of the Comers. In Texas, Klanswomen sued Judge Comer for interfering with the legitimate business of the women's Klan, and Gill Comer promptly banished them from the order. In Michigan, clashes between the women's and men's Klans ultimately ended in alien civil courts when the WKKK hired a lawyer to recover a portion of their treasury that Klansmen had seized.[54]

Such conflict makes it apparent that the vaunted claims of the WKKK that they were organized by women and for women were not entirely accurate. Men who led the KKK, especially James Comer and Hiram Evans, had a great deal of influence within the women's order. Yet to dismiss the women's order as nothing but a puppet auxiliary of the men's order does not capture the reality of the relations between the KKK and the WKKK. Klanswomen protested when Klansmen overstepped the boundary between supporting and dominating the women's organization. Whether WKKK klaverns judged men's actions to be acceptable varied considerably. Some women's Klans saw themselves as the helpmates of the men's group, serving coffee and refreshments at Klan rallies and coordinating Klan social engagements. Others sought a more independent route and complained mightily when they were treated as second-class citizens within the Klan. The spotty historical record left by both organizations makes it impossible to determine the precise conditions under which women's Klans pushed for additional autonomy or settled for a wifely role in the Klan. It is clear, though, that autonomy of the WKKK—like the understandings of gender ideology itself—was far from a settled question in the 1920s Klan movement.

ATTACKS ON KLANSWOMEN

It was not only within the Invisible Empire that the role of Klanswomen was controversial. Anti-Klan forces, too, seized on the existence of Klanswomen to ridicule and condemn the second Klan. If the Klan juggled reactionary politics and some support for gender equality, anti-Klan Progressives often used misogynistic vitriol. As early as 1922 opponents of the Klan derided the KKK by suggesting that Elizabeth Tyler was its true leader. After the WKKK was created, anti-Klan forces pointed to Klanswomen as the ultimate proof of the moral bankruptcy of the Invisible Empire.

Drawing on dualistic images of women as virgins or whores, Klan opponents portrayed Klanswomen in two ways. Either Klanswomen were politically innocent and naive and thus susceptible to the political and sexual enticements of Klansmen or Klanswomen were politically savvy and sexually promiscuous women able to manipulate Klansmen for their own purposes. In either case, anti-Klan forces pointed out, Klan meetings gave a ready excuse and Klan meeting halls a convenient location for "assignation purposes" between Klanswomen and Klansmen.[55]

Klan opponents used the same duality to describe married Klanswomen. Some were the unfortunate dupes of overbearing Klan husbands who insisted that their wives join the Invisible Empire. Others were aggressive women married to pathetic henpecked husbands who allowed their wives to neglect duty to home and family to pursue political goals. In either case, anti-Klan forces agreed, Klan membership was devastating to marriage and family life.

Although Klan opponents greatly exaggerated the marital problems of Klanswomen, there is evidence that some non-Klan husbands resented their wives' involvement. A Muncie, Indiana, man told interviewers for the Lynds' Middletown study that his divorce was due to "the g-d Klan," adding that "I couldn't stand them around any longer." In another divorce suit, a man blamed his wife's devotion to the WKKK for her neglect of the children and home, despite his pleas that she abandon Klan work.[56]

Two major figures in the anti-Klan movement, George Dale of Muncie, Indiana, and Ben Lindsey of Denver, Colorado, exemplify how anti-Klan activists used women's participation as a basis for attacking the Invisible Empire. Both Dale and Lindsey suffered personal assaults by the KKK for their anti-Klan work. Yet to recount the terror of the Klan's attacks each man seized on the image of violent Klanswomen.

George Dale, publisher of the *Muncie Post-Democrat*, waged a bitter protracted war on the Klan in the Klan stronghold of Muncie, Indiana. Dale charged that Klan members dominated the Delaware County courts and that the city administration of Muncie was subservient to Klan interests. His newspaper published lists of those reputed to be Muncie Klansmen, among them many of the city's officials and business leaders.[57]

Dale became incensed when he discovered that the Delaware County Klan was recruiting women and children into the organization. Klan parades through Muncie in 1923 gave women a prominent—and provocative—role. As Klanswomen passed by, if male bystanders did not remove their hats in respect they faced physical threats by Klansmen. Dale was indignant. "All men who have a spark of manhood left in their veins," he thundered, should refuse to salute.[58] At that, the Klan counterattacked in force. Klansmen physically assaulted, reviled, and threatened Dale and his family. When he did not end his editorials against the Klan, Dale found himself in legal trouble, repeatedly arrested by a Klan-dominated police and held in contempt of its judiciary.

Klansmen in the municipal administration caused most of his legal troubles, yet Dale's account focused on the role of Klanswomen. In an editorial entitled "Bloodthirsty Women," Dale depicted the audience of Klanswomen at his 1923 trial as "bob-haired Amazons" demanding his death. His account attacked both the politics of Klanswomen and their usurpation of men's rightful places:

> Women of the Ku Klux Klan had been busy the day before telephoning to their sister Amazons of Hate to be on hand bright and early in the court room. Figuratively speaking a victim was about to be crucified and the gentle creatures crashed the court room door in hordes in order to dabble in the blood of the captive. . . . One young woman, a tall, coarse featured, bob-haired brunette who stood in the crowd at the south side of the court room inquired audibly, "Why don't they take him out and hang him?"[59]

Dale particularly objected to women who "abandoned" husband and children for Klan politics. He recounted one such morality tale, involving Edna Walling, a "young wife" whom unscrupulous Klan recruiters convinced to join the organization in spite of her Roman Catholic background. Shocked by her allegiance to the Klan, her old friends promptly shunned her. Then a full-fledged Klanswoman, Edna cashed a bad check, was arrested, and deserted by her new Klan friends. Had she maintained her rightful "place in the home" instead of affiliating with an "unscrupulous political camp," Dale concluded, Edna Walling would not have been disgraced.[60]

Dale also assailed the masculinity of Klansmen and the husbands of Klanswomen. In his editorials Dale ridiculed men who were forced to tend to children while their wives cavorted with sister Klanswomen, suggesting that Klan wives had become the real household heads. "It is real fun to see men waiting with autos at the Kamelia [WKKK] meetings, to take the boss home. It sure takes a fat head Koo to wait around for hours with a machine full of kids waiting till midnight to take Ma home."[61]

Men deserted wives who joined the women's organization over their husbands' objections, Dale claimed, and wives fled husbands who "enlisted in the army of Satan." Even when divorce was not the outcome, he argued, the Klan undermined marriages by giving men a convenient and unverifiable excuse for all-night absences from the home. Conformity to the rules and rituals of Klankraft, for women and men alike, placed yet another concern above the institution of marriage, "with the inevitable result" of divorce.[62]

Benjamin B. Lindsey, a Denver judge internationally recognized as an authority on juvenile court systems, came under attack from the Denver Klan for his support of companionate marriage, lenient divorce laws, and birth control and for his opposition to the Klan. A Klan candidate narrowly lost to Lindsey in a judicial election, then filed for a recount of the votes, claiming electoral fraud in a predominantly Jewish section of Denver. The Klan candidate lost the recount but appealed the decision through the courts and was awarded the judicial post by the Colorado Supreme Court in 1927, two years after his death from suicide. In disgust, Lindsey burned the records of his court in a "shame bonfire" and moved out of state.[63]

Lindsey's account of his battle with the Klan, like Dale's, made special note of the role of Klanswomen. The antagonism shown him by the women's Klan angered Lindsey, in light of his support for judicial and legislative issues to protect women and children. "Like screaming furies," Lindsey wrote, women of the Klan led the assault on his position. "The conduct of the women at meetings cannot be likened to anything but that of women before the Tribunal at the French Revolution, demanding the blood of their victims." He recounted that one woman screamed in his face at an anti-Klan meeting, addressing him as "you cur, you dirty cur . . . you are not 100 percent American, you are against the Klan."[64]

Lindsey, like Dale and others who actively opposed the Klan of the 1920s, made the participation of women in the Klan an easy target for denouncing the order. Just as Klansmen wrestled with the presence of women within the order, men outside the Klan had reservations and objections to women's active role in politics. Women who overstepped the traditional boundaries of feminine involvement in politics represented to anti-Klan activists the fundamental corruption and degeneracy of a movement of aggressive women and henpecked men.

The symbolism of womanhood had power for the second Ku Klux Klan, as it had in the original Klan. But the Klan's decision to admit women as Klan members changed the terms for discussing gender issues. The abstraction of white womanhood gave way to the reality of actual women, whose political agendas in the Klan did not always correspond to those of Klansmen. Gender issues—the roles of women and men in family and politics—intruded into Klan politics. On this terrain competing forces within the Klan contended for power. But battles over gender took different forms among the leaders and the rank and file. Among leaders, conflicts over gender often hid conflicts over personal access to the financial spoils of the organization. On the local level, however, debates over gender issues reflected very different concerns. The next chapter explores some of these concerns by examining the Indiana Klan's use of sexuality and morality to recruit women into the Invisible Empire.

CHAPTER III

Battling the Seductive Allurements

To many who enlisted in the fiery crusade of the 1920s Klan, racial, religious, and national antagonisms were *moral* issues. The Klan, its leaders and members insisted, did not preach hatred and intolerance of any group. It sought only to defend traditional moral standards against the seductive allurements of modern society. And thus the Klan battled those groups—primarily Jews, Catholics, and blacks—who it claimed promoted vice and immorality.[1]

Such claim to moral righteousness is a common feature of political movements. Its political power is twofold. First, wrapping political issues in the mantle of moral concern obscures underlying political agendas. Throughout U.S. history, groups have framed—and thereby concealed—conflicts over racial inequities, definitions of family, and community power, among others, as questions of morality. Second, the cloak of moral concern amplifies political passions. From the Klan's crusade of racial hatred in homogeneous communities of the 1920s to its vicious contemporary campaigns against gay rights, moral concern personalizes and gives urgency to political issues remote from the particular lives of their adherents.

Although morality is a common political symbol, each political movement constructs it differently. Even the first and second Klans differed considerably in their definition and use of morality. The first KKK, like its immediate successors such as the Guardians of Liberty, linked sexual morality to racial and religious hatreds by depicting Jewish, Catholic, and black men as sexual savages who sought to quench their insatiable sexual appetites with white Gentile women. These political movements defined gender as a central aspect of morality: white women were victims of immoral black, Jewish, and Catholic men.[2]

Morality remained inextricably tied to ideas of gender and symbols of white womanhood in the second Klan, but this Klan incorporated ideas and rhetoric from women's rights to define its moral terrain. Caught between conventional and modern views of women's rights, it played on both images in presenting itself as an agency of moral reform. The Klan ranted against the victimization of white Protestant women by Jewish businessmen, sexually sadistic Catholic priests, and uncivilized black men. At the same time, however, it aimed its promise—to enforce marital monogamy, punish wife beaters, and restrict alcohol, gambling, and other vices—at abuses by white Protestant husbands. The second Klan used its predecessor's imagery of women's victimization by immoral forces to inflame white Protestant men's political passions. It addressed female recruits, in contrast, with a language of rights, arguing that vice and immorality denigrated white Protestant women and that Klanswomen had the right, and the duty, to end it.

Many white Protestant women heard the Klan's message about morality and embraced it readily. Klanswomen across the country marched under banners proclaiming We Stand for True Godliness, Purity, and Loyalty; We Are the Foe of Vice, the Friends of the Innocent; Love Thy Neighbor as Thyself but Leave His Wife Alone; and Wife Beaters Beware. Women's Klan chapters often described their mission in self-righteous terms, as safeguarding public virtue and as keeping "the moral standards of the community at a high plane." The underlying message of klannish morality was effective, too. Klanswomen and Klansmen across the country responded to the Klan's appeal and launched a frenzied assault upon "immoral" Jews, Catholics, and blacks.[3]

The Klan's morality campaigns succeeded in normalizing fear and hatred of minorities. When the second Klan attacked racial, ethnic, and religious groups, it did so by portraying them—especially minority men—as ruthless beasts who operated outside the moral code that shaped civilized life. In this way, the Klan deepened an existing perception among white Protestants that nonwhites and non-Protestants were strange, alien, and inexplicable. Disguising a viciously racist, anti-Semitic, and anti-Catholic agenda as a moral crusade was particularly effective in homogeneous white Protestant communities in which racial and religious minorities posed no immediate economic or social competition to the majority population. It allowed the Klan to denounce Jews, Catholics, and blacks as evil, even as devils, and as a potent threat to white Protestant moral values.

MORALITY, BIGOTRY, AND WOMEN'S RIGHTS

The Klan's morality crusade, like contemporaneous movements for temperance and moral reform, attempted to integrate the language of women's rights with an agenda of support for conventional moral standards. The Klan differed, however, in the ferocity of its insistence that women show their support for women's rights by lashing out against immigrants, blacks, Catholics, and Jews. How did white Protestant women come to identify their interests as women with the Klan's racist, anti-Catholic, and anti-Semitic agenda? The life history of Bishop Alma Bridwell White, an evangelical preacher, women's suffragist, and influential Klan spokesperson, exemplifies a common process whereby women integrated these seemingly disparate political ideologies.

Bishop White's transformation from minister to Klan propagandist is detailed in voluminous autobiographical and political writing, including thirty-five books, two hundred hymns, and six edited periodicals. In these works, White traces her Klan partisanship to a lifetime of indignities and inequitable treatment suffered because of her sex.

According to White, even her birth was a disappointment to her large and struggling rural Kentucky family who desperately wanted another son. At the age of sixteen, eager to escape her family, she embraced spirituality and tried to join the ministry. Few Protestant denominations accepted female ministers, however, so White's pastor urged her to marry a minister and pursue religion as a clergyman's wife. She did, marrying Kent White and preaching in his Denver church.[4]

Alma's preaching—described as "heavenly dynamite" by her many followers—was so successful that she soon outgrew her role as minister's wife and began to hold revivals in gold mining camps and rural areas throughout the West. Freed from her husband's watchful eye, Alma preached her own version of holiness and attacked official

Protestantism as "hopelessly apostate." Not surprisingly, Protestant ministers, including her husband, were irate that an unauthorized preacher—a woman at that—was attacking established religion. Alma wrote, "It was most humiliating to churchmen to have a woman wield the sword of truth, when no recognition had been given her by ecclesiastical authorities, and she was supposed to have no place except that of a servant."[5]

In response, Alma left the Methodist church and organized her own holiness sect, the Pentecostal Union church (renamed the Pillar of Fire, in 1917) with forty pastors and evangelists. The Pillar of Fire (POF) claimed to be the true descendant of pure Methodism with its doctrines of conversion and sanctification, faith healing, and propriety of women and men as preachers. From her POF post, Alma preached the literal accuracy of the Bible and declared war on "immoral modernism," including Protestant ministers who used their religious positions to conceal a lust for women, tobacco, and money. She decried the social tragedies caused by the "incorrigibility of sexual passions," arguing that "sex infatuation" leads to crime and depravity. She was equally passionate about men's weakness for liquor, which ruined the lives of their dependents, and insisted that the liquor industry was supported by Catholic politicians.[6]

Alma was intensely involved with every detail of the POF. She conducted daily revival meetings, missions, and afternoon prayer meetings, often in the family's parlor and living room. As primary evangelist for the new church, she traveled extensively, often pushing herself to physical collapse. Within two years the fledgling movement had a Bible school and a church auditorium in Denver; several years later it added a new headquarters in New Jersey that boasted an auditorium, a dozen farm houses, a college, two preparatory schools, and a printing plant. The POF never grew to be a very large religious movement but it eventually established seven divinity schools, two radio stations, and a liberal arts college. White herself received considerable fame as the first female bishop of a Christian church in the United States.[7]

In the midst of her spectacular religious success Alma's marriage collapsed. Declaring that he was irritated at being known as "Mrs. Alma White's husband," Kent joined a rival pentecostal sect and publicly repudiated the POF. Kent, Alma wrote, believed that "on account of sex he should be the head [of the family], that it was the wife's duty to submit to a place of subordination."[8] Rather than treat the end of her marriage as a private shame, Alma publicized her marital troubles

in a lengthy book of verse, *My Heart and My Husband,* which included copies of the couple's letters and legal papers:

> I loved him more than tongue can tell,
> Alas! my love he spurned,
> And far away in distant lands
> From me his face he turned.

In rhyming couplets, Bishop White painted a picture of a man whose
sense of masculinity was undermined by the preaching success of his
wife and who turned to a cult to humiliate her:

> The leaders of his cult had said
> That woman should submit
> To man's own wish and purposes
> And waver not a whit.
> "Yea, glory of the man is she
> With no mind of her own,
> When meekly she sits by and waits
> For his will to be done."

Even visionary religious men, Alma deplored, had no desire to expand
women's roles in their vision of the ideal church:

> The women in this new regime
> Must meekly sit and learn;
> Should they attempt to speak in church
> Their message men should spurn.[9]

Faced with both marital and religious friction over her conduct,
Alma became a public advocate for women's rights in the church and
in secular society. Discrimination between the sexes, she argued, was
utterly in opposition to the principles of the New Testament. Laws
that favored men over women were "unjust and tyrannical, and calcu-
lated to block the wheels of progress and bring the wrath of God upon
nations."[10]

By the early 1910s White's desire to promote women's rights and
morality turned her efforts in a viciously anti-Catholic and anti-
Semitic direction. In a political shift that would later cause her to promote the Ku Klux Klan, White argued that the Catholic church was
the major world force opposing women's suffrage and gender equality,
exemplified by the extreme degradation of women in Latin America
and in those European nations controlled by the Catholic church.
Women had been barred from the electorate for most of U.S. history,
she argued, because Catholic politicians feared that female voters
would remove them from office. White credited Protestantism with the

women's suffrage amendment, "the triumph of the Cross in the liberation of women." She also argued for passage of the Equal Rights Amendment (ERA) to remove the remaining barriers to women's progress. Prophetically, she cautioned that passage of the ERA would be difficult.[11]

White saw her periodical, the *Good Citizen,* as a mouthpiece for "exposing political Romanism in its efforts to gain the ascendancy in the U.S.," a weapon "against immorality and crime, the white slave traffic, the liquor curse, the oppression of women, cruelty to children, and other kindred evils" and a vehicle "to expose science, falsely so-called, and the foolish theories of evolution." The same doctrines were the basis for her popular sermons, a mishmash of admonitions against whipping children ("a tyranny under the cloak of parental authority"), pronouncements in favor of women in the ministry, diatribes against scientific modernism, and brutally anti-Catholic convictions.[12]

Although White never publicly announced her membership in the Klan, she lectured across the country on behalf of the Invisible Empire and wrote three books heralding the Klan's contributions to Americanism and morality. One book even featured a letter of commendation by Hiram Evans and a cartoon of the Statue of Liberty removing a Klan hood over the caption "Liberty Found Under the Hood of the K.K.K."[13]

White's lectures on behalf of the Klan broadcast old rumors of Catholic sexual depravity, including allegations of "papal prisons" where unwilling girls were kept isolated and in bondage and stories of nuns used as slaves for priests. The only hope for these pathetic victims of Romanist debauchery, White argued, was the sympathy of other women who could use their newly won vote to "liberate the victims of their sex" and who could join the Klan and go in person to rescue girls trapped behind convent walls.[14]

White was also violently anti-Semitic. She charged Jews with secretly financing the Catholic empire, making immoral films, keeping motion pictures and other "vile places of amusement" open on Sunday, and procuring young Protestant women to work in movies, dance halls, sweatshops, department stores, and white slave dens. The Jewish-owned fashion industry, White argued, foisted immodest clothing on women through "the powerful edicts of fashion." In moral standards, White thundered, a Jewish man had "no code to restrain him in his dealings with Gentile women." White's portrayal of how Jewish men victimized Protestant girls was deliberately provocative:

A girl in the rural district dreams and reads of adventure. Her parents are usually unsophisticated as to the pitfalls that await their daughter in large cities and when a smooth-talking seducer comes around and offers her a lucrative position in the theatre they are captivated by the prospects of a bright future.[15]

The evils of Catholicism and Judaism took up most of White's work on behalf of the Klan, but she also embraced white supremacy as a way to defend her audience against racial integration and miscegenation. White supported the Klan's racist agenda, even when it contradicted the principle of equality between white women and white men. She evoked white men's fears of losing both racial and male supremacy, for example, with a warning that black men were organizing societies in which all members pledged to marry white women.[16]

Even though White attributed most of women's oppression to Jewish, black, and Catholic men, she was not optimistic that white Protestant men would join with their female counterparts in the fight for women's equality. Protestant men, she feared, were likely to be "unyielding" in opposition to gender equality since they benefited directly from the current situation. White noted that even Protestant male clergy who used women as missionaries, as servants in church kitchens, as advocates for increasing wages of male preachers, and as beggars for church enterprises did little to support women's rights.[17]

White's anti-Catholic, anti-Semitic, and racist message fit well into the Klan's efforts to convince white Protestant women that their collective interests as women, as well as their racial and religious interests, were best served by joining the Klan. Although the motivations of individual Klanswomen are impossible to determine, it is clear that many WKKK leaders and at least some local klaverns found this combination appealing.

MORALITY CRUSADES AND ANTI-VICE ACTIVITIES IN INDIANA

Ideas of women's rights were incorporated into the Klan's morality agenda in a number of ways. Klan propagandists like Alma White used morality to link political intolerance to women's rights by arguing that Catholics, Jews, and blacks promoted degeneracy and encouraged women's subordination. Others went further, proclaiming the Klan's willingness to protect the rights of white Protestant women against any threat, even those emanating from white Protestant men.

But to a great extent the Klan's use of moral issues relied on traditional notions of women as victims and women as susceptible to immoral behavior. The situation in Indiana is a case in point.

Indiana was a particularly fertile field for the bigoted appeal to morality used by Bishop White and other Klan spokespersons. That it was may seem odd, for Indiana in the 1920s was one of the most racially, culturally, and religiously homogeneous states. The history of racism and intolerance in Indiana, however, suggests that the Klan's appearance in the state simply made visible deep racist and bigoted attitudes that many of the state's white native-born Protestants had long held. Indiana's tradition of racism, anti-Catholicism, and moral vigilantism fit well into the Klan's political agenda.

Slavery was abolished in Indiana before the 1863 Emancipation Proclamation, but pro-slavery and overt racist sentiment was common among whites throughout the nineteenth and early twentieth centuries. Much of this sentiment was codified in Indiana law. An 1831 law, for example, required blacks moving to Indiana to post a bond against being a public charge and for a pledge of good behavior. The 1851 Indiana Constitution prohibited blacks and mulattoes from coming into the state and penalized those who encouraged them to do so. Neither statute was enforced often, but both indicate the climate of hostility toward blacks.

Blacks constituted less than 5 percent of the Indiana population in the late nineteenth and early twentieth centuries. In the counties where the 1920s Klan became strongest, the nonwhite population was negligible (except in Marion County, which includes Indianapolis). Many whites I interviewed could not recall having ever seen a black person during their childhood, except at a distance during trips to large cities. The small size of the state's black population, however, did not diminish the fear and loathing in which blacks in Indiana were held by the majority white population. Indiana had the most drastic measures against interracial marriage of any Northern state; lynchings in the rural areas of Indiana terrorized the black population. Twenty black persons were lynched between 1865 and 1903, some by masked mobs. No one was ever convicted for the deaths. As late as 1930 in the industrial town of Marion, Indiana, a white mob lynched three black men.

After 1910 the black population of Indiana grew, increasing by 50 percent between 1910 and 1920 and again by 39 percent in the 1920s, periods when the white population increased at a much slower rate. In the capital city of Indianapolis the black population climbed from sixty thousand to eighty thousand between 1910 and 1920. Yet even in 1920 Indiana was remarkably homogeneous. Ninety-five percent of the population was native-born, 97 percent white and 97 percent Protestant. Many towns barred black residents. Sundown laws that prohibited blacks from remaining in town after sunset were enforced, though often unwritten, in nearly every small town in Indiana.[18] My informants easily recalled the racial separation in various parts of the state in the early twentieth century.

> Huntington County was one that had the rule on the statutes that the ground was given to the county for the county courthouse as long as no black person stayed overnight in the county. And they had that rule on the statutes.
>
> They used to have a sign on the railroad [in Elwood]: "Nigger, don't let the sun set on you here."
>
> They didn't like colored. . . . A town like Linton, Indiana, at that time, a colored man supposedly couldn't stay in Linton overnight.[19]

Indiana's cities and towns, housing, schools, social life, and work were strictly segregated by race. Blacks were excluded from most skilled occupations and could obtain mainly menial, unskilled, and low-paid jobs. Between 1896 and 1932 not one black candidate was elected to the state legislature and not one piece of legislation beneficial to blacks was enacted in the state. Although black children had access to public schooling after 1865, Indiana schools were segregated. Blacks and other nonwhites were routinely denied entry to most public places, a situation that nearly all whites I interviewed perceived as unproblematic: "In [town], 'til after World War II, there wasn't any place for a nigger to eat, except in every restaurant, they would let him eat in the kitchen, or back room somewhere."[20]

Anti-Catholicism also had a prominent place in Indiana history. The Know-Nothing party, with its anti-Catholic oath of admission, enrolled sixty thousand members in Indiana in the 1850s. Forty years later, many of the state's Protestants joined the American Protective Association (APA), whose members pledged not to vote for Catholics or patronize Catholic-owned businesses. The APA also sponsored tours by women lecturers claiming to be "escaped nuns," who spread stories of illicit sexual activity between Catholic priests and nuns. These anti-Catholic movements created fear and hatred of Catholics among Indiana's white Protestants.[21] A former Klansman from a small town in northern Indiana noted that the racist and anti-Catholic message of the 1920s Klan differed little from attitudes that were commonplace during his childhood in the late nineteenth century.

> For them [the Klan] to say, we want to get rid of the niggers, we want to get rid of the Catholics, it didn't mean a thing to us. . . . I can remember quite well the stories that you hear sitting on the porch . . . and the lights are low or no lights, and . . . people gathered in groups, friendly groups. They'd talk about religion, and they'd talk about Catholics . . . the Catholics were considered horrible people. . . . They would talk about Catholics killing people and destroying their bodies.[22]

Indiana had a tradition of terroristic and vigilante movements posing as morality crusades. The most prominent of these was the "white caps," a secret terrorist network that operated from 1850 until the Indiana general assembly prohibited it in 1889. Whitecappers—often prominent local men whose costumes disguised their identity—picked out those they viewed as morally unsuitable for the community. Common targets included errant wives or (less often) philandering husbands, fornicators, and prostitutes, as well as those suspected of stealing livestock.

Masked bands of whitecappers first visited and threatened their victims. If threats did not change the offending behavior, a whipping followed. Women who violated the moral code imposed by whitecappers received particularly sadistic treatment. A contemporary observer described the "moralistic blood lust [in which] these helpless women were stripped naked and flogged with a pathological zeal that left many of them nearly dead."[23] Another contemporary described the whitecappers in Morgantown, Indiana:

> If unsatisfactory or unclean blacks lived in town, they left a bundle of switches on the porch of their house with a sign that said, "Get out." If a man didn't take care of his wife and children, a bundle of switches was left on his porch. If he didn't care for them, he got switched.[24]

A similar vigilante network operated in the Horse Thief Detective Association (HTDA), the direct predecessor of the Indiana Klan. The HTDA began in 1865 as a secret organization ostensibly working to recover stolen property. By the early 1920s it claimed a following of fifteen thousand Indiana men who used violence to break up youthful sexual encounters ("petting parties") and close illegal liquor manufacturers and distributors. When the KKK was organized in Indiana, HTDA members were urged to join the Klan.[25]

Morality crusades patterned after earlier efforts by the APA, white-cappers, and HTDA were the Klan's entrée into many communities in Indiana. The 1920s Klan was extraordinarily successful in bringing a wide range of white Protestants who feared liquor or sexual promiscuity or gambling into an organized political force with common targets: nonwhites, immigrants, and non-Protestants. The call to morality fired political passions while obscuring white Protestants' real differences in sentiments toward sexuality, alcohol, and leisure time activities. A resident of Indianapolis recalled the excitement of joining the Klan's crusade: "It gave people a feeling that they were doing the right thing . . . really felt like they were doing the Christian duty."[26]

Klan recruiters portrayed themselves as a movement of righteous Protestants beleaguered by forces of immorality. Thousands of cards were distributed on street corners and in churches and lodges by Klanswomen and Klansmen seeking new recruits for the crusade. Each small calling card bore the terrifying message:

> Remember, every criminal, every gambler, every thug, every libertine, every girl ruiner, every home wrecker, every wife beater, every dopepeddler, every shyster lawyer, every K of C [Knight of Columbus], every white slaver, every brothel madame, every Rome-controlled newspaper—is fighting the KKK.[27]

The Klan's claims to support women's rights and its efforts to recruit women did not prevent it from directing its morality crusades in Indiana to Klansmen and urging them to fight on behalf of white Protestant women. It invoked women to justify nearly every action that the Klan took against vice and corruption. When the Klan fought against prostitution, gambling, "bawdy houses," pool halls, dog and horse racing, and slot machines, it did so in the name of women who faced financial ruin by wayward or erring husbands: in gambling houses, "men are robbed, by shrewd house men of their weekly payroll, and their poor wives and children must suffer hunger and real need in order to please these bands of thieves."[28]

The Klan claimed to oppose liquor for the same reason: women were vulnerable to physical abuse and economic ruin at the hands of drunken husbands and fathers. Klan chapters threatened, raided, and assaulted bootleggers and moonshiners and condemned those (outside the Klan) who used alcohol. Some Indiana chapters even gathered evidence for the arrest of local druggists who sold alcohol-based preparations. Despite its self-portrayal as an antiliquor group, KKK klaverns often protected bootleggers and moonshiners, raiding only those who did not pay for the Klan's protection.[29]

At least initially, campaigns against vice were popular. Across Indiana, Klan members were recruited by local elites who introduced the group as a community reform organization. The Klan placed ads in local papers announcing its "clean-up campaign" and warning officials of repercussions if they failed to take action against gambling houses and liquor. Too, the Klan's ability to define itself as the major barrier to vice appealed to Protestant clergy, who recruited for the Klan from among their congregations.[30]

Klan chapters frequently threatened those it regarded as violators of the moral code through letter or visit. Physical attacks on offending persons were less common since the Klan's reputation for violence made threats extremely effective. A resident of rural Warren, Indiana, recalled that "in spite of no record of violence there was a general feeling of fear, mystery, and power associated with the Warren Klan. Young girls were warned never to get into a car with men—especially men wearing white hoods!"[31]

The earliest victims of the Klan's assault on vice were individuals and establishments with few defenders among the middle class or elite of a community. Town loafers and undesirables—a net wide enough to hold drunks, disorderly house operators, rumrunners, the unemployed, criminals, racial and ethnic minorities, even horseshoe players—were easy targets. Places frequented by the lower class or minorities—cheap "blind tigers" (illegal saloons) and brothels—were also convenient targets for a crusade against vice. Sometimes Klan violence hid personal vendettas as moral enforcement. Men asked their Klan brothers to threaten or assault those who competed for a desired woman's love and sexual favors. One Klan chapter even intervened in a child custody case, kidnapping a child from the custodial grandparents for the Klansman-father.[32]

In the 1920s the Klan's use of morality as a political crusade came to encompass more than a statement that non-Protestants and non-whites caused social decay. Now, drawing from ideas of women's rights advocates like Alma White, the Klan claimed it would pursue immoral behavior, even that committed by white Protestant men. The Klan's claim, meant primarily as a public relations ploy, was vastly overstated. No serious attempt to end immorality among white Protestant men occurred; the primary victims of the Klan's hate crusade remained Jews, Catholics, and blacks. Nonetheless, Klan violence

against white Protestant men on behalf of white Protestant women—
even if sporadic—is interesting for what it reveals about the politics of
morality in the Klan. As part of their purported defense of morality,
Klan chapters threatened and punished those whom it labeled as
openly violating the marital code. Although both Klansmen and Klanswomen engaged in threats, and even violence, on behalf of morality,
those beseeching the Klan's aid were usually women.[33]

Many of those menaced by the Klan were men who deserted their
wives or took up with women in adulterous affairs. Klansmen sought
to strengthen their own reputations as upright husbands and fathers
by singling out delinquent men for public reprobation. Through channels of neighborhood gossip, local women targeted philandering men
for Klan punishment. Klan chapter no. 40 of Logansport, Indiana,
sent a letter to Frank Fennemore warning him of the consequences
that would follow his continued transgressions:

> We are sending you a warning. . . . Why are you neglecting your wife and
> children. Those women you are spending your money on care nothing for
> you. . . . You are a poor example to your children. . . . We have warned
> you before by signs. You will be punished further. Go to church. Take your
> wife and family, spend your money for their comfort and leave women and
> whiskey alone.[34]

KKK locals advertised their assistance to women in dealing with
problematic husbands. Husbands who deserted wives and family, the
Klan promised, could be returned by force. At least some women responded to the Klan's offer. The powerful midwestern Klan leader
D. C. Stephenson, for example, circulated a detailed description and
likely whereabouts of C. C. Yoke after Yoke was accused of running
off with a female companion, leaving his crippled wife and seven-year-
old daughter destitute. All Indiana Klansmen were asked to search for
the deserting husband so that he might be returned to his wife and
daughter. Women also asked the Klan's assistance with financially irresponsible husbands. A woman in Glenwood, Indiana, wrote to the
Klan asking its help in collecting support money from a husband who
had deserted her with "two little boys to take care of." Others appealed to the Klan for help with husbands who spent badly needed
money on liquor and gambling.[35]

Men were the more frequent—but not the exclusive—target of the
Klan's threats and violence. It purported to be equal in its enforcement
of moral standards for men and women, but women's transgressions

were more likely to evoke a sadistic response by the Klan. Some incidents were relatively minor, like that of a Greene County, Indiana, WKKK chapter that threatened a local woman who was said to meet the daily train in order to seduce men. Others were more serious, like those in which furious Klansmen stripped "fallen women" of their clothes and whipped them.[36] Klansmen regarded white women with a mixture of paternalism and misogyny. In their proper role, white women were victims; out of their place, white women transgressed the most sensitive of moral codes. This complex attitude could lead to bizarre results, as in a 1927 incident in rural Alabama. Led by a Baptist minister, a Klan group flogged a divorced mother who had married a divorced man. After the beating the assailants took up a collection for their victim, giving her money and salve for her wounds. The minister then informed her that she had not been punished in anger but rather "in a spirit of kindness and correction, to set your feet aright."[37]

The Klan proclaimed neglect of one's family to be another violation of its moral code. Mothers accused of neglecting their children were subject first to a warning, then to violent punishment. In Indianapolis a mob of Klansmen beat a woman after she was arrested for child neglect. The highly publicized situation in Oklahoma where groups of Klansmen administered violent Klan justice to straying men and where Klan locals routinely sent letters accusing men of abusing or failing to support their families, was extreme but not unique. In Indiana, too, the local Klan called men to account when it deemed their behavior unacceptable. In a small town in north-central Indiana, "They took one guy out, and laid the leather to him, because he wasn't taking care of his family. Well, he got a job right quick and started working."[38] Likewise in Henry County, Indiana, four Klansmen seized a man from the public square and terrorized him for neglecting his family and associating with the "wrong people." A woman informant in central Indiana described the Klan primarily as an agency of redress for wronged women, whereas a woman in northern Indiana remembered that the Klan's threats did not always meet with success. Each woman reminisced:

> Well, wasn't their original purpose to kind of straighten out people? Like, say, that . . . some man would beat up his wife. Then, the Klan would come around . . . and beat him up.[39]

> The tombstone maker in the town, who was of German descent . . . had spanked or beat his little boy. . . . And, so the Klan went down and they

were going to discipline him and beat him up a little bit and he was a great strong fellow and he threw them out. So, they sent a second committee and he threw them out and they decided to leave him alone.[40]

There were few standards for selecting Klan victims. Women and men who were hostile to the aims of the Klan or who were not native-born white Protestants were the most likely targets. Even Klan members, however, might be singled out by fellow Klansmen or Klanswomen for not living a proper klannish life. One such incident in Williamsburg, Indiana, involved a Klansman who was accused of spending money on illegal liquor in lieu of providing adequately for his wife and children. After an evening visit by his Klan brothers the man changed his ways. A former Klansman from west-central Indiana explained that the Klan was able to make use of powerful political connections to locate its victims. "They used to take men that would leave their wives and not provide for their wife. They would get a hold of that fellow and sometimes horsewhip him." Asked how the Klan got its information, he said, "Well, a lot of lawyers were members of the Klan and the judge and those people. They were members of the Klan."[41]

Another aspect of the Klan's moral code concerned the chastity of white Protestant women themselves. Like its predecessor, the second Klan vowed to defend women's sexual purity. The impetus for this aspect of the Klan's moral crusade came primarily from the KKK, although the women's Klan was occasionally involved.

Young women were the particular objects of male Klan protectiveness. The KKK press roused intense public fear with suggestions of a vast sexual traffic in young white women, alleging that tens of thousands of girls were snatched into a sexual netherworld each year. The northern Indiana Klan attempted to stop a scheduled boxing match near Chicago on the grounds that Jack Johnson was a professed "negro white slaver." Making a similar appeal, a Klan pamphlet posed this chilling question to potential recruits: "Do you know that annually there are 50,000 girls, from approximately 50,000 American homes, whose virtue is sacrificed upon the altar of vice? [That] there are thousands of girls of foreign birth who were once sent to this country's shores and sold as slaves to the godless passions of men?"[42]

Klansmen's vigilantism in defense of girls' virtue, though, often mixed with other concerns, such as fear of female sexuality and attention to the interests of local elites, as in this story related by a southern Indiana former Klansmember.

The Klan asked a chap by the name of Neth who was a minister . . . to leave town and he did. . . . In addition to being a minister of the church, he taught two or three classes in high school. . . . But this high school girl, she decided she kind of liked Neth, and so she was always a'hanging around, and the real problem was the girl was just pretty much of a tramp, anyway you'd figure it. So, but . . . nevertheless her dad was a rather prominent businessman in town and so on, and they thought that Neth and this girl was a gettin' too thick and so they advised him to leave and he did.[43]

Many Klan actions, in which both Klansmen and Klanswomen participated, were aimed at curbing the sexual temptations of young women and men. Two areas were of particular concern: dance halls and automobiles. Both allowed young people a measure of privacy away from the watchful eyes of parents and other adults. Both gave young people a chance to indulge in liquor and sex. Both, the Imperial Wizard warned, subjected the weak to unnecessary and dangerous "seductive allurement."[44]

In town after town in Indiana the Klan tried to make a public issue of dance halls and other "vile places of amusement." In some areas the Klan appealed to local authorities to intervene for the sake of public morality and the protection of town youth from sexually suggestive dances. An Indianapolis Christian church minister, later a Klan lecturer, generated much publicity by condemning as "immoral" the mayor's support of public dancing. In Hammond, Indiana, the Klan announced that it would monitor all dance halls, pool halls, picture shows, and other places of amusement for the town youth in order that the "moral conditions" of such places (and presumably also of the youth who frequented them) be improved. In taking this action, the Hammond Klan claimed, it was responding to protest from an aroused citizenry, citing complaints from local women about "brazen male mashers" and impassioned "love grips" in the "cheaper movie houses" of the town. Similarly, in South Bend the Klan engineered a police raid on a local liquor establishment and claimed, in an article entitled "Klan Plays Part of Good Samaritan to Modern Magdalene," that three white teenaged girls were being held prisoner there.[45]

In other Indiana towns the Klan acted more directly, destroying and burning buildings that permitted youth dancing. The Pittsburg, Kansas, chapters of the KKK and WKKK summed up the feelings of many Indiana Klansmen and Klanswomen when they demanded the closing of all public dance resorts since "most of the cases of assault between the sexes have followed dances where they got the inspiration for rash and immoral acts." Many times, the condemnation of dance halls only thinly veiled anti-Semitic attitudes. The Klan implied and sometimes openly declared that Jews benefited financially from places of amusement and thus were responsible for the "misuse of girls" and "promiscuous petting" that these places encouraged among the young.[46]

Automobiles offered an even more direct threat to the moral standards of young persons. Often, the Klan's first public action in a community would be a campaign to "clear the highway of spooners." Parties of masked and hooded Klansmembers (presumably, but not certainly, men) patrolled highways and back roads in search of young couples in parked automobiles. In some communities Klan delegations simply reported to parents and police the names of those found parked at the sides of roadways. In other areas couples caught in an embrace faced a more immediate punishment, including threats and beatings by night-riding Klan posses. The Klan's fervor made people fearful of using the roadways in many areas. Indeed, the Klan's enthusiasm for breaking up "petting parties" by searching all cars on highways caused several motor clubs to blacklist the entire state.[47]

The Klan reserved its greatest terror for nonwhite men who were "involved with" white women. To the Klan of the 1920s, dating and marriage across racial or ethnic lines evoked the same images of white female exploitation and usurpation of white men's privileges that fueled the Reconstruction-era Klan. Nonwhite, foreign-born, and non-Protestant men who were caught with white women faced fierce reprisals by the Klan, including whipping, beating, kidnapping, and even lynching. White women who consorted with Jewish, immigrant, or black men met similar fates. In Muncie, Indiana, a Klanswoman even accused blacks and Catholics of a conspiracy, claiming that Catholics had discovered a powder that would bleach the skins of black men so that they could marry white girls.[48]

ANTI-CATHOLICISM AND PORNOGRAPHY

Although the Indiana Klan presented itself as an agency of moral reform, the Klan's real message was clearly different. At the same time as it proclaimed itself the force of morality and sexual purity, the Indiana Klan offered audiences graphic tales of female enslavement and sexual exploitation, usually by Catholic priests but also by black and Jewish men.

Typical of such stories was the Klan's attack on a photoplay picture it described as "coarse, degrading, and insulting to the white race." In fact, the Klan's fury over the play centered on its "tendency to create aspirations in the lives of negro people." As was true in much Klan propaganda, it referred to illicit sexual aspirations and to black men: "the revolting spectacle of a white woman clinging in the arms of a colored man is simply beyond words to express." To make the threat of black men's sexual aspirations more threatening, the Indiana Klan press charged that when the picture played in Texas, a bulletin board adjoining the theater bore the message, "White-skinned ladies will flirt with black-skinned men when their husbands are away."[49]

Similarly, the Indiana Klan justified its anti-Semitic attitudes as a defense of Gentile womanhood against the avarice of Jewish men. Jewish businessmen, according to the Klan, were attempting to destroy the very foundations of Christianity by seducing and raping Protestant girls. A typical Klan publication argued that its anti-Semitic policies were simply giving voice to the disgruntlement of many Protestants who "are tired of the outrages inflicted upon innocent girls by Hebrew libertines."[50]

The most common target of the Indiana Klan, however, was Catholics. Anti-Catholic lectures, stories, and books that proliferated in the 1910s were recycled with few changes by the Klan a decade later. The Klan circulated thousands of copies of an alleged Knights of Columbus initiation that was the secret blueprint for a Catholic take-over of the country. In the purported pledge, aspiring Knights of Columbus promised to "wage relentless war, secretly and openly, against all heretics, Protestants, and Masons." The document detailed the Catholic initiates' vow: "Burn, waste, boil, flay, strangle and bury alive these infamous heretics; rip open the stomachs and wombs of their women and crash their infants' heads against the walls in order to annihilate their execrable race [or] secretly use the poisonous cup, strangulation cord, the steel of the poiniard, or the leaden bullet."[51]

The most powerful anti-Catholic allegations made by the Indiana Klan concerned sexual practices of priests and nuns. Klan publications and lecturers described an international network of convent prisons that enslaved young Protestant women, exacting forced labor and sexual favors from the girls and turning them into compliant Catholic adults. According to Gill Comer and the WKKK, Romanists prevailed upon innocent Protestant couples to sign over their children to the religious upbringing of Catholics. Occasionally, boys were the alleged target of Romanist avarice, as in the tale of fifty-two boys snatched from a Methodist Episcopal orphanage by a Catholic-incited police raid and placed in Catholic homes from which they fervently endeavored to escape. But it was mainly Protestant girls who were alleged to be ensnared by Catholic institutions, allowing the Klan to claim that it was safeguarding the virtue of 100 percent females.[52]

Indiana Protestant preachers commonly adopted the klannish term for the Roman Catholic church and titled lectures on the Klan's battle with the Catholics "The Beast vs. the Invisible Empire."[53] In Muncie, Indiana, the Lynds' *Middletown* reported that "local Klansmen vowed they would unmask 'when and not until the Catholics take the prison walls down from about their convents and nunneries.'" One of the Lynds' informants, indicating a copy of a common Klan periodical, declared, "Look at this picture of this poor girl—look at her hands! see, all those fingers gone—just stumps left! she was in a convent when it was considered sinful to wear jewelry, and the Sisters, when they found her wearing some rings, just burned them off her fingers!"[54]

To make initial contact in a new territory, the Klan sent lecturers posing as former nuns and former priests to titillate audiences with details of Romanist sexual depravity and to prepare the way for the Klan's troupe of Protestant minister-lecturers. The tactic was so successful that the same "nun" and "priest" lecturers returned to areas over and over, drawing massive crowds. Lurid stories of Catholic depravity were rumored in public and discussed openly and in great detail in assemblies restricted to Klan members.

The Klan's genius at self-promotion was evident in its Indiana lecture tours. Publicly distributed Klan newspapers described the "torture and abuse of Protestant girls in the Roman Catholic hell holes" of Catholic convents that observers would relate since the girls themselves demurely declined to reveal intimate details of their abuse in a public forum. Memories of the sexual tales spread by the Klan are still fresh in the minds of former Klansmembers and contemporaries of the 1920s Klan movement in Indiana.

> They were saying that the Catholic priests and nuns were having sexual relationships and they'd kill the babies. They'd have abortions. All that kind of stuff. They ripped the stomachs of the nuns open and would take the baby. All that kind of business. Just horrible things.

> They would never come out and say things but they would imply a lot of things. And, then you would draw your own conclusions about how the Catholics and priests and nuns behaved. In fact, you know, the convent at

Huntington and the friary was right there. Of course, the friary didn't belong to the Catholics anymore. But, there actually was an underground passage between the two. And, of course, the whole community made a lot of that.

Where the [convent] academy was, they had their own graveyard to bury their dead from the babies that was born to the girls there in that thing. . . . I was curious where the graveyard was [but] I didn't ask anybody.[55]

One of the most successful Klan emissaries was Helen Jackson, billed as an "escaped nun." Jackson traveled across the country, regaling her sex-segregated audiences with tales of sexual horrors behind convent walls. She claimed to have firsthand knowledge of infanticides and abortions forced on nuns by the priests who fathered their babies. Displaying little leather bags, Jackson told her riveted audience that these were used to dispose of the convents' murdered newborns and aborted fetuses. In small towns of the West and Midwest, she regaled thousands of avid listeners with tales of Catholic sadomasochistic practices, including one incident in which a cross was burned on her own back. One informant recalled an anecdote of convent life from Helen Jackson's speech: "When they misbehaved, they were soaked in the bathtubs where, they didn't have kotex in those days, it was just cloth that was washed out in tubs and soaking with those pots. That was the most hideous thing, it just hit me."[56]

Jackson's autobiography, *Convent Cruelties,* was sold at Klan rallies (see photograph 10). It also was advertised in Klan publications, with a suggestive cartoon of a girl being whipped by nuns. Provocatively subtitled—"A providential delivery from Rome's Convent Pens: a sensational experience"—the volume traced Jackson's alleged imprisonment by sadistic Catholic officials in a convent in Detroit, Michigan, and in a House of the Good Shepherd in Newport, Kentucky. Jackson maintained that she was constantly humiliated by other nuns, forbidden any contact with the outside world, subjected to torture by immersion in cold water, forced to drink vile substances, and ordered to work unceasingly at ironing and embroidery. She also claimed that she had witnessed the tortures and imprisonment of other girls, some of whom were Protestants abducted into the Romanist slave den. Appended to the volume were affidavits from other "escaped nuns" who provided their own tales of imprisonment and abuse in Catholic convents and homes.[57]

Helen Jackson frequently traveled with L. J. King, who billed himself as an "ex-Romanist." King had made his living for years on the anti-Catholic lecture circuit, claiming to be a former priest. Like other anti-Catholic evangelist lecturers of the 1910s, King specialized in highly emotional harangues. With his audiences separated by sex, King regaled the crowd with horrid tales of Catholic sexual tortures dating from the European Inquisition. In modern times, King thundered, these same perversions continued, fostered by priests whose "unnatural" pledge of celibacy drove their sexual desires in depraved directions.[58]

In the early 1920s L. J. King enlisted in the Klan and joined forces with Helen Jackson on the Klan lecture circuit. King's propaganda—on the implications of the unmarried clergy and the sexual exploits of the mysterious Catholic church—was ideal for the Klan's anti-Catholic agenda: "Every priest and nun connected with the [school] system is chained to a life of celibacy in defiance of nature and clad in a strange, unsanitary costume."[59]

Jackson and King held revivals on behalf of the Klan in many small towns in Indiana, setting up headquarters in a local restaurant or hotel and meeting nightly for two or three weeks—as long as a month—drawing crowds of hundreds and even thousands. In a single visit the pair would deliver lectures with titles such as "My Visit to the Nunnery at St. Louis, Missouri," "See Bottle Convent Booze," "The Fruits of the Confessional," and "Priest Hans Smytt Murders Two Girls." On the Klan circuit, King expanded on Jackson's personal account, regaling audiences with highly detailed tales of imprisonment in convents and sexual debauchery between Catholic nuns and priests. He described convent dungeons with bolted doors, iron-barred windows, and high massive walls that imprisoned hapless girls, making suicide their only escape.[60]

King and Jackson vividly described the grotesque tortures to which nuns were subjected for the sexual pleasure of priests, including tales of nuns confined in coffins filled with human excrement. A favorite legend recounted by the pair was the tale of Maria Monk and the nunnery of the Hôtel-Dieu in Montreal, a famous anti-Catholic diatribe dating to the early nineteenth century. Indeed, nearly all my respondents recalled owning a copy of Maria Monk's story, and most could recount its "awful disclosures" of convent life, including the murder of illicitly conceived infants.

> It was a horrible tale. My grandmother and I read it when we were in Florida one winter. And, she laughed about it. She thought it was horrible too,

but she let me read it, and it was just a horrible thing. It was just like all these things they had in that messy newspaper [*Fiery Cross*]. You know, incredible things.[61]

Jackson and King were expert at picturing even innocuous Catholic rituals as sordid and perverse. Their stump speech on the "abomination of secret auricular confession" is an example. King claimed that the secret confessional of the Catholic church was nothing more than "a school of licentiousness, seduction, and adultery." Priests encouraged innocent young girls to participate in confidential sexual fantasies in the confessional by means of suggestive questions whispered outside the hearing of male relatives or husbands. Secret confessions also provided the pretext for illicit love making between priest-confessors and nuns in convents, leading to abortion or infanticide.[62]

King's lectures and his annual, *The Converted Catholic and Protestant Missionary,* included many stories of women victimized in Catholic rectories, homes, and convents. These ranged from innuendo of sexual torture and intrigue to case histories of girls condemned to a life of drudgery, deprivation, and cruelty in convent "prisons." Before her lectures, Jackson would read from letters by local Klan chapters that charted successes in liberating Protestant girls from "Rome's slave pens" and encouraged others to free girls imprisoned in their localities. The traffic in white women, King seethed, was increasing "to fill up the place of poisoned, deluded, outraged, starved, raped, and murdered victims of priestcraft in the nunnery, to feed the lust of the adulterous bachelor, overfed, drunken priesthood of the Romish fake."[63]

The magnetism of King's and Jackson's oratory is evident in the account that the daughter of an active Indiana Klanswoman and Klansman gave of how her parents "practically broke out in tears about some of the things that were being taught to the children in the school . . . all these things that went on in the priest's home and the nun's home and all these babies that were buried underneath the mother's houses."[64]

Even girls who avoided the terror of the convent life, the Klan suggested, were not safe. Jackson, King, and other Klan lecturers charged priests with attacking girls in school dormitories and in church sanctuaries; with being drunk, stupid, or intolerant; and with gambling and promoting law breaking. Sometimes the finger of blame pointed toward priests in general; at other times it accused particular priests or convent schools.[65]

MORALITY AS A POLITICAL TERRAIN

The Klan's success in bringing sexual morality into the political agenda gave it great public credibility (and an enormous following) among white Protestants who applauded the Klan's efforts to subvert the immoral intentions of Catholic clergy, Jewish businessmen, and black and immigrant men and to uphold morality within white Protestant families. Tales of sexual perversity also normalized hatred of the Klan's enemies. The Klan's accounts of sexual depravity among Catholic clergy and the wanton sexual exploitation of youngsters by priests and nuns led many white Protestants to view Catholics as far removed from accepted standards of moral and ethical behavior.

When the Klan had established Catholics as strange and inexplicable beings, few stories about them seemed implausible. And the Klan was expert at generating rumors for gullible audiences. In reaction to news that the 1917 U.S. dollar bill was covered with secret Catholic symbols, loyal Klan members dutifully tore off a corner of the bill where the pope's picture was said to be hidden. Indiana Klan members heard, and often believed, accusations against the Catholic church that ranged from plotting the assassination of President Abraham Lincoln, to fomenting World War I in order to strengthen the papacy, to leading the massacre of American Indians.[66]

As befitting an organization built on xenophobia, Klan propaganda was hysterical on the topic of the Italian pope and Vatican City. The pope, known in Klan parlance as the "dago on the Tiber," was identified with the biblical Delilah, putting the Samson of the United States to sleep in order to carry out her evil plans. Many Klanswomen and Klansmen in Indiana firmly believed that the arrival of the pope as emperor of the United States was imminent. Rumors circulated that a palace was being built in Washington, D.C., to allow the pope to oversee his empire.[67]

A major theme of the Klan's anti-Catholicism was that of a church under foreign leadership. Catholics in the United States—citizens as well as immigrants—were accused of being spies for the Vatican. The police forces of the major cities, the Klan asserted, were dominated by Catholics who owed their allegiance to the pope in Rome. The Klan's opposition to the World Court was based on a similar belief—that the Vatican would manipulate the World Court as a tool for "romanizing" America and forcing "papist aliens" into the United States. Ignoring its own hierarchical structure, the Klan argued that the strict lines of authority in the Catholic church were antithetical to democracy and individual freedom. Catholics, according to the Klan, came from the lower classes and criminal elements of Europe and were forced to do the bidding of the pope.[68]

Typical of the way that many Protestants in 1920s Indiana regarded Catholics is the account given by a woman in Muncie when attempting to convince an interviewer for the Lynds' ethnographic work, *Middletown,* to join her in the local Klan. She insisted that the pope started the first Klan in order to divide and conquer Protestants, a convoluted logic meant to underscore the malevolent intentions of the Catholic empire.

> It's about time you joined the good people and did something about this Catholic situation. The Pope is trying to get control of this country, and in order to do it, he started the old Klan to stir up trouble among the Protestants, but instead of doing that he only opened their eyes to the situation, and now all the Protestants are getting together in the new Klan to overcome the Catholic menace.[69]

The Catholic fraternal order, the Knights of Columbus, was a frequent target of Klan propaganda, which typically insisted that the Knights were the secret military arm of the pope. According to the Klan, the Knights planted Catholic girls in Protestant homes as maids and child helpers who then filed weekly reports with the Vatican on the activities and conversations of Protestant families.[70]

Protestants in Indiana also commonly believed that Catholics were arming themselves for a massacre of non-Catholics, using guns and ammunition stockpiled in the basements of Catholic churches. Rumors circulated throughout the state that Catholics buried a rifle under the local church each time a Catholic boy was born, for his later use to defend the papal empire that would rule the United States by the time the child grew to manhood. A woman in central Indiana recalled that "stories floated here that the Catholic church, that the basement was really an armory, getting ready for a revolution . . . the Catholic church was getting ready for a civil war in this country, they were going to take over the government."[71]

The Klan's success in making morality a matter of public discussion in Indiana ironically turned public attention to the sexual practices of Klan leaders themselves—an attention that the Klan could ill afford.

The downfall of D. C. Stephenson, and consequently of the Indiana Klan itself, shows this most graphically.

Stephenson attracted constant allegations of sexual impropriety and exploitation. He had married a number of times, leaving a string of divorced or deserted wives and children in various states and a reputation for immorality long before Hiram Evans recruited him as a KKK kleagle for Indiana. As a Klan leader Stephenson was enormously successful, building Indiana into the most powerful state Klan in the country. He controlled the influential Klan paper *Fiery Cross* and dictated much of state politics. The ultimate demagogue, Stephenson appealed to xenophobia and hatred of minorities. He predicted that a wave of black labor would sweep up from the South to work for a dollar a day, live in squalor, and commit horrible crimes against virtuous white women. He declared that Catholics were nothing but a slavish army for the pope's world conquest and that Jews had an international banking conspiracy against the interests of Gentile businessmen and farmers.[72]

A major part of Stephenson's success was his personal charisma and proficient stage management. Calling himself "the Old Man" or "State," Stephenson traveled in an airplane, descending from the heavens draped in a purple cloak to deliver fiery orations that whipped audiences into a frenzy. In his most famous appearance, in Kokomo, Indiana, men stripped the rings from their fingers to toss at Stephenson. Eerily foretelling Stephenson's downfall, witnesses claimed that Stephenson dipped into this cache of rings to reward special women friends. Indeed, Stephenson's reputation for harassing and attacking women was legendary in Klan circles. A friend acknowledged Stephenson's weakness for liquor and women: "When he was in his cups no woman was safe from him." As he gained more power, his sexual exploits and profound hatred of women drew more notice and Stephenson's mansion home in Indianapolis became famous for late-night parties and orgies.[73]

After stunning Klan electoral successes in Indiana in 1924, Stephenson decided that he no longer needed to take orders from Evans and broke with the Klan hierarchy. Evans struck back at Stephenson's vulnerabilities by circulating stories that Stephenson was a lecher and a drunkard. Local klaverns further embroidered these rumors. The Evansville KKK, Stephenson's home klavern, formally charged Stephenson with "gross dereliction" for the attempted rape of a local "virtuous young woman." Further, they charged that Stephenson was guilty of numerous other instances of immoral behavior in Columbus (Ohio), Columbus (Indiana), and Atlanta. Secretly tried on the charges, Stephenson was found guilty and banished officially, though not in fact, from the Invisible Empire.[74]

Stephenson's fall came the following year. A twenty-eight-year-old social worker, Madge Oberholtzer, was invited to Stephenson's mansion, drugged, and forced to accompany Stephenson on a train to Chicago. On board the train, Stephenson raped and brutalized Oberholtzer, chewing and biting her tongue, breasts, back, legs, and ankles. Near Chicago she was taken off the train and moved to a hotel but received no medical treatment. She managed to leave the hotel long enough to go to a drugstore, purchase bichloride of mercury tablets, and swallow them. When Stephenson realized that Oberholtzer had attempted to kill herself, he rushed her back to his Indianapolis mansion where, again, she received no medical treatment. Finally released to her parents, Madge recited a story that caused Stephenson's arrest for mayhem, rape, kidnapping, and conspiracy. When Madge died a few weeks later of the combined effects of injuries and poison, a charge of second-degree murder was added.[75]

Indiana papers avidly covered the resulting trial. At the same time a woman arrived in Indianapolis, publicly denounced Stephenson as her deserting husband, and sued him for desertion and child support. Stephenson argued that Klan forces loyal to Evans had engineered both incidents. Evans, he claimed, had bragged that "when you want to 'get' a man, just hang a woman on him," a policy Evans had used successfully against Clarke in the early days of the second Klan.[76]

Debate even in Indiana's non-Klan newspapers revolved around the moral character and reputation of Oberholtzer, more than that of Stephenson. Anti-Klan forces highlighted Oberholtzer's respectable middle-class upbringing, noting that she had been engaged to be married in the past, but that her wedding plans had been shattered by the World War. Witnesses testified for Oberholtzer that she was "a nice girl" and did not deserve the fate that befell her. Klan forces, on the contrary, cast suspicion on the motives of this unmarried woman who frequented statehouse parties and who voluntarily entered Stephenson's home in the evening. A former Klansman in central Indiana expressed a sentiment common among Klansmembers: "It's too bad she died, but what did she go up there with him for? Why was she shacking up with him and so forth?"[77]

For bystanders the trial was exhilarating. Most of those I interviewed could remember the trial vividly and relished relating lurid details of the crime. Male and female informants made similar comments. All expressed some skepticism about Oberholtzer's story. At best they saw Madge as a willing victim; at worst, as a woman who plotted to seduce and destroy Stephenson and the Indiana Klan. A man remembered the incident:

> Him and Madge Oberholtzer. You know, he didn't kill her. He just maimed her. . . . D. C. Stephenson, I never will forget seeing him down here at the big parade, and this lady that he maimed. She was a very fine looking lady. I've seen her. And, I know they sent him, D. C. Stephenson up for raping her. I don't think he raped her. I think she was willing, but he bit her nipples off. That's how he maimed her and she killed herself.[78]

An Indiana woman saw the incident similarly. "That was a gruesome trial you know, this girl might have been a party girl, I supposed she was or she wouldn't have been on that train but even back in those days you know, murder wasn't very pretty."[79]

A dying declaration by Oberholtzer swayed the jury and Stephenson was convicted, sentenced to life imprisonment, and served twenty-five years in the state penitentiary. The Indiana Klan, once the strongest in the Invisible Empire, collapsed precipitously. By 1928 only four thousand in Indiana claimed Klan membership, down from a high of almost half a million. Klan partisans mounted petition campaigns to secure Stephenson's release and continued to provide a forum for his politics. Many of them believed Stephenson's lengthy sentence was simply a tactic to silence a man who knew too much about the Klan's role in Indiana politics. Others disputed the charge of murder brought against Stephenson, insisting that his actions merited no more than a "drunk and disorderly" arrest. Stephenson was pardoned in 1956 on the condition that he leave the state. In 1961 he was again arrested in Indiana for attempting to force a sixteen-year-old girl into his car and was sent back to prison.[80]

Once the most powerful force in Indiana, D. C. Stephenson and his Klan movement were destroyed by publicity about sexual atrocities and moral bankruptcy. It was ironic, but perhaps inevitable, that the tactics that built the Indiana Klan also led to its collapse. Stephenson's arrest and trial for manslaughter thrilled the very audiences who once responded to pro-Klan pornographic tales by "escaped nuns" and "converted priests." Even Oberholtzer's suicide attempt echoed the alleged fate of Protestant girls forcibly entrapped in Catholic convents.

The politics of morality in the Indiana Klan ultimately turned against the Klan itself. But the use of sexuality as a political terrain by the Klan movement was highly effective, if finally unstable. When the Klan drew on racist, anti-Catholic, and anti-Semitic innuendoes and tales of immorality and depravity, it mobilized large numbers of indignant white Protestants. Sexuality and morality meant home and family, the symbolic foundation of most white Protestant communities in Indiana. Stories of exotic sexual debauchery among Catholic clergy, Jewish businessmen, and black migrants from the South gave white midwestern Protestants an easy way to affirm their allegiance to home and family life by simply distancing themselves from such extremes of profane sexuality. The real issues that divided men from women and parents from children in the Midwest of the 1920s—issues of women's rights and families shattered by geographic mobility, for example—could be forgotten or ignored in the common white Protestant reaction to strange and remote sexual crimes.

The women and men of Indiana who joined the Klan movement for greater public enforcement of morality responded to different aspects of the appeal. Some women might have seen the Klan's fight against alcohol, gambling, and extramarital sexuality as a means to empower women against abusive husbands. Other women and men were excited, as well as alarmed, by stories of sexual atrocities. Still others found the Klan's public affirmation of standards of conventional morality reassuring. For all these groups, sexuality was a convenient boundary between "us" and "them." The outlandish stories of Klan lecturers lack credibility in retrospect, but they were effective in setting a boundary between ordinary and odd, normal and bizarre. The Klan's condemnation of "Rome's slavery dens" or secret burial grounds for coercively aborted infants expressed public sentiment without threatening the private lives of white Protestants in Indiana.

In the end, the Klan fell victim to this use of sexuality as a political symbol.[81] The secrecy of the Klan—like that of Roman Catholic hierarchy and ritual—made it vulnerable to suspicions of evildoing and corruption. Klan leaders understood the political significance of sexuality and turned it against rival Klan forces through rumors of sexual exploits by leaders of the Invisible Empire. Too, the avid public curiosity about private sexuality that served the Klan well as a recruiting device could not be contained when the Klan itself was the target. Like the temperance and purity movements, the Klan supported public efforts to control private conduct. By its success in making sexuality and drunkenness public issues, the Klan invited public scrutiny of sexual misdeeds and alcohol consumption among its own leaders, ultimately undermining itself. The experience of the 1920s Klan suggests that sex campaigns, then and now, create an awesome political momentum but an unstable foundation for an enduring political agenda.

1.   Klanswomen, August 1924. (Courtesy W. A. Swift Photograph Collection, Archives and Special Collections, Bracken Library, Ball State University)

2. Official attire for a non-officer Klanswoman. (From *Catalogue of Official Robes and Banners*, WKKK, ca. 1923)

3. Banner of the St. Louis, Missouri, WKKK chapter. (From *Catalogue of Official Robes and Banners*, WKKK, ca. 1923)

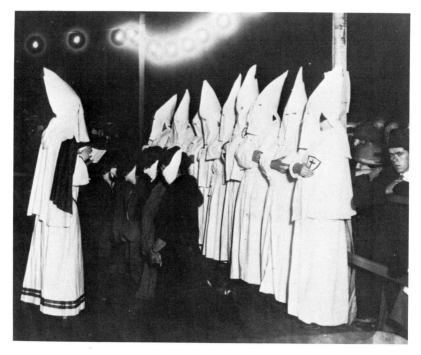

4. Initiation of new members in the first public appearance of the WKKK on Long Island, July 15, 1924. (Courtesy Library of Congress)

Go to Church Sunday

One of the foremost duties
of a Klanswoman is to
WORSHIP GOD

Every KLANSWOMAN Each Sunday
Should Attend the Church of Her Choice

5. Card for distribution by WKKK klaverns. (Courtesy George R. Dale Papers, Archives and Special Collections, Bracken Library, Ball State University)

"THE AWAKENING"

Presention By Dick Dowling Klan No.25
Port Arthur, Tex. June 2.5 to July 3 rd. Inclusive
A JAMES H. HULL PRODUCTION.
© 1924 MDP-IT

6. Entertainment staged by the Port Arthur, Texas, Klan, 1924. (Courtesy Library of Congress)

7. Banner for WKKK parades. (From *Catalogue of Official Robes and Banners,* WKKK, ca. 1923)

AMERICA
for
AMERICANS

AS INTERPRETED BY THE
Women of the
KU KLUX KLAN

CREED
OF
KLANSWOMEN

Yesterday—Today and Forever
God and Government
Law and Liberty
Peace and Prosperity

8. A WKKK statement of principles. (Published by the Women of the Ku Klux Klan, Little Rock, Arkansas, ca. 1924)

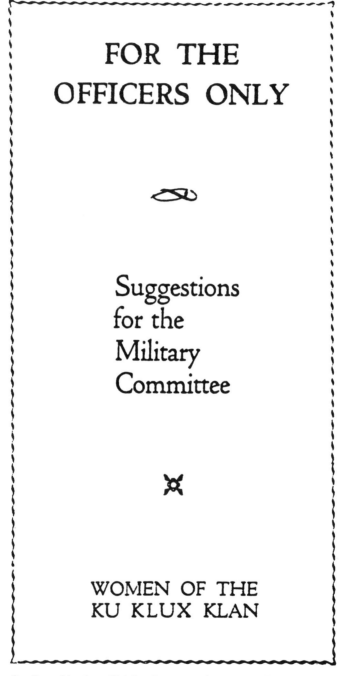

FOR THE
OFFICERS ONLY

Suggestions
for the
Military
Committee

WOMEN OF THE
KU KLUX KLAN

9.   Pamphlet for officials of WKKK chapters. (Published by the
Women of the Ku Klux Klan, Little Rock, Arkansas, ca. 1924)

Convent Kidnaping

10. Anti-Catholic cartoon. (From Helen Jackson, *Convent Cruelties,* 1919, 27)

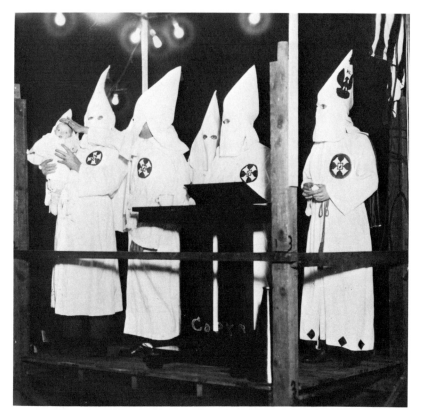

11. Christening of eight-week-old baby in Klan ceremony, 1924. (Courtesy Library of Congress)

12. Funeral in Muncie, Indiana, ca. 1923; mostly Klanswomen in attendance. (Courtesy W. A. Swift Photograph Collection, Archives and Special Collections, Bracken Library, Ball State University)

13. Ku Klux Kiddies in parade in New Castle, Indiana, August 1, 1923. (Courtesy W. A. Swift Photograph Collection, Archives and Special Collections, Bracken Library, Ball State University)

14. Klanswomen in New Castle, Indiana, August 1, 1923. (Courtesy W. A. Swift Photograph Collection, Archives and Special Collections, Bracken Library, Ball State University)

15. Women in Klan parade, Grants Pass, Oregon. (From the Collection of Lloyd Smith, Grants Pass, Oregon)

PART II

Women in the Klan

CHAPTER IV

Joining the Ladies' Organization

A former Klanswoman from Greene County, Indiana, wrote about the time a woman came to her village and invited the "better known and educated women" to a session where she lectured on the value of education, the meaning of the flag, cross, and Bible and the need to uphold Americanism. The visitor, actually a WKKK kleagle, then asked whether they would be willing to band together in secret and carry on these "high traditions." The Greene County woman responded:

> Why not? It seemed a fun thing to do with our friends. The next meeting we were told to be ready and wear uniforms when called upon. The uniforms were white robes, tall peaked hoods with eye holes, so no one could be recognized. What a thrill when we were told to assemble at a certain place wearing our robes, then marching with others also unknown to us. A huge cross, set up in the village, flared up in the darkness, crowds had assembled to watch. How they knew, I was not informed. As the cross burned we marched quietly down the roadway. A hush fell on the crowd. They seemed to sense a force of something unknown. It created a fear, as if like a child being told to be good or the bogey man will get you. Usually after the march an orator stood on a platform to proclaim the issues before the KKK and how many were supporting the movement.[1]

Hundreds of thousands of women poured into this "ladies' organization" in the mid-1920s. What motivated them to adopt the Klan's agenda of racial and religious hatred as their own? Part of the answer lies in the Klan's appeal to women through the symbols of home, family, and women's rights. But this answer is incomplete. Not all white

101

Protestant women accepted the Klan's call to defend white and Protestant supremacy. And Klanswomen construed the message of the Klan crusade in various ways. To understand the WKKK, we need to look at the lives of individual members, both leaders and rank and file, before the WKKK was organized. What characterized the lives of these women in the 1910s and earlier? What organizational or political routes led them to the Klan?

This chapter addresses these questions through an analysis of the life histories of more than one hundred members of the Indiana women's Klan. Their collective biographies are intended to show the specifics of recruitment into the WKKK and further our understanding of how women become involved in right-wing political movements.

Two assumptions characterize the scanty research on women in right-wing or reactionary politics. One is that women who enlist in right-wing movements do so for nonpolitical reasons. Right-wing women, according to this stereotype, are little more than the pawns of politically engaged men. They follow the political leanings of husbands or fathers or are swayed by charismatic male leaders. The assumption, however, is rarely tested in studies of political movements.

The second assumption is that most women (or men) who participate in extremist right-wing politics like those of the Klan are socially marginal. People without strong occupational, social, familial, or cultural bonds to the mainstream of society, according to this theory, are more likely to join political movements to change the status quo. The assumption of social marginality guides most popular ideas of the male Klan. Writers portray Klansmen as isolated and personally unstable men from lower-class or downwardly mobile sectors of society who focus their resentments against society on racial, ethnic, and religious minorities.

However, the assumption of social marginality has several problems. Studies of occupations, class backgrounds, and family situations of men in the 1920s Klan find that the Klan drew as many members from the middle class and working class as it did from the lower class. The same may be true of Klanswomen. In addition, the theory suggests that only irrational individuals join political movements outside the mainstream, a description that fits neither the informants I interviewed nor the Klansmembers that other scholars describe. Disturbingly, many Klansmembers were intelligent and well informed on some topics—if also bigoted, intolerant, and prejudiced. Finally, women's place in a theory of marginality that defines social ties as those that structure men's lives—jobs, workplace networks, fraternal associations, political parties—is unclear. The connections that bind women to the mainstream of society (or whose absence denotes their marginality) are poorly understood.

A more promising approach is to drop both assumptions and focus instead on the experiences and political views that brought women into the Klan crusade. Indeed, the collective biographies of Klanswomen in Indiana show a common history of involvement in mainstream politics, and in civic, religious, and social groups before they joined the WKKK. I explore these routes into the women's Klan below.

ROUTES THROUGH TEMPERANCE AND EVANGELISM

The most common avenue into the Indiana WKKK was through the temperance movement. Many rank-and-file Klanswomen, and some of the WKKK's most prominent spokeswomen, had been activists in the Women's Christian Temperance Union or held strong temperance beliefs. From our vantage point it may seem incongruous that a woman who was a temperance activist, Quaker minister, and clubwoman would lead midwestern Klanswomen into battle against Catholics, Jews, blacks, and immigrants. Yet the life and politics of this notable Klanswoman, Daisy Douglas Barr, showed little disjuncture before and during the heyday of the 1920s Klan movement. Barr's work as a temperance activist as well as a Republican party stalwart and active clubwoman overlapped—in ideology as in personal networks—with Indiana's Klan movement.

The political efforts of women like Daisy Barr must be seen within the context of the temperance movement of the late nineteenth century. As WCTU historian Ruth Bordin argues, temperance in the United States was "a 'safe' women's movement," one that did little to challenge existing gender arrangements. Through the WCTU women could express grievances against abuse and mistreatment at the hands of drunken husbands, but the movement did not require that participants overstep the bounds of women's accepted domestic role. It attacked alcohol primarily as a threat to the sanctity of the home and family and drew heavily on women's church networks. The Klan-dominated paper *Fellowship Forum* expressed a similar evaluation of the WCTU, stating that the group "believes in women's rights but isn't feminist."[2]

The WCTU did not share the vicious, hate-mongering attitudes of the later Klan movement. Indeed, the WCTU had black members and a commitment to work with immigrants and ethnic minorities. But ultimately, Bordin argues, the WCTU "could not really rise above its white Protestant middle class origins." By the 1890s the WCTU bowed to increasingly popular nativist sentiment and stressed alleged connections among Catholics, immigrants, and alcohol.[3]

In some states, antiliquor forces like the WCTU wielded a great amount of political power through electoral and legislative success. For many individuals, especially midwestern Protestant men, Prohibition was the single strongest influence on party alignment and voting choice. Among the champions of the Prohibitionist cause in Indiana was the Anti-Saloon League (ASL). This powerful national organization was built on a network of evangelist and mainstream Protestant churches and claimed responsibility for the Wright Bone Dry Law in Indiana, which made it a felony to have liquor in an automobile and prevented judges from suspending the sentences of those convicted of violating the law. Notwithstanding its denials, the Indiana ASL had strong ties with the Klan and served as a conduit for many to enter the KKK and WKKK.[4]

Religious evangelism influenced Barr and other Klanswomen of the 1920s. In the climate of the early twentieth-century Midwest, the transition from religious to political activist was an easy one. Religion nearly always shaped politics, and politics often shaped religion. As an Indiana historian comments, "religion was the fundamental source of political conflict in the Midwest . . . [forming] the issues and the rhetoric of politics."[5]

The life history of Daisy Barr (born Brushwiller) illustrates the combination of religious evangelism with zeal for combatting moral corruption and alcohol that led into the women's Klan in the 1920s. The granddaughter of a pioneer and Methodist minister in Grant County, Indiana, Barr was born in the small town of Jonesboro in 1876. According to her autobiography, her parents (like those of Alma White) were greatly disappointed by her birth, as they had hoped for a son to carry on the Christian ministry. Like Alma White, Barr surmounted early obstacles to pursue a path toward the ministry. She was moved first to give oral testimony of her spiritual commitment at the age of four at a Friends' meeting. At eight and again at twelve, Barr felt a personal call from God to the ministry. At sixteen she began preaching at a Friends' meeting.[6]

Barr's commitment to the gospel, combined with a natural talent for elocution, quickly made her a celebrated Quaker minister. She was ordained in 1896 and held memberships and offices in meetings in Indiana at Upland, Westland, Greenfield, Muncie, Lewisville, Fairmount, and New Castle. Contemporaries of Barr's remember her "rare intellectual attainments" and great power as an orator and preacher. The *Minutes of the Yearly Meetings of Friends* noted Barr's "personal magnetism and zeal, together with natural eloquence [that] attracted large numbers and many were won to Christ through her preaching."[7] Recalling Barr's preaching in a small town outside Indianapolis, a woman informant extolled her excellence as an orator: "She was a marvelous speaker. Oh, I just sat there . . . she just had you spellbound . . . she talked about the Bible of course. And made everything very plain, very clear and very interesting. She had a marvelous crowd."[8]

Daisy married Thomas Barr in 1893 and bore a son, Thomas, Jr., in 1895. Daisy's husband was a man of many and varied careers, including teacher, school principal, deputy sheriff, meat inspector, clerk, and bank examiner. Like Daisy, he was a member of the Friends' church and, in the 1920s, a member of the Klan, although he never achieved the prominence his wife did in either organization.[9]

Daisy Barr's social activism and public acclaim began in the early 1910s during her ministry at the First Friends' Meeting of Muncie. At the time the Quakers were emphasizing social purity and temperance as means of social reform. Barr adopted this social agenda and quickly became a leading figure in Muncie politics. Her organizing talents first came to notice in 1911 during a local antialcohol campaign when she recruited her own sisters and an evangelist singer to campaign for the dry cause in both white and black Muncie churches. A contemporary remembers the exhilaration of Barr's crusade, in which even children had a part. "And they even had yells . . . when the young people would get together and I remember every one of them: 'Easy Daisy, Who's a Daisy, Daisy Douglas Barr.'"[10]

Barr was very successful in organizing women for temperance, attracting sixteen hundred women to a single meeting. She became president of a female affiliate of the Muncie Dry League and active in the temperance union. As her fame as an organizer grew, Barr was in high demand to speak and to preach. She traveled throughout Indiana as an evangelist and a propagandist for the cause of temperance, setting up "protracted meetings" for as long as ten days in a single community with the support of local churches.[11]

Like other temperance advocates, Barr argued that alcohol had particularly devastating effects on women. Women were forced to bear the brunt of men's enchantment with alcohol, which "stings his family, degrades his wife, marks his children, and breaks the heart of his mother." Barr's oratory combined opposition to alcohol with a call for passage of the women's suffrage amendment, a message that many of her female followers took to heart. "I just thought she was marvelous. You know, she had a silver tongue. She could really talk. Some of the women [influenced by Barr] were active in helping to get women the vote."[12]

Both as evangelist and political organizer, Barr emphasized the effects of all social vices on the lives of women. Of special concern were the temptations faced by young working girls in the city. Loneliness, poverty, and contact with unsavory elements in factory life, Barr warned, lured young women into a life of prostitution. To combat these temptations Barr organized a Young Women's Christian Association (YWCA) in Muncie, to supplement the branch of the Young Men's Christian Association (YMCA) established earlier by the local elite.[13]

Barr advocated rights as well as protection for women. She used her fame as an evangelist to encourage advocates of women's equality to join the church. One sermon told of a woman who was interested in women's progress and who was brought back to spiritual faith when she entered Barr's tabernacle to support the female ministry.[14]

Barr was adamant in her call for the admission of women to the ministry. In an article in the widely circulated *Indianapolis News*, she was insistent:

> One can hardly imagine, under our present day progress, that most of the religious denominations in our own country still refuse the rite of ordination to women applicants. Women have entered the professions of law, medicine, teaching, art, music and even are wrestling with the sciences. . . . And yet the relic of our barbarism and heathenisn [*sic*] dogmas, when the belief was current that women had no souls, is still evident in the fact that other doors are open, while the holy ministry still bars her free entrance.[15]

When local newspapers in Muncie agreed to reprint her sermons Daisy's political fortunes soared. The combination of pulpit and newspaper gave Barr a powerful forum for her views, which included denunciation of the Sunday retail trade, opposition to the sexual double standard, and a diatribe against church members who used racial slurs. By the mid-1910s her political opinion had weight throughout the city. In 1913 she was appointed president of the powerful Humane Society, a post from which she lobbied the city to create a position for a policewoman who would reform and convert prostitutes. When the mayor appointed an antitemperance Catholic, Barr took her campaign against prostitution in a direction that she could control more directly, by establishing a home for prostitutes. The resulting Friendly Inn opened in 1914, with Barr as its president.

Barr appealed to the Muncie public to support the Friendly Inn so that the community's crackdown on vice would not ruin the lives of girls working as prostitutes, whom she portrayed as victims—as well as perpetrators—of crime and immorality. Without the Friendly Inn, she warned, women deprived of a home and means of support by Muncie's cleanup campaign would be "thrown on to the streets, either to starve or infect the community with a scattered evil instead of a segregated one." The Friendly Inn, however, was plagued with problems. It had difficulty finding a suitable matron to guard and reform the "unfortunate and wayward" inmates. For their part, prostitutes refused to remain in the home to be cured. The strictures Barr placed on admission to the Friendly Inn—to accept only those who were not addicted to drugs, drink, or cigarettes, who had not been procurers or proprietors of vice resorts, and who were free of "loathsome and infectious diseases"—limited its usefulness to prostitutes. The Friendly Inn closed the same year.[16]

In the late 1910s Barr's interests changed, in a direction that would shape her later work in the Klan. During a dry campaign in Muncie she became acquainted with the traveling evangelist Milford H. Lyon and spent a year in his crusade as the superintendent of work among women. Lyon's method of evangelism in unconventional locations showed Barr a way to reach those who did not attend church. She preached in factories, halls, garages, streets, shops, and businesses as in tabernacles, sharpening her ability to relate to people from a variety of social classes.[17]

Barr's entry into electoral politics, and into the Klan movement, began in the early 1920s. She was active in the Women's Department Club and the Women's Republican Club and rose quickly in the Republican party (GOP), serving as the first female Republican vice-chair of the state of Indiana during the administration of Governor Warren

McCray. Her political influence in the Republican party helped her husband gain a position as deputy state bank commissioner, a post to which he was appointed by the Klan-backed governor, Ed Jackson.[18]

Several factors led Barr into the Klan. First, she was adamantly opposed to alcohol. The Klan championed the cause of Prohibition and promised to rid communities of bootleggers, moonshiners, and drunkards. This stance probably accounts for the seemingly anomalous presence of several Quaker ministers (both women and men) as preachers and organizers in the Indiana Klan. Local Indiana histories claim that kleagles were instructed to visit Friends' meetings first to gain recruits when they arrived to organize a new community.[19]

Second, the Klan appealed to Barr's desire to end social and political corruption. Barr's work with the Friendly Inn and other cleanup campaigns had little success in ending prostitution, gambling, and vice. The Klan promised success in such endeavors. Since it was not bound by legal restrictions, the Klan claimed that its concerted drive would rid a community of social evils and corrupt influences in short order.

Third, even as a temperance leader and revivalist Barr held political views consistent with those of the 1920s Klan. She demanded curbs on immigration, proclaimed the superior rights of the native-born, and called for the protection of women against what she saw as immigrant, Catholic, and Jewish purveyors of vice and corruption. A sermon from the 1910s foretold Barr's xenophobic rhetoric and use of womanhood as a code for white native-born privilege:

> I am utterly disgusted that a man from the foreign land can come here and be made an American citizen in 12 months, when it takes an American born man 21 years with the public schools of our country back of him to become a franchised citizen. . . . The New Patriotism is a patriotism that will take care of the womanhood and its young . . . no nation ever rises above its womanhood.[20]

Opportunism and greed also probably played a part in Barr's attraction to the Klan. After years of preaching and organizing Barr had the ability, and the extensive network of personal contacts, to succeed in the Klan. For its part the Klan had much to offer Daisy—jobs for her husband, wealth and power for herself.

Stephenson brought Barr into the Klan as head of the Queens of the Golden Mask (QGM), a female counterpart of his Indiana KKK. Insisting on tight control of her organization, Barr hired field representatives to travel Indiana to recruit for the QGM. Under Barr and Stephenson, the Indiana KKK and QGM grew so rapidly that they threatened Evans's hold over the national Klan organization and caused a battle for control between Stephenson and Evans. As a result, the QGM was dissolved and Barr defected to Evans's camp. Her talent as a women's organizer was now firmly established and Barr's fortunes in the Klan continued to rise.[21]

Barr quickly gained national stature in the Klan movement. She was the only woman to speak at the first annual meeting of KKK Grand Dragons in July 1923 at Asheville, North Carolina. There Barr read a poem, "The Soul of America," which suggested that the Klan represented the very essence of the American nation: strong, righteous, just, pure, and all-seeing.[22] That same month, Barr and Evans entered into an agreement whereby Barr would organize chapters of the WKKK in Indiana, Ohio, Kentucky, West Virginia, Pennsylvania, New York, Michigan, and Minnesota in exchange for four dollars of the five-dollar initiation fee paid by new members.[23]

As head of the Indiana WKKK and as an organizer for many state WKKK realms Barr was an immense success. Already well known throughout the Midwest as a preacher, Barr attracted large crowds of women to secret organizing meetings for the WKKK in the same towns and cities in which she had been a revival speaker. In large cities like Indianapolis Barr spoke jointly with Evans. In smaller communities she was the featured speaker. In five months Barr spoke at WKKK gatherings in nearly every corner of Indiana, led dozens of WKKK contingents in Klan parades, and personally recruited seventy-five thousand Indiana and Ohio women into the WKKK.[24]

Barr used her position as a Quaker preacher to great effect in Klan organizing, telling a group of women in Marion, Indiana, that if Christ were on earth at the present time he would certainly join the Klan. Barr was sophisticated in her understanding of the role that spectacle and social life could play in the appeal of the Klan. Her speeches were dramatic and her presentations carefully staged and crafted. Moreover, in each community she sought ways to integrate Klan life with the social life of the resident white Protestants. In Marion, for example, she attempted to turn the Ambulance Choir into a Klan choral group.[25]

Barr's work in the Klan was not without problems. In one highly publicized incident in 1923, Barr was forced from one of her most prominent civic positions—the Indiana War Mothers—under a cloud of accusations about her Klan connections. Several years earlier Barr had been elected president and honorary State War Mother of the Indiana chapter of the American War Mothers (AWM), a national organization of women that originated in the wartime drive for food conservation. Barr pressed women to act on their political and civic obligations as mothers of servicemen. Motherhood, Barr insisted, was an inherently political role, as seen in the "patriotism [that] has always lived in the hearts of mothers."[26]

Barr rose quickly in the American War Mothers, showing the talent and enthusiasm for political life that had served her well in local Muncie politics. She undertook an investigation of the state's veterans' hospitals, demanding better hospitals for the state's soldiers. She also traveled to France to investigate the postwar situation and returned to campaign against the United States' forgiving any wartime debts owed by foreign nations because of France's "spirit of ingratitude for the service of the Americans." Alice Moore French, the first head of the Indiana War Mothers, recalled that in Barr's early days in the organization, "everything looked hopeful [as] Mrs Barr was a popular evangelist of the Friends Church and [of] our Indiana War Mothers."[27]

The political aptitude that caused her rise in the AWM also led to her downfall in the organization. By 1923 it was clear to the members that Barr was using her AWM connections to recruit kleagles for the WKKK. Although some in the AWM may have found Barr's work in the Klan consistent with the AWM philosophy, its leaders worried that Barr's public appearances for the Klan while still president of the Indiana War Mothers could spell disaster for the organization. Barr's highly publicized address in March 1923 to five hundred cheering Klanswomen in Franklin, Indiana, was the last straw. French demanded Barr's resignation, arguing that she was "using the AWM to introduce the Ku Klux Klan as a more exciting and easy way to make money." Barr resigned to devote herself to the work of the Klan.[28]

Barr was also caught in internecine Klan battles. As she became more and more powerful in the Klan, Barr clashed with Evans, as she had with Stephenson. According to Barr, it was Evans who sponsored the lawsuit filed against her and several others by Mary Benadum, a Klanswoman in Muncie, Indiana. Barr also charged Evans with responsibility for a lawsuit filed in the Grant-Delaware Superior Court by the WKKK. This suit claimed that Barr had failed to remit $1 for each of forty thousand members she had recruited (a number derived by rifling Barr's files in the WKKK Ohio office) and demanded

$45,085 in restitution. Further, the suit charged Barr with depriving the WKKK of revenue by selling Klan robes from an unauthorized source at a personal profit that a dissident Klansman estimated at $1 million.[29]

Anti-Klan newspapers had a field day ridiculing Barr's battles with Hiram ("Hi") Evans, so soon after her legal tussle with Mary Benadum ("Ben"):

> Daisy Doodle's sued again
> By Hi this time, and not by Ben.
> Perhaps you think that Daisy's flighty,
> But she got it all at ten per nighty.
> A million bucks she got, 'tis said
> And gave to the wizard nary a red.
> So the goblins cussed and the dragons swore
> They'd get the dough or a bucket of gore.[30]

That same year Barr was indicted by an Ohio grand jury when one of her WKKK field organizers, operating under Barr's control, embezzled the WKKK treasury in Zanesville, Ohio.[31]

Barr left Indiana in the wake of the Stephenson scandal that brought down the Klan in Indiana. In 1926 she ran for Congress from a district in Florida but withdrew her name before the election. After that Barr dropped from public sight. In 1938 she was killed in an auto accident in Indiana.

Lillian Sedwick, a much less prominent WKKK figure than Daisy Barr, paralleled Barr in her entrance to the Klan through the temperance movement. Sedwick, born in 1880, received her political education in the WCTU for which she served as state superintendent, county director of the young people's branch, and local president of its northeastern union. In addition to the temperance movement, Sedwick was active in a number of civic organizations. She was a member of the Queen Esther chapter, Order of the Eastern Star; White Shrine of Jerusalem; Southeastern Rebekah Lodge; the International Order of Odd Fellows; and the Betsy Ross Federation. She was a member of the Methodist Episcopal church. She married Thomas Sedwick (a railroad yardmaster), raised three daughters, and attended Moores' Hill College in Indiana.

In the 1920s Sedwick became an active and powerful member of the WKKK in Indianapolis and in 1926 was elected president of the Marion County (Indianapolis) WKKK. Throughout her time in the Klan Sedwick maintained a simultaneous career in electoral politics. A year before being elected to the WKKK presidency, Sedwick gained a seat on the Indianapolis board of school commissioners on the United Protestant ticket, a slate openly supported by the Marion County KKK and WKKK. The Exalted Cyclops of Marion County presided at a huge pre-election rally in which Klan-backed candidates for mayor, city council, and school board were presented to the public, amidst Klan-led prayers and speeches. That year Klan-supported candidates swept a number of Indianapolis electoral offices, including that of mayor.

As a member of the majority faction but the only woman member on the school board, Sedwick exerted much political power in Indianapolis. In 1926 she gained control of the board's instruction committee, which allowed her great influence over the appointment of county schoolteachers. Sedwick and her allies on the school board did not begin, but did intensify, racial segregation in the schools of Indianapolis. Three years earlier the Indianapolis school board had voted to establish separate high schools for black and white students and the following year had redrawn district boundaries to exclude more black pupils from majority-white elementary schools. The election of the Klan slate coincided with agitation from the Klan, Klan-affiliated racist groups like the White Supremacy League, and the Indianapolis Federation of Community Clubs demanding that schools be completely segregated by race and that instruction in the New Testament be mandatory in public schools.[32]

ROUTES THROUGH ELECTORAL
AND SUFFRAGE POLITICS

Another path to the 1920s women's Klan in Indiana was politics. In the postwar, post–Bolshevik Revolution era of "red scares" and heightened nativism in the United States, political leaders, civic associations, and even movements for women's equality often supported an agenda of repressive patriotism and xenophobia. This was true in Indiana where women's organizations had a history of militant antiradicalism and isolationist sentiment before, and independent of, the WKKK. In early 1923, for example, a number of state women's associations, including the Business and Professional Women and the League of Women Voters, worked with the Indiana Bar Association to counteract radicalism in the state. Local women's clubs frequently sponsored speeches about the racial peril of unlimited immigration and the threat to Prohibition posed by foreign-born residents. A common topic at women's church and missionary societies was how to define and protect "true" Americans. Speakers constantly evoked images of threatening and mysterious outsiders as they beseeched listeners to defend the "real American home," "the real American woman," and "true citizenship." In this context the WKKK's call for preservation of 100 percent Americans was not extraordinary.[33]

The lives of Mary Benadum and Vivian Wheatcraft, both reputed organizers of the Indiana WKKK, illustrate a path into the Klan through electoral politics and civic involvement. In Benadum and Wheatcraft the Klan acquired women with impressive connections and extensive histories of political involvement. Certainly one key to the success of the Indiana WKKK was this ability to target as organizers women who were well known and respected in their communities.

Mary Benadum was born in 1890 and attended public schools in Delaware County, Indiana. She graduated from Valparaiso University (which the KKK tried unsuccessfully to purchase as a Klan college in the 1920s). Benadum taught public school for twelve years in Muncie. She was active in Republican party politics, serving as precinct committeewoman, president of the Delaware County Women's Republican Club, and vice-chair of the tenth district (Indiana) Republican central committee. A renowned lecturer and public speaker, Benadum belonged to the Methodist church and the Business and Professional Women's Club of Indiana. Her husband was Clarence E. Benadum, a noted attorney who served as prosecuting attorney for Delaware County.[34]

Her social prominence notwithstanding, Mary Benadum was a very vocal public leader of the WKKK. She organized Klanswomen as a force in electoral politics, canvassing door to door for Klan candidates and engineering large turnouts of women on election day to vote for Klan-backed candidates. Benadum, like Barr, heralded women's newly won political enfranchisement. Speaking before three thousand women at a Klan rally in Youngstown, Ohio, Benadum envisioned imminent victory for the Invisible Empire through the power of women's ballots: "It has been wonderful already what part women have played in politics. It is being made cleaner and are [sic] almost purged from rottenness."[35]

Benadum and Barr battled for control of the central Ohio WKKK, setting off public conflict. In 1924 Benadum led her faction of the WKKK into a melee with the WKKK faction of a rival organizer—

probably Barr—in Alliance, Ohio. It was finally quelled by the police after one woman was seriously injured and Benadum was treated for nervous shock.[36]

A more serious confrontation between Barr and Benadum emerged in the courts. Benadum filed suit against Barr in circuit court in Muncie in early 1924. The suit asked $50,000 in damages for an alleged defamation of Benadum's character by Barr, Thomas Barr, Clarissa Spangler (Barr's Muncie agent), Gertrude Hawkins (a WKKK organizer in Delaware County), and Hazel Dickens (a personal representative of the Barrs). Benadum claimed that Hawkins and Spangler, acting on behalf of Daisy Barr, told a meeting of five hundred local WKKK women that Benadum had "gone South" after stealing $3000 from the WKKK treasury. Moreover, Benadum charged that she was prevented from attending two meetings of the Muncie WKKK—one with two thousand women in attendance—at which she planned to refute the charges. Benadum claimed that she had earned "the respect and esteem of the citizens of Muncie and Delaware County" during a decade of teaching school and that her reputation was impaired by Barr's slanderous accusations. In court Barr replied that James Comer and Hiram Evans had contrived the suit to strengthen their control of the women's Klan. The suit was withdrawn when Benadum and her husband moved to Ohio to take positions as kleagles in the WKKK and KKK, respectively.[37]

Benadum's public exposure in the WKKK did not end her career in electoral politics. Even after the Klan collapsed, she remained active in the national and Indiana state Republican organizations. As a Republican party official, Benadum traveled through Indiana in the 1940s, speaking on behalf of local, state, and national Republican candidates. She also chaired the successful 1952 senatorial reelection campaign of Indiana's William Jenner, who then recommended her appointment to a judgeship in the United States Tax Court.[38]

Vivian Wheatcraft, like Mary Benadum, was a highly controversial leader in the Indiana WKKK. She came to the WKKK with extensive experience and, like Benadum, made her time in the Klan a stepping-stone rather than a check to later political involvement. Wheatcraft first became active in politics in 1920 as the vice-chair of the Johnson County (Indiana) Republican Committee. In 1921 she advanced to the vice-chair position in Indiana's fourth electoral district and two years later was elected by the Republican state committee as state vice-chair. In addition, she was instrumental in organizing the Indiana Statehouse

Women's Republican Club and served as president of the Indiana Women's Republican Club.

In 1924 controversy erupted over Wheatcraft's role in state politics. The state industrial board attempted to place Wheatcraft as director of its department of women and children, edging out the occupant, Margaret Hoop. When Hoop refused to cede her position, Wheatcraft was appointed director of intelligence and education for the state fire marshall's office. The following year Wheatcraft succeeded in wresting the directorship from Hoop and during the 1924 campaign headed the women's committee for the state Republican party.[39]

Governor Jackson fired Wheatcraft from the state fire marshall's office in 1925, claiming that Wheatcraft had engaged in political activity on behalf of Senator James E. Watson and his allies while she worked in the fire marshall's office. Long affiliated with the Watson faction of the Indiana Republican party, Wheatcraft then became head of the women's organization in the reelection campaign of Senator Watson. In that position, Wheatcraft built a formidable women's political organization and informally managed the Watson campaign. Watson owed much of his political success to Wheatcraft's organizing talents. When she boasted, "I taught women how to vote," the estimated 60 percent of the female vote cast for Watson bore out her claim.[40]

In 1926 the Republican committeewomen of Vigo County demanded that Wheatcraft be removed as vice-chair of the Republican state committee for defaming women in the Indiana GOP. Wheatcraft told an interviewer for the *Baltimore Sun* that Watson's senatorial reelection success derived from "a poison squad of whispering women." Alluding to Klan involvement in the state Republican party, Wheatcraft claimed a "victory of gossip" through "scores of skirted lieutenants" and declared that her "little black book" contained the names of five women in each county who were members of a so-called poison squad of whispering women through whom she could spread any gossip across the state in twelve hours. Wheatcraft compared her women's network to the "Whispering Women of the Piave" whose defeatist propaganda contributed to Italian military defeat in 1917.[41]

Wheatcraft was caught up in the scandals that followed Stephenson's conviction. From prison, Stephenson (who was pressuring the governor for a pardon) confirmed the Klan's involvement in campaign payments to Governor Jackson and other Republican officials. Wheatcraft, then the vice-chairman of the Republican state committee, was linked to a $240 check dated October 6, 1924, that she claimed Stephenson gave her to pay the salary of Mrs. Allen T. Fleming as a field worker in the Republican women's organization in the campaign of 1924. Fleming denied the charge, insisting that she was a party worker before October 1924 and never worked under Wheatcraft. Wheatcraft was also accused of working in Watson's campaign while still holding office in the GOP central committee, in violation of the spirit, if not the actual letter, of the state's Corrupt Practices Act. Like others in the Klan, however, Wheatcraft continued her political career undaunted by the fall of the Klan in Indiana. The Republican congressional committee hired her in 1926 to organize women in Maine.[42]

Others entered the Klan through non-electoral political experience. Klanswomen often had backgrounds in racist nativist movements, in women's suffrage, and even in progressive politics. These odd routes into the Klan were possible for two reasons. Some leaders of the women's suffrage movement used nativist and racist arguments and rhetoric, calling for votes for white women to counter the votes of black and immigrant men.[43] In addition, the Klan masked its right-wing political agenda under layers of support for the rights of the "common" man and woman. Because of this, the Klan appealed to women from very different points on the political spectrum. Ann Carroll, a racist leader from Indianapolis, and Lillian Rouse, a progressive leader in rural Indiana, exemplify the diverse mixture in the women's Klan of Indiana.[44]

Ann Carroll, a WKKK leader in the large and powerful Marion County klavern, was an outspoken racist leader in Indianapolis for years before the Klan started to build its Indiana realms. At one level Carroll was the model of respectable civic involvement. She was a charter member of the Indianapolis chapter of the League of Women Voters, a member of the Methodist church, Center Civic League, Rebekah Lodge, and other civic improvement associations. At another, Carroll was the force behind the White Supremacy League of Indianapolis in which she served as president in 1922. A fierce proponent of white privilege, Carroll was a vocal Klanswoman; when the Indiana WKKK collapsed she ran unsuccessfully for the Indiana state House of Representatives as an unaffiliated right-wing candidate.[45]

Lillian Rouse, in contrast, came to the women's Klan in a rural county in east-central Indiana through women's suffrage and progressive politics. Rouse was more highly educated than most rural Indiana women at the turn of the twentieth century, having earned a high school diploma. Both literature and politics interested her; she regularly read the *Literary Digest* and (in the 1930s) *The Progressive* and fancied herself open to "offbeat" and progressive politics. Indeed, she described herself as a socialist, pointing to her support for government aid for the elderly and a guaranteed living wage. She saw no contradiction between those positions and the Klan, although she admitted that she favored restricting those eligible for government assistance.

Rouse came from a family of suffragists and herself supported women's suffrage. She was an active member of the WCTU and its young people's affiliate. Although both she and her husband were in the Klan, they saw their choices as distinct. Her husband had little formal education (in fact, she taught him to read as an adult) and less progressive politics than his wife. He expressed only mild support for women's suffrage and women's employment and little interest in activist politics except for the Klan, which he regarded as a social club. Lillian Rouse, however, saw the Klan as the logical outcome of her desire to be an informed, active citizen and recalled the WKKK as "a club stressing good government."[46]

Of course, there were women in the 1920s whose motivations to join the WKKK had less to do with politics, religious commitment, or civic involvement than family and personal situations. Examples are Ellen Curtis, a member of a klavern in a small town in north-central Indiana, and Nancy Taylor, a Klanswoman from south-central Indiana.[47]

Ellen Curtis was raised in a pioneer family in southern Indiana that held membership in the Friends' church and taught its children to value education and culture. She attended college and married a man who had to leave college after three years to manage his father's farm. Curtis's life, which had revolved around social life, reading, and cultural activities, narrowed considerably when she became a farmer's wife. The isolated rural county in which they settled and raised children offered her little. Activities considered appropriate for married women—the Home Economics Club and church auxiliaries—did not appeal to her. When a WKKK klavern was organized in the county, Curtis was immediately attracted. As her daughter recalled, "this Klan thing really meant something to her in kind of a social way. There wasn't anything social in her life before like that, except her family."

The seeds for Curtis's attraction to the Klan were already in place in the 1920s. Her mother-in-law, an early and active suffragist and clubwoman, was rabidly anti-Catholic, referring to Catholics as "bead-rattlers." Although Curtis herself was not involved in the WCTU or other temperance activities, she had an inclination to temperance, refraining from joining the WCTU only because of her husband's "little drinking problem." Until the advent of the women's Klan, Curtis's political life was limited to voting and expressing her support for the right of married women to work outside the home. Klan activities awoke her interest in politics; like her husband, a precinct committeeman, she became involved in local politics. She did not sustain this interest after the Klan collapsed in the late 1920s. She seldom again read political magazines and rarely held political positions that differed from those of her husband.[48]

For Nancy Taylor, a Quaker minister, involvement in the Klan, by her own admission, was motivated by the money she was offered to become a lecturer-minister on behalf of the Indiana WKKK. Little in Nancy Taylor's biography suggests that she would become a Klanswoman. Taylor was the first social worker in her small town, which adjoined the community in which she ministered at a Friends' church. Orphaned at a young age, Taylor married a successful local businessman who paid the expenses for her travels around the country on behalf of parentless children. She was appointed to the state board of charities for her work on behalf of orphaned and deserted children and was an advocate of women's suffrage and of temperance. Taylor freely acknowledged that she joined the Klan for financial reasons. For several years, she combined her social welfare work with her advocacy of the Klan and, when the Klan collapsed, continued her work for charities.[49]

RANK-AND-FILE KLANSWOMEN

These life histories of WKKK leaders in Indiana suggest that prior involvement in temperance, religious evangelism, electoral politics, or women's suffrage were common routes into the 1920s women's Klan in Indiana. But we do not know whether they were routes only for women who achieved prominence and leadership positions within the WKKK. Thus we also need to examine the anonymous rank-and-file members of the WKKK.

Ideally, an analysis of the personal and political backgrounds of nonleaders of the WKKK in Indiana would require data on a random sample of Klanswomen. Unfortunately, in a secret organization like the WKKK this is impossible. No comprehensive or even partial listing of Klanswomen survives. I relied instead on four indirect methods to identify rank-and-file Klanswomen in Indiana.

I first included those members of the WKKK who used their names publicly as leaders or spokeswomen for the WKKK. This source detected only women who were willing to have their names publicly associated with the Klan, women with an unusually great commitment to the Klan, a prominent position in the Klan, or the ability (through secure family position) to suffer the consequences of public recognition.

As a second source, I considered women to be WKKK members if their Klan membership was reported in either of the influential anti-Klan papers, *Tolerance* (Chicago) or *Post-Democrat* (Muncie, Indiana). This is a more tenuous identification, as these papers used sources for identification that cannot be traced and no doubt included rumor and personal allegation as well as stolen Klan membership lists. In fact, I could glean little information aside from names and addresses about most of the women identified in the newspapers.

Third, I identified women in the Hartford City, Indiana, WKKK through a complete surviving receipt book of the local Godfrey Klan no. 93 for 1924 to 1932. It listed the WKKK treasurers and minor local officers, together with occasional names of non-officer members. I then traced the backgrounds of these women by searching the city directories of Hartford City for thirty years prior to the Klan.

The fourth, and single best source of information about anonymous Klanswomen, came from newspapers' obituaries. The WKKK publicized funeral rituals of its members in the *Fiery Cross*. Many local Indiana papers sympathetic to the Klan also published descriptions and photographs of Klanswomen's funerals.[50] Biographical information about Klanswomen named in funeral rituals I traced through local newspaper obituaries, county histories, genealogies and biographies, indexes, and records at local historical societies and libraries. In this way, I obtained information about the lives of women whose Klan membership was secret throughout their lives—and who died between 1923 and 1925. Of course, relying on obituaries for biographical information introduces some atypicality since the probability of death is related to such factors as occupation, social class, and, most important, age. In the 1920s, however, the mortality risks of childbirth and infectious disease meant that the deaths did not occur only at advanced ages. Thus, among women identified as Klanswomen, the age at death ranged from 19 to 82 with an average age of 43.3 years.

Using these four methods, I found a total of 118 Indiana Klanswomen with significant biographical information, in addition to those already profiled in the biographies. With these data I could begin to analyze several common assumptions about what women joined the WKKK in Indiana.

First, many Klan histories assume that women joined the Klan in the 1920s only through and because of their husbands' Klan membership. The data on Klanswomen in Indiana suggests that this was not necessarily the case. Of 118 women, 19 (16 percent) were clearly identified as single and never married at the time of their death in the mid-1920s; 7 women (6 percent) were clearly identified as widowed. The marital status of the remaining 92 is less clear, as they were identified as "Mrs.," a term used for currently married, widowed, and divorced women. Even under the extremely conservative assumption that every woman identified as "Mrs." was then married and residing with a husband who was a Klansman, only 78 percent of the identified women had the possibility of joining the WKKK because of their husbands' KKK membership.

Another way to test the assumption of women following husbands into the Klan was to assess the joint membership status of men and women. This required using only those women identified in *Tolerance,* a newspaper that listed Klan membership by address separately for men and women for a few cities. Nineteen women were listed in *Tolerance* as belonging to the WKKK in Rushville or Michigan City, Indiana. Of these, only five had husbands listed as belonging to the KKK.

More impressionistic evidence also supports the conclusion that all women did not follow husbands into the Klan. One woman was described, derogatorily, by the *Post-Democrat* of Muncie as busy campaigning for the WKKK in Michigan while her poor beleaguered husband stayed at home in Indiana doing the housekeeping. And, of course, men followed women into the Klan as well as the reverse. An Indiana KKK kleagle commented, for example, that the "ladies' organization" was responsible for two men who joined his klavern during the past week "because their wives preached KKK to them from morn' to night."[51]

There are other indications that the pattern of recruitment of Klanswomen was similar to that of Klansmen. Twenty-five (21 percent) of the women had paid occupations, a conservative estimate of the true number working for wages since data on occupations were not always provided in the obituaries and rarely reported in newspaper accounts. In addition, a number of women not included by these sources among employed women were listed in Klan records as being paid for work done part-time on behalf of the Klan.[52] Among women whose occupations can be identified, seven (28 percent) held professional or proprietary jobs. These included two physicians, a chiropractor, a nurse, a realtor, and two shop owners. Twelve women (44 percent) worked full-time in politics, either as party officials, political office holders, or organizers for the women's Klan. The remainder held other occupations, including those of dressmaker, laborer, and clerical worker.[53]

Although it is impossible to generalize from such a small number of cases, most Klanswomen probably were middle class or working class. Data from Indiana rank-and-file Klanswomen and WKKK leaders suggest that Klanswomen, like Klansmen, were not marginal members of society.[54] For twenty-four of the identified Klanswomen, information is available on the occupations of their husbands (who were not necessarily themselves in the Klan) in the mid-1920s. Eight of these husbands (33 percent) had professional or business jobs, including fire chief, physician, and town mayor. Two were farm owners, two were in the military, three were salesmen, two had skilled occupations, six were semiskilled or unskilled workers, and one was a bootlegger.

Biographies of WKKK leaders indicate that civic and religious involvement was a route for women into the Klan's world. It was for rank-and-file Klanswomen as well. Virtually all women whose church affiliation was recorded were "active churchwomen," participating in women's auxiliaries of church societies. The Quaker affiliation of two Indiana WKKK leaders was matched by none of the other women. The most common affiliations were Methodist, Baptist, Christian, and Methodist Episcopal, consistent with research on the religious membership of Klansmen.

Most rank-and-file women of the Klan also belonged to political, civic, or fraternal organizations in addition to their Klan membership. Indeed, through these associations many women likely became interested in joining the women's Klan. Many belonged to the women's auxiliaries of male fraternal societies or Masonic lodges (Degree of Pocahontas, Pythian Sisters, Rebekah Lodge, Eastern Star). Other associations listed in the biographies include civic societies (League of Women Voters, Civic League), patriotic societies (American War

Mothers), leagues of exclusivity (Daughters of the American Revolution, Homeowners Union) and the Women's Christian Temperance Union.

The connection between civic involvement and Klan membership again underlines the continuity of Klan philosophy with the political culture and attitudes of many Indiana women in the early 1920s. City and rural county newspapers of the time were full of notices for meetings of women to discuss immigration restrictions, the virtues of Protestantism, Prohibition, national pride, declining public morality, the "godlessness" of public school teaching, the impending threat posed by immigrating radicals, and how to exercise newly granted voting rights in a patriotic, God-fearing direction. In some sense, the women's Klan posed few—if any—new political ideas. Rather, the WKKK consolidated and made exciting a political philosophy that had long penetrated movements for women's suffrage, temperance, and civic improvement.

CHAPTER V

A Poison Squad
of Whispering Women

The 100 percent American women of the WKKK created an organization that was enormously and disastrously successful. It extended from one end of Indiana to the other, recruiting women from cities, small towns, and farms. Women from a variety of white Protestant backgrounds found a common purpose in white supremacist politics; in the WKKK, they also found camaraderie and friendship. In complicated, often subtle ways, the social and political activities of Indiana Klanswomen advanced the Klan's agenda of racial and religious hatred.

DIFFUSION OF THE WKKK IN INDIANA

The order's activity was first reported in early 1923 in central Indiana, in the communities of Clarks Hill, Muncie, Franklin, Indianapolis, and Shelbyville. These initial locations, and the dispersion of WKKK klaverns thereafter, defy any simple interpretation of the appeal and growth of the women's Klan in Indiana. WKKK chapters formed in large industrial cities as well as in small towns and rural communities. Although early WKKK organizing efforts, and the majority of chapters overall, concentrated in the central part of the state, WKKK klaverns existed in nearly every region of Indiana, from the northwestern corner near Chicago to the southeastern edge bordering Louisville, Kentucky (Map 1).

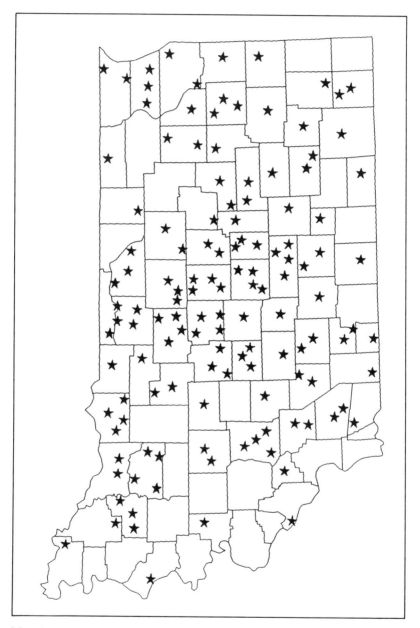

Map 1.   Locations of Indiana WKKK chapters. (Courtesy John Watkins, Department of Geography, University of Kentucky)

Many rallies and local chapters of Indiana's women's Klan clustered within a fifty-mile radius around Indianapolis. For the most part,
the communities in this radius were not suburbs of Indianapolis but
retail and commercial centers for surrounding farms or small manu-
facturing towns. Although small, these communities were not isolated
from the capital city of Indianapolis. An interurban railroad ran from
Indianapolis to outlying towns in the 1920s and my informants
confirm that travel to the capital for shopping and visiting was frequent.

These geographical clusters of WKKK activity and chapters occurred for several reasons. First, although organizers like Daisy Barr
swept the state on speaking and recruiting tours, the bulk of membership recruiting for the WKKK, as for the KKK, was done through personal contacts. Women told female relatives and neighbors and Klansmen told wives about the Klan crusade, spreading the women's Klan
from large WKKK centers like Indianapolis through nearby towns and
rural communities. Second, when professional organizers came to address a WKKK rally they often recruited new members from the surrounding communities as well. Within a two-week period in mid-
1923, for example, Barr spoke at WKKK rallies in the adjacent
southern Indiana towns of Seymour, Crothersville, and Brownstown.[1]
Third, women from established klaverns, along with their Klan bands
and guard companies, traveled to nearby areas to help organize new
klaverns or participate in rallies and parades, creating regional centers
of WKKK strength in Indiana.[2]

Although the exact size of the women's Klan in Indiana is impossible to assess, historians estimate the total membership of Indiana's
WKKK as a quarter-million during the 1920s, or 32 percent of the entire white native-born female population of the state. This figure is
somewhat deceiving, however, since many women were WKKK members only for short periods, making membership estimates at any
specific point lower than cumulative totals.

Membership estimates for a specific year exist for only a few county
and local WKKK chapters. The Indianapolis WKKK had approximately 10,000 members in 1923, or 12 percent of the native white
adult female population of the city. In 1924 the Kokomo WKKK had
2,500 members and the Hartford City WKKK had 750 members, representing 31 percent and 43 percent of the native white adult female
populations of those communities. That same year WKKK chapters in
Martin and Blackford counties each had 500 members, or 17 percent

and 13 percent of the adult white female population of their respective counties.[3]

In the absence of surviving membership rosters, the size of local and county WKKK klaverns can be estimated through reports of WKKK initiations ("naturalizations"), meetings, and parades. Table 1 gives the number of Klanswomen recorded at WKKK events from 1923 to 1925 as well as 1920 population figures for the towns and cities in Indiana where the events were held. It lists the total eligible (native-born adult white female) population and computes WKKK attendance as a percentage of the population eligible for WKKK membership. The percentage is biased downward to some extent by the inclusion of Catholic and Jewish women among native-born white women, but their numbers were small for most communities in Indiana.

These attendance figures must be regarded as very tentative estimates. Although most reports of WKKK activities are taken from county and local histories and non-Klan newspapers, some are from the Klan press (especially the *Fiery Cross*), which was noted for exaggerating attendance and membership figures.[4] The figures cannot be used for precise comparison across communities since estimates are drawn from a number of unrelated sources with differing sources of bias. Though attendance figures tell us how many Klanswomen at-

TABLE 1   ATTENDANCE AT WKKK EVENTS

Site of Event	Attendance	WKKK-Eligible Population[a]	Attendance as % of WKKK-Eligible Population
Advance	375	672[b]	55.8
Alfordsville	300	672[b]	44.6
Auburn	100	1,484	6.7
Billingsville	2,000	672[b]	100.0[c]
Brazil	300	2,536	11.8
Brightwood	500	672[b]	74.4
Carlisle	300	672[b]	44.6
Clinton	41	1,875	2.2
Columbia City	450	1,218	36.9
Columbus	200	2,894	6.9
Frankfort	41	3,727	1.1
Franklin	700	1,654	42.3

TABLE 1   (*continued*)

Site of Event	Attendance	WKKK-Eligible Population[a]	Attendance as % of WKKK-Eligible Population
Greencastle	500	1,249	40.0
Greenfield	100	1,431	7.0
Hobart	550	750	73.3
Indianapolis	10,000	86,885	11.5
Kirklin	500	672[b]	74.4
Knox	100	672[b]	14.8
Kokomo	2,500	8,172	30.6
Lebanon	200	2,091	9.6
Linwood	400	672[b]	59.5
Logansport	1,000	6,375	15.7
Marshall	25	672[b]	3.7
Medaryville	100	672[b]	14.9
Morocco	114	672[b]	17.0
Muncie	500	10,300	4.9
Oakland City	165	672[b]	24.6
Odon	250	672[b]	37.2
Peru	250	3,780	6.6
Rockville	65	672[b]	9.7
Seymour	195	2,322	8.4
Shelbyville	800	3,098	25.8
South Bend	32	14,363	0.2
Summitville	200	672[b]	29.8
Terre Haute	1,400	18,493	7.6
Valparaiso	600	1,942	30.9
Waterloo	300	672[b]	44.6
Washington	1,000	2,620	38.2
Waynetown	15	672[b]	2.2
Wheatland	35	672[b]	5.2

SOURCE: Population figures are from the U.S. Census, 1920, "Population—Indiana," tables 1, 8, 9, 10, 11; WKKK attendance figures are from historical and newspaper accounts.
[a]Total number of adult white native-born women.
[b]Number of WKKK-eligible women is estimated for communities with total populations of fewer than 2,500. Numbers shown are maximum estimates.
[c]This event drew from the surrounding area.

tended an event at a particular site, they do not necessarily show that those women lived at that place or were officially members of the women's Klan. Women traveled around the county, and sometimes across the state, to attend WKKK rallies and meetings. Nevertheless, so little is known about the women's Klan that it is instructive to examine even these imprecise estimates of attendance at WKKK events.

Most women probably joined the WKKK because it coincided with their political beliefs, as it did for one woman who summed up the 1920s Klan: "They were right, were always doing good, and they should be here today."[5] For some, however, the appeal of the WKKK was social. Women's klaverns frequently gave parties for themselves, to meet visiting WKKK dignitaries, to welcome new members or new kleagles, or to bid farewell to departing kleagles. WKKK klaverns from one city invited nearby women's klaverns to teas, parties, and picnics as well as to meetings and rallies. Like church auxiliaries and civic clubs, the WKKK promised friendship; more than these other groups, the WKKK delivered excitement and entertainment. When the Vigo County WKKK sponsored a women's minstrel show and an Aunt Jemima Glee Club at the county fairground outside Terre Haute, it provided both a social event with like-minded women and an enticing break from the monotony of small-town life.[6]

The sense of belonging and collective importance instilled by the women's Klan was evident in the first statewide meeting of the Indiana realm of the WKKK, held in a woods one-half mile outside Mooresville from July 13 to 15, 1923. Klansmembers came to the Mooresville woods from klaverns throughout the state, camping in the woods for the three-day meeting and celebration. By all accounts the WKKK event was a great success for the WKKK and for Mrs. J. Walter Greep, the organizer of the Mooresville WKKK, who planned the state meeting. Newspapers reported that fifty thousand people—divided equally between women and men—attended the meeting, overwhelming the town of eighteen hundred. Two hundred men from the local Horse Thief Detective Association were pressed into service to help with traffic and parking of an estimated twenty thousand automobiles.

WKKK's statewide meeting, like many of its events, combined pomp and pageantry with politics. Christian and Methodist church ministers from Mooresville and Carlisle gave welcoming addresses. Physicians staffed a first aid station. Women from local Protestant churches prepared massive quantities of food and drinks, which they hauled to the wooded spot. Bands and quartets entertained while

Daisy Barr, another speaker from the Indiana WKKK, a Baptist minister, and a Klan lecturer from New York City (the head of the Cavalier Motion Picture Corporation) addressed the crowd on a variety of issues, including problems faced by the white race. That evening three hundred women and seven hundred men of the Klan marched through Mooresville in a mile-long parade headed by state WKKK officers on decorated floats, followed by Klanswomen from each chapter in the state, more floats, bands from a number of cities in Indiana, and a drum and fife corps. The parade ended with a $500 fireworks spectacular and a naturalization ceremony for fifteen hundred female recruits, six hundred of whom received the WKKK's second-degree obligation.[7]

The WKKK was also a vehicle for women's friendships. Friendships made in the WKKK might last a lifetime. One informant in Blackford County claimed that the women's Klan remained active in the early 1930s, long after the men's Klan had disbanded and that some of the Klanswomen continued to get together socially into the 1960s to talk and play cards. Another informant recalled her klavern where "everything was orderly, our little chapter was a friendly association. A fund was kept on hand to purchase a flower cross for funerals."[8] The same was true of other women's klaverns. Although membership rolls were closely guarded and in some klaverns masks were worn even before sister Klanswomen, members insisted that they could identify sister Klanswomen by their physiques, style of walking, and shoes.[9]

Despite the emphasis on social life and social cohesion, many women's Klan chapters in Indiana hummed with internal strife. The Klan's propaganda stressed klannishness and a sisterhood that transcended the petty divisions of the alien world, but such lofty ideals did not necessarily carry over into practice. As the *Muncie Post-Democrat* wrote about the Logansport chapter, "Klanswomen will not associate with sister Klanswomen who they wouldn't associate with before they joined the Klan."[10]

Moreover, issues of morality and "character" with which the Klan assailed its enemies reverberated within the Klan itself. Women who joined the WKKK because of its staunch opposition to moral decay and legal liquor often looked aghast at the women who arrived as local organizers. Accusations that WKKK leaders were of "bad character" or "bad reputation" and thus unfit to direct associations of virtuous church-going women arose in women's Klans and did the organization little good.[11]

Recruitment into the WKKK through personal contact was not always based on friendship or ideological compatibility. Indeed, the desire to recruit more members often reached a fevered pitch. Members
meant money for recruiters and prominence and funds for local Klan
chapters. When targeted recruits were not convinced by a description
of the Klan's fiery crusade, women turned to cajoling, even to threatening, female friends and relatives to get them to join the Invisible Empire. Women who refused often found themselves cut off from their
friends.[12]

Even with internal frictions, the diffusion of the WKKK throughout
Indiana was extraordinary. Table 2 lists all Indiana communities be-

TABLE 2   CHARACTERISTICS OF COMMUNITIES WITH WKKK CHAPTERS

| Community | Total Population | Adult Women | | |
		Total	Total Native-born White	% of Native-born White
Anderson	28,767	9,118	8,515	93.4
Attica	3,392	1,069	1,010	94.5
Auburn	4,650	1,538	1,484	96.5
Bedford	9,076	2,747	2,621	95.4
Bicknell	7,635	1,837	1,554	84.6
Brazil	9,293	2,800	2,536	90.6
Clinton	10,962	2,647	1,875	70.8
Columbia City	3,499	1,244	1,218	97.9
Columbus	8,990	3,005	2,894	96.3
Connersville	9,901	3,074	2,843	92.5
Crawfordsville	10,962	3,563	3,426	96.2
Decatur	4,762	1,473	1,423	96.6
Elkhart	24,277	7,684	6,977	90.8
Elwood	10,790	3,075	2,895	94.1
Fort Wayne	86,549	28,307	25,151	88.9
Frankfort	11,585	3,798	3,727	98.1
Franklin	4,909	1,760	1,654	94.0
Greencastle	3,780	1,326	1,249	94.2
Greenfield	4,168	1,454	1,431	98.4
Greensburg	5,345	1,943	1,906	98.1
Hartford City	6,183	1,822	1,734	95.2
Hobart	3,450	999	750	75.1

TABLE 2   (*continued*)

Community	Total Population	Adult Women		
		Total	Total Native-born White	% of Native-born White
Huntington	14,000	4,452	4,265	95.8
Indianapolis	314,194	105,628	86,885	82.3
Jeffersonville	10,098	3,460	2,859	82.6
Kendallville	5,273	1,762	1,673	94.9
Kokomo	30,067	8,847	8,172	92.3
Lafayette	22,486	7,734	6,967	90.1
Lebanon	6,257	2,137	2,091	97.8
Logansport	21,626	6,912	6,375	92.2
Marion	23,747	7,574	7,027	92.8
Martinsville	4,895	1,625	1,602	98.6
Michigan City	19,457	5,298	3,802	72.8
Mitchell	3,025	873	829	95.0
Muncie	36,524	11,235	10,300	91.7
New Castle	14,458	7,820	7,073	90.4
Noblesville	4,758	1,645	1,546	94.0
North Vernon	3,084	982	913	93.0
Peru	12,410	4,064	3,780	93.0
Plymouth	4,338	1,480	1,427	96.4
Rockport	2,581	854	755	88.4
Rushville	5,498	1,898	1,787	94.2
Seymour	7,348	2,415	2,322	96.1
Shelbyville	9,701	3,281	3,098	94.4
South Bend	70,983	20,013	14,363	71.8
Sullivan	4,489	1,413	1,371	97.0
Terre Haute	66,083	21,087	18,493	87.7
Tipton	4,507	1,427	1,414	99.1
Valparaiso	6,518	2,190	1,942	88.7
Wabash	9,872	3,173	3,020	95.2
Washington	8,743	2,721	2,620	96.6
Winchester	4,021	1,385	1,361	98.3

SOURCE: U.S. Census, 1920, "Population—Indiana," tables 1, 8, 9, 10, 11.

NOTE: This table includes only WKKK chapters in cities and towns with total populations of 2,500 or more. These data are not available for communities with 1920 populations of fewer than 2,500.

tween 1923 and 1925 with total populations of 2,500 or more that had WKKK chapters, together with each community's population, number of women twenty-one years of age or older, and number (and percentage) of adult native white women. For these communities the percentage of the female population that was native-born and white varied from 70.8 percent to 99.1 percent, with an average of 92.0 percent. Although comparable statistics are not available for communities with WKKK chapters in which the total population was less than 2,500, it is likely that small towns had more homogeneous racial and ethnic composition than larger communities did.

The women's Klan cannot be easily explained in terms of local economies or size of community—WKKK klaverns were found in small towns, small cities, and large urban areas. Of the 131 Indiana communities with WKKK chapters, 79 had populations smaller than 2,500 in 1920, 32 had populations between 2,500 and 10,000, and 20 had populations larger than 10,000, including most of the large urban areas of the state.

ORGANIZING KLAVERNS

It is instructive to examine in detail the organization of local Klan chapters. Although great secrecy usually surrounded organizing efforts, the beginnings of the women's Klan were well documented in two Indiana communities. In Franklin, a small town twenty miles south of Indianapolis, a local newspaper gave extensive and largely sympathetic coverage to Klan organizing efforts in the community and in the surrounding area. Kokomo, a midsized commercial city fifty miles north of Indianapolis, was the site of one of the largest Klan assemblies in the nation in 1923, an event that subjected its Klan to extensive press coverage.

FRANKLIN, INDIANA

Like many Indiana Klan strongholds, the small town of Franklin in Johnson County was homogeneous. Of 4,909 residents, 4,589 (93 percent) were native-born white, 35 (less than 1 percent) were foreign-born white, and 285 (6 percent) were black. The vast majority of the adult population was literate (97 percent of men and 98 percent of women), and virtually all children under sixteen years attended school.

The first public meeting of the KKK in Franklin was in late February 1923 and featured Daisy Barr. Ads in the *Franklin Evening Star* invited men and women to hear Barr lecture on "The KKK, I am for it" and watch an accompanying motion picture. Underlining its enthusiasm for the upcoming event, the paper noted that this was the same speaker who "conducted a successful revival in the Tabernacle Christian Church here four years ago and [who] is well known in Franklin."[13]

At the time of Barr's visit the Klan sent minister-lecturers to Protestant churches in the area surrounding Franklin to convert local ministers to the Klan cause. Ministers spoke from pulpits and in local high schools and gyms to capacity crowds of women and men on the Klan's potential to clean up the community and the schools. Ministers proclaimed that local public schools were hiring priests as teachers to convert unsuspecting Protestant children; the Klan guaranteed that it would stop such practices. In the words of one Franklin minister who enlisted in the Invisible Empire, the Klan stood against Romanist domination and for "the laws of the state, the laws of the United States, and the American flag."[14]

Within a month Klan ministers held seven highly attended lectures in the Franklin area. Music and entertainment accompanied political discussion. Apparently these talks produced a number of recruits for the men's KKK. In the countryside around Franklin, the Klan burned fiery crosses at night to announce the success of its initial recruitment drive. One month after its first visit to the area, the Klan was established in Franklin.[15]

The women's Klan of Franklin was not far behind. While Barr was lecturing in Franklin, ads in the local newspaper warned against imposter women's organizations and gave a Franklin box office number for the authentic women's Klan. Apparently Barr's secret women's meetings were more successful than those of rival organizations. Barr drew five hundred local women to hear about starting a local women's Klan and soon established an official WKKK in Franklin.[16]

The next few months witnessed much WKKK and KKK activity in Franklin. A joint meeting of the Klans of Franklin and Columbus (a town to the south) on March 9 ended with the first Klan parade through downtown Franklin, featuring five hundred masked and robed Klansmembers. A Klan speaker several weeks later attracted three thousand people. The audience, described as one of the largest ever assembled for a public meeting in the county, was made up almost equally of women and men, all cheering wildly as the anonymous speaker swore that with the Klan's ascendancy to power, Anglo-Saxon and Negro blood would never again mix. Moreover, the Klan would curtail the financial power of American Jews who, the speaker charged, owned 80 percent of the nation's wealth, some by profiteering in World War I. Catholic exclusivity and political power, too, needed to be checked as Catholic weddings, Catholic cemeteries, and allegiances of U.S. Catholics to a foreign pope threatened to undermine Protestant supremacy.[17]

Despite the overt racism and nativism of this appeal, the Franklin Klan worked hard to portray itself as a philanthropic organization and to counteract what it claimed to be a "campaign of misrepresentation" in the county. Klan leaders insisted that in only five weeks the order had done a great deal of charity work among the sick and needy of Franklin, including donating sums ranging from $32 to $250 to families whose breadwinners were stricken ill. Moreover, the Klan claimed it had presented $5 baskets of food to fourteen local families, awarded large American flags to three Protestant churches, and even given $25 to a "colored" woman whose home was damaged by fire.[18]

In May the women's Klan decided to announce itself to the local public. To signal the event the WKKK set burning crosses throughout Franklin and the surrounding countryside, including one erected and set ablaze on a downtown street. The resulting publicity heightened speculation and interest in the promised parade of Klanswomen, held the following month. Typical of Klan parades, Franklin Klanswomen assembled at the county fairgrounds and marched through downtown in a show of force meant to inspire awe and intimidation among the spectators. Newly naturalized local Klanswomen marched on foot, preceded by officers of the state WKKK who rode horses draped with American flags. Bystanders must have appreciated the Klanswomen's display; the local newspaper commented on the "generous applause among the spectators on the sidewalks when large flags passed by." The only reported incident of tension during the parade occurred when one male spectator failed to doff his hat to a Klanswoman parading with a flag, but the assembled Klanswomen quickly made him comply. At the conclusion of the parade, the WKKK initiated between five hundred and two thousand women into the order.[19]

Buoyed by its triumphant march through Franklin, the WKKK began to flex its political muscle in the area. The effects soon were evident. Within weeks after the WKKK parade, the Johnson County school board introduced and adopted a resolution mandating the teaching of the Bible and the U.S. Constitution in the public schools, a move applauded—and very likely prompted—by the Franklin women's Klan.

The following month the local women's Klan made another spectacular public appearance at a countywide rally. In what was described as the largest crowd in the history of the county, ten thousand people assembled to witness masked Klanswomen and Klansmen parade through Franklin, accompanied by two local bands and a marching band from Indianapolis. "Almost the entire route of the march," the paper noted enthusiastically, "was lined with spectators in the hundreds . . . enthusiastic in their applause for the various spectacular features of the parade." Following the parade, Klanswomen assembled for a rally and an address by Mable Brown of the Indiana state office of the WKKK, who was a national speaker for the organization. In a "fiery, eloquent speech," Brown addressed the topic, "The 100 percent American Women," to a vast crowd of cheering Klanswomen. Her talk concluded with the spectacular fanfare for which the Klan was noted, including a hot-air balloon ascension and a parachute leap. As dusk fell the WKKK inducted another large class of Franklin women.[20]

KOKOMO, INDIANA

The beginning of the Kokomo (Howard County) WKKK, probably the largest and most active chapter in the state, is less visible than that of the Franklin WKKK. The first trace of the Kokomo organization was at the famous July 4, 1923, Klan spectacular at which Daisy Barr spoke. Yet evidently the WKKK had been active in town for awhile, as Barr's address pledged an army of committed women to the Klan cause in what she termed "this moment of danger." At the July event the Kokomo WKKK staffed a first aid station and food tables for an estimated fifty thousand to two hundred thousand women, men, and children who congregated at Melfalfa Park in Kokomo. The Klanswomen's task of arranging food for visiting Klansmembers was no small one; the mountain of food included six tons of beef, hundreds of pounds of hamburger and hot dogs, five thousand cases of pop and near-beer, two hundred fifty pounds of coffee, and thousands of pies. Buffet tables extended two blocks long bulging with food prepared and served by local Klanswomen.

The scale of the Klan's Kokomo event was staggering. Special reserved train cars brought Klansmembers from all over the state to Kokomo. Eight hundred men and women arrived on a single reserved train from Elkhart and Michigan City wearing purple hats and Klan robes. A boys' band from Alliance, Ohio, traveled three hundred miles to play at Kokomo, giving concerts in every city along the way to publicize the event.

At the rally the Klan rose to new heights of spectacle and display. Besides the usual Klan fare of bands, speeches, and dinner, the Kokomo event featured a boxing exhibition, a baby show, pie-eating contests, fireworks, and prayers by local and visiting ministers. A parade of masked Klansmembers, including five hundred wearing the robes of the WKKK, wound its way through town, headed by a contingent of marching girls carrying huge American flags between them, floats of Klanswomen and girls, a fife and drum corps from Muncie, bands from cities throughout Indiana and Ohio, and Klansmembers on twelve-foot-high stilts. The coup de theatre, however, was D. C. Stephenson's dramatic arrival to Melfalfa Park. Draped in a purple robe, Stephenson disembarked from an airplane marked with the legend "Evansville KKK No. 1," ascended the speaker's platform, and was greeted by an enthusiastic crowd of supporters cheering and throwing money and jewelry onto the platform.[21]

Immediately after the Fourth of July event the Kokomo chapter of the WKKK seized the opportunity for publicity by pledging $1,000 to the Howard County hospital. In a public announcement, two women from the WKKK admitted that "no definite arrangements had been made for the raising of the sum" but expressed confidence that the cash would be turned over to the hospital in a short time. In fact, only enough money was raised to begin construction and the county was forced to take over the project. Moreover, the American Trust Company of Kokomo, the local "Klan bank" where both Klan treasuries and donations for the hospital campaign were kept, collapsed and was closed by the bank examiner in 1927 because of financial misdeeds by its officers.[22] But the hospital drive and July 4th spectacle drew attention to the Kokomo WKKK and prompted the state office to dispatch an organizer to build on the community's momentum. The organizer decided to have an informal meeting to give members and potential recruits an opportunity to get acquainted and learn about the organization. On July 25 the meeting was held, complete with a rally and initiation ceremony that rivaled the July 4th event for pageantry and attention to detail. The evening began with a parade of Klanswomen through downtown Kokomo in a procession led by fifteen women on horseback and followed by floats, lines of Klanswomen in white robes and yellow masks marching two abreast, and three hundred masked but unrobed initiates.[23]

The parade wound its way to a city park. There, to the accompaniment of music from the girls' Klan band of Muncie and the Kokomo Klan drum corps and band, the initiates marched into a ring three hundred yards in diameter guarded by members of the Kokomo KKK and illuminated by an electric fiery cross and red flares. The initiates were blindfolded and led to a throne where four robed but unmasked members of the women's order solemnly read the ritual to the group of supplicants. A large fiery cross was then ignited at the rear of the throne, illuminating a tableau featuring a woman draped in an American flag holding another cross and wearing a headdress to represent the goddess of liberty. Framed by this tableau, the initiates listened to the vows of the women's Klan and, after murmuring their responses, received instruction in the organization's secret work. The line of guards then opened and the public was allowed to approach the stand and congratulate the new initiates. Two officials from the men's state organization also addressed the group, one a minister from Lyons who declared that "the women would have a larger and better organization within a year than the men."[24]

The following week the Kokomo WKKK put on a mammoth picnic for Klan families in the area and, two weeks later, staged another large demonstration and parade. The parade began at night in a local park, led by robed and masked Klanswomen on horseback and featuring the Muncie girls' band, a large electric fiery cross, and many floats. Crowds along the route applauded heartily at the spectacle, especially at the floats representing the ship of state and the goddess of liberty. A unique touch was given by a formation of Klanswomen marchers who paraded in the shape of a cross, carrying red flashlights pointed heav-

enward and thus forming a fiery cross in the sky. The parade also included three hundred women in full Klan regalia, a male drum corps,
and a section of Klansmen on foot and on horseback.[25]

After the parade a class of four hundred women candidates was initiated into the mysteries of the order under an electric fiery cross, with
other crosses burning in the distance. At the conclusion of the ceremony the public was allowed to come forward and hear two speakers
address the subjects of Americanism and the principles of the Klan.
One speaker praised the WKKK for its rapid and consistent growth.
The other speaker discussed the Cavalier Motion Picture Company's
efforts to correct the misimpressions generated by anti-Klan pictures.[26]

These successes were followed by a number of highly visible WKKK
events, including a barbecue lunch and march of two thousand Klanswomen, Klansmen, and their children, led by a women's drum corps
on September 22; a public address on the principles of the WKKK by
a national speaker from the women's Klan on October 12; and a large
public meeting at a local armory that included the initiation of a class
of sixty-seven Klanswomen on November 16.[27] The Kokomo WKKK,
whose membership and attendance at events rivaled the Kokomo
KKK, even organized a guard company of its own, known as Company C, which it presented to the public for the first time on July 4,
1924, to protect a WKKK rally. Company C routinely guarded the
park during WKKK meetings and kept order during WKKK parades.[28]

In late 1923 the women's Klan of Kokomo received its official charter from the national WKKK. In nearly every respect it had become an
established part of the white Protestant community in Kokomo. The
WKKK rented a headquarters in the Independent Sewing Machine
Company and routinely sponsored rallies, parades, and meetings, either for women only or with men and children. Both the men's and
women's Klans held weekly rallies and initiations in Melfalfa Park: the
WKKK on Monday evenings, the KKK on Tuesdays. One WKKK
meeting, held in a Baptist church outside the city, drew one thousand
Klanswomen to hear a woman speaker. Most of the audience, and the
speaker as well, were unmasked, signifying their sense of security in
the community.[29]

The Kokomo WKKK had both social and political aspects. When
the WKKK organizer moved from Kokomo in December 1923, local
Klanswomen gave her a lavish and public surprise farewell party in
Melfalfa Park, at which she received a silver tea service and a serenade

by the WKKK Quartet of nearby Logansport. Klanswomen also sought to spread the message of the Klan crusade to surrounding areas. In March 1924 a delegation of Klanswomen from Kokomo traveled to the small town of Sharpsville to meet a fledgling WKKK chapter in that community and explain the charter of the organization. Kokomo women also traveled to Logansport to hold joint events with that city's WKKK, including a large rally addressed by Daisy Barr.[30]

The development of the women's Klan in Franklin and Kokomo was fairly typical of the pattern in other Indiana communities. Famous speakers like Daisy Barr were dispatched by state or national Klan organizations to attract initial interest and ministers were quickly cultivated as local spokespersons and recruiters. Likely recruits were identified through personal contacts and church and political affiliations. They then were invited to mysterious secret meetings to discuss local "problems," which ranged from municipal corruption and vice to curriculum in public schools and the presence of Catholics, Jews, or blacks in certain occupations or neighborhoods. Once a core of local women enrolled (and paid dues), a WKKK chapter was declared and publicly announced through burning crosses, rallies, and parades. From that point, women's Klans typically moved in two directions— one public, the other very secret. Publicly, WKKK chapters sponsored marches, speakers, social events, and outdoor gatherings. Secretly, women's Klans worked in economic boycotts, campaigns of political sabotage, or, as in the case of Franklin's WKKK, attempts to change the public school system.

INTERNAL WORKINGS OF A KLAVERN

Indiana's Klanswomen used a variety of techniques to intimidate and destroy the perceived enemies of white American Protestantism. Rallies featuring professional organizers like Barr built solidarity and commitment within the Klan by intensifying racial hatred and religious bigotry. Klanswomen's ostentatious charity drives, in contrast, attempted to deflect public attention from Klan violence. Many WKKK klaverns worked to change local policies. Other WKKK activities were aimed at demonstrating the political muscle of Indiana's

Klan; as a former Klanswoman from central Indiana noted, "our attendance at rallies or marches showed others the force and number of
Klan members."[31]

It is impossible to determine how much of the WKKK's efforts were
directed toward each type of activity: solidarity building, charity, and
politics. Some evidence suggests, though, that building solidarity and
maintaining the Klan organization itself overshadowed ostensible
charity work and political activities in many of Indiana's WKKK klaverns. This is evident in the financial transactions of the Godfrey
WKKK of Hartford City whose financial account books from December 1924 through October 1932 have survived. The group's treasurer
made detailed notes on only a minority of expenditures, but these are
revealing. Based on $1,459.87 of detailed expenditures, this local sent
a staggering $965.42 (66.1 percent) of monies collected locally to the
realm and national WKKK as dues and imperial taxes. Another
$257.37 (17.6 percent) was spent for local organizational mainte-
nance, primarily office rent and office supplies, and $139.00 (9.5 per-
cent) for salaries of the local treasurer and secretary. Supplies for cross
burnings and parades consumed only $41.68 (2.9 percent) of the de-
tailed treasury, with a mere $10.00 (0.7 percent) distributed to char-
ity. In contrast, $46.40 (3.1 percent) was spent on entertainment and
commemoration of births and deaths in members' families.[32]

The solidarity-building activities of Indiana's WKKK did not in-
volve parties and entertainment alone. Racial and religious hatred also
created cohesiveness among Klanswomen. An unusually detailed account of this process appeared in a 1923 newspaper report on a
WKKK rally in the southern Indiana town of Seymour. Several weeks
before the rally the WKKK made its inaugural appearance in Seymour
at a combined WKKK-KKK event with four hundred Klansmen, one
hundred Klanswomen, and (variously reported) twenty to seventy-five
female initiates.[33] Apparently it was the success of this initial event
that prompted a professional WKKK organizer to set up a major
WKKK rally in Seymour. Publicity for the event promised a speech by
a 100 percent American woman who, from descriptions of her oratorical style ("like a sermon") and the content of her talk, may have been
Daisy Barr.

The evening of the rally, several hundred people assembled at a
shelter house at a local park. As was common in some Klan meetings,
the welcoming addresses did not explicitly mention the name of the
Klan but only commended the audience for coming to hear about the

problems that faced America. No one in the assembled crowd, however, could mistake the intention of the meeting. Both the woman who chaired the meeting and the speaker were robed in the well-known attire worn by WKKK officers.

The speaker's address was a classic example of the WKKK's attempts to unify white Protestant women by fueling social hatred. Her talk began with vivid descriptions of the forces that were seeking to undermine white Protestant American culture—a somewhat unusual opening as Klan speakers often tried to appear tolerant in public and reserve messages of racism and prejudice for closed private meetings. At this talk, however, the speaker was unrestrained. Sensing her audience's predisposition to believe nearly any story about the sinister qualities of immigrants and Catholics, she regaled them with tale after tale of diabolical works by Romanists and aliens.

A detailed knowledge of the audience's fears and prejudices allowed the speaker to condemn the Klan's enemies in terms that were oblique yet fully comprehensible. When she called for "united Protestantism in the conduct of governmental affairs," her listeners understood the unspoken message that Catholics had too much political influence. When she demanded a ban on all but native-born officeholders, her audience easily envisioned foreigners being swept into political office throughout the country. When she counseled eternal warfare against liquor, the gathered crowd understood that powerful Catholic politicians supported illicit and immoral traffic in liquor. When she demanded "absolute separation of church and state," her audience pictured the dire effects of Catholic teachers on the impressionable minds of Protestant children.

The strength of the Klan's appeal to Indiana's women lay in part in its ability to use such cataclysmic predictions to empower white Protestants. Insisting that white Protestant women need not sit idle while foreigners, Catholics, and nonwhites burrowed their way into the nation's statehouses, schools, and homes, the rally's speaker played on this theme. By working together and with dedication, women could ensure the privileges and rights of white native-born Protestants. Women's efforts, she thundered, could save the home from those insidious forces that besieged it. Women's efforts could cleanse politics of its corruption. Their efforts could assure the purity of the white race by segregating and "uplifting" the Negro race. Women's efforts could purge Catholic influence and make Bible study mandatory in public schools.

When the speaker referred to "women's efforts" she obviously meant the WKKK. Only the Klan claimed the size, strength, and courage to destroy the evils threatening white native-born Protestants. Armed with the right of suffrage and the Klan's political vision, white Protestant women were unstoppable. In the past, she noted, women had worked together for political purity, white supremacy, and militant Protestantism but only now were the efforts of all women united under one organizational banner. This appeal in Seymour, as elsewhere, was highly effective. White-robed Klanswomen offered each woman in the audience a card to fill out if she was interested in becoming a member of the WKKK. Many responded.[34]

A second activity of Indiana's Klanswomen was the ostensible charity drive—meant to bolster the claim that the WKKK was primarily devoted to good works. Charity drives not only legitimated the Klan but also allowed it with little accountability to raise large sums of money from sympathetic donors. Klan papers constantly appealed to readers to send money for its charity funds; the WKKK seized on this as their special province. In the charter granted to the WKKK of Hendricks County two years after it began operating, the particular obligation of Klanswomen to charitable works was made explicit: "Aside from the fraternal benefits of such an organization, the first duty of the ladies of the Ku Klux Klan is to the community in which they operate. This duty is first manifested in charity and aid extended the unfortunate."[35]

Although WKKK and KKK locals in Indiana collected money to aid orphans, sustain the livelihood of widows, and assist families who faced financial hardships, the Klan's charity was always directed at "worthy" individuals and organizations. Often this meant fundraising for Klan members and families or for organizations populated by Klansmembers. KKK chapters bequeathed aid to Klan families in financial trouble or to lodges and fraternal societies favored by Klansmen. WKKK locals preferred women in desperate situations and widows as beneficiaries of their charitable works, with distribution of Christmas baskets by robed and hooded Klanswomen to poor families an ever-popular event.[36]

When the WKKK made a donation, no matter how small the amount or effort, it heralded its generosity with extensive publicity. The Logansport women's Klan endlessly praised its efforts in sponsoring a Christmas party for children from the local orphans' home while the Brazil women's Klan boasted of its activity in unspecified "charity work." The WKKK of Fillmore widely publicized its contribution of a single basket of clothing to a needy girl, and the WKKK of Plymouth spoke enthusiastically of its one visit to entertain patients at a children's infirmary. At times the desire for legitimacy and publicity led the Klan in bizarre directions, as in the contribution by the Delaware County Klan to a local black Baptist church, a contribution quickly returned by its incredulous intended beneficiaries.[37]

The particular obligations of Klanswomen toward the unfortunate did not stop with fundraising for bereft families and orphaned children. The women's Klan donated money to local YWCAs, citing the "noble work of the YWCA" in making the ideal of "pure womanhood" possible. Klanswomen also acted in the timeworn fashion of middle-class paternalism to change the lives of women in unfortunate circumstances. As Barr opened her Friendly Inn of the 1910s to fallen women and prostitutes, the women's Klan of Indiana marked unwed teenage mothers for its assistance by arranging for adoptions of their babies.[38]

The charity of the women's Klan was not always appreciated, of course. Catholic churches and largely black denominations often refused to accept offers of Klan money in order not to validate the Klan as an equitable dispenser of charity funds. Even white Protestant groups sometimes resisted the Klan's largess. When the WKKK of Roachdale, Indiana, attempted to make a donation to the community's milk fund by presenting cash to the president of the community club at the community supper, they were distressed to find their donation rejected. Making the best of a potential publicity disaster, the Klanswomen turned the money over to the township trustees to purchase milk for public school children.[39]

But charity and socializing were secondary to the real purpose of the WKKK and KKK in Indiana—that of defending white Protestant supremacy. Often a fine line separated the Klan's goodwill campaigns from its political terrorism. This was most obvious in the Klan's activities for hospitals and public schools. When the WKKK and KKK made philanthropic gestures toward public schools or raised money to build Protestant hospitals, they warned Protestants that Catholics and foreigners had invaded the most basic institutions of public life. The crusade of nearly every WKKK chapter to present flags and Bibles to the public schools of their county and to build Protestant-only hospitals in communities then dependent on Catholic hospitals roused images of Catholic teachers secretly indoctrinating Protestant youth or Catholic doctors and nurses insisting on religious conversion in exchange for hospital treatment.[40]

WKKK chapters competed among one another to bring Protestant values to the public schools. When one WKKK klavern presented a Bible to every public school in the township, another donated a Bible to every school in the county, or a flag *and* a Bible to every school. Some schools received copies of *Stories of the Bible* together with their flags and Bibles. Others received multiple copies of new Bibles for the use of their students or placards with the Ten Commandments for every schoolroom.[41]

The way schools received their Bibles, flags, and books was important. The favored manner of donation was a public ceremony of presentation and acceptance. The WKKK of Coal City succeeded in this endeavor: it presented its gifts to the school principal on stage during intermission of the school play. Less successful was the WKKK of Terre Haute whose presentation involving one hundred Klanswomen was marred by the school board's refusal to allow the Klanswomen to don robes for the ceremony.[42]

Many Indiana Klan chapters received favorable publicity by announcing lavish fundraising drives to assist or build local Protestant hospitals. Although few, if any, such fundraising promises were fulfilled, the WKKK and KKK made lavish predictions that it would collect sums of $50,000 and more for hospitals and schools in Indiana's cities and towns. If nothing else, these fundraising drives replenished the treasuries of Klan locals and realms.[43]

Another deft publicity tactic pioneered by the men of the Klan and then adopted in identical form by the women's Klan was the church visit. Within a three-month period thirteen WKKK chapters reported making church visits in small Indiana communities, involving between five and seventy women. In a church visit, robed and masked Klanswomen would interrupt a Protestant service, stride up the center aisle, and present the minister with a sum of money. Ostensibly the money was for church work, in keeping with the Klan's pledge of militant Protestantism, but money easily found its way to the minister's personal funds. The minister's role was to act surprised, if pleased, by the visit of the Klanswomen. Often the drama was prearranged with cooperating ministers who viewed the proffered purse as payment for espousing Klan doctrines from the pulpit.[44]

While the school, hospital, and church campaigns of Indiana's WKKK and KKK chapters demonstrated the Klan's muscle, they delivered the message in indirect terms. Other political actions by Klanswomen more directly abused and harassed the enemies of the Klan. WKKK chapters in Indiana bombarded public schools with protests and calls to reform a school system that Klanswomen insisted was permeated with foreign, Catholic, and even Bolshevik influences. Klanswomen fought to remove Catholic encyclopedias from public school libraries, campaigned against the teaching of German (the language of the wartime enemy), and constantly pressured for a cabinet-level Department of Education to monitor and shore up the public school system and thereby undermine parochial education. Women of the Klan in many Indiana counties met with township trustees to urge compulsory Bible reading in public schools.[45]

Klanswomen in Indiana also were active in the effort to "cleanse" public schools of the corrupting influence of non-Protestants. The innocent minds of Protestant children, Klanswomen insisted, were being filled with Romanist doctrines. A number of Indiana's WKKK klaverns worked to have Catholic teachers, even Catholic school superintendents, fired. The Anderson WKKK, for example, mounted an effort to get two Catholic teachers fired. After being bombarded with letters from the women's Klan demanding her resignation, one teacher left town. The other teacher resigned after "several other small incidents happened," but she refused to leave town. In Muncie the Klan worked to remove a Catholic teacher with thirty-seven years' experience but without success.[46]

Klanswomen in Indiana also devoted a great deal of time and effort to electoral politics. Thanks in no small part to the work of WKKK klaverns, the Klan's electoral success in Indiana was enormous. Although the Klan rarely promoted or endorsed women for office, Indiana Klanswomen upheld their charter to "use the power of the ballot in the hands of its collective membership as a factor in higher citizenship." In public, Klanswomen insisted that they would consider candidates of all political persuasions and faiths, but in closed meetings Klansmembers vowed to vote only for other Klansmembers or for aliens backed by the Klan.[47] One Klanswoman speaker told a crowd in Marion that the WKKK would never accept Jews, foreigners, or Catholics either as Klansmembers or as political officeholders. The Klan existed "for the purpose of uniting the church, the Protestant people. . . . We don't take any foreign people, we don't accept Jews. There is a place for these people and they must not think they can come over here and have a hand in our government."[48]

Each local WKKK and KKK klavern was required to establish a political committee as part of Stephenson's "military machine." These local committees collected information on each political candidate's race, ethnicity, religion, family background, and attitude toward the Klan. They sent questionnaires asking candidates their positions on abolishing parochial education, limiting immigration, and prohibiting liquor. After considering this information, WKKK and KKK chapters each made endorsements and informed the others of their selections.

Once a candidate received the backing of the WKKK and KKK, the Klan set its formidable political machine into motion. Klanswomen distributed thousands of handbills containing the Klan's assessment of the candidates or flyers that simply listed religious preferences of candidates and their spouses. Klan slates were distributed at the polls, attached to clotheslines by clothespins, left on porches, and printed in Protestant church bulletins. Klan locals also circulated mock premarked ballots indicating which candidates had the support of the Invisible Empire. In many areas every eligible voter received the Klan's political propaganda before election day.[49]

The size of the Klan in Indiana made it a significant force in nearly every electoral race, especially in 1924. Politicians vied with one another for the Klan's endorsement, promising to appoint only Klan members and sympathizers to patronage offices. Klan candidates in primary elections signed pledges to withdraw from the general election race if another Klan candidate received more votes. A politician who antagonized or ignored the Klan faced near-certain defeat in most areas of Indiana. Local klaverns mailed copies of the *Fiery Cross* to prospective voters; on the eve of the 1924 election over two hundred thousand copies were distributed. Further, secret decrees issued from local klonklaves and state klonciliums doomed many unsuspecting candidates who aimed their campaigns at the regular party vote.[50]

As part of the Klan's ward organization, Klanswomen acted in ways time-honored in partisan politics. Their military machine registered voters, got voters to the polls, and worked to ensure that they voted according to the Klan's desires. Klanswomen drove the precincts looking for women who had not gone to the polls because of childcare responsibilities. Acting in concert, one Klanswoman babysat a sympathetic voter's children while another Klanswoman drove her to the voting place.[51]

The Indiana Klan's electoral strategy paid off in 1924. Klan-backed candidates won the governorship, many mayoral contests including those in Indianapolis, Evansville, and Kokomo, and numerous local offices of sheriffs, district attorneys, and others.[52] In the legislature, however, the Klan's record was mixed. Although many Klan-backed candidates were elected to the state legislature, they fought one another as much as they battled Klan enemies. Klan-supported legislators introduced an "Americanization" program to ban religious officials and parochial school graduates from teaching in public schools, mandate state-selected textbooks and Bible reading in the public schools, grant college credit for Bible study outside school, and release students from school to attend Bible education classes. The only bill that passed was a relatively innocuous provision requiring all students to study the U.S. Constitution.[53]

Though the Klan could elect members and supporters in Indiana, its electoral efforts were less effective than another political tactic: the boycott. This technique drew on women's traditional role as manager of the family's consumption. A boycott brought even the act of shopping into the fight for racial and religious supremacy. It infused the ordinary tasks of Klanswomen's lives with political content. Acting individually but with a collective direction, Klanswomen could force Jews, Catholics, or blacks out of their communities or into financial bankruptcy. Indiana Klanswomen avidly took to the task.

Daisy Barr set the tone for the WKKK's crusade of selective shopping in weekly addresses to Indianapolis Klanswomen. At each meeting, attended by as many as fifteen hundred women, Barr read the roll of Indianapolis WKKK and KKK members who were engaged in local retail or service trade. These businesses and products had the WKKK seal of approval. These, and only these, were to be patronized by Klanswomen; all others were "Catholic or Jew" (or "alien") and should be rejected. Barr was particularly indignant about "Jew-owned" stores and claimed that "Jews had 75 percent of the money of the United States." This situation would change, however. "When the women should be as strongly organized as the men," she raged, "THEY WOULD HAVE THE POWER and then GOD HELP BLOCK [Jewish businessman] AND HIS SLACKER SON. THERE WILL BE NO JEWISH BUSINESS LEFT IN INDIANAPOLIS."[54]

Organizing Klanswomen as consumers had an immediate and phenomenal effect. Businesses with Jewish owners, ranging from large department stores to small shops and professional services, went bankrupt throughout Indiana. Jewish professionals and business owners fled communities in which they had lived for decades.[55]

The consumption campaign of the WKKK gave many communities their first indication of the strength of women's klaverns and the extent of pro-Klan sentiment among local women. Shopping at one place over another allowed women to exercise considerable political clout without overstepping even the most conventional definition of their roles as mothers and wives. Moreover, the political content of the act was elusive. Women could act on racist, anti-Semitic, or anti-Catholic sentiments in a completely invisible fashion. It was not necessary to attend klaverns, become an official WKKK member, or even discuss the Klan to participate in the Klan's economic crusade. Shopping, after all, involves myriad subjective choices about quality, price, and convenience—any woman could justify her selections, if need be, without revealing sympathy with the goals of the Klan. For many women in Indiana who declined to join the WKKK because of fear of being identified with the Klan or because of reluctance to be involved with a political movement, the economic strategy of the WKKK was perfect.

The diffusion of information about approved and boycotted businesses operated through a shadowy network of Klanswomen and Klan sympathizers. Informal conversations among women—dismissed as insignificant gossip by contemporary men and Klan historians—fueled one of the Klan's most powerful weapons. Rumor did not spread randomly; the WKKK used tightly organized bands of Klanswomen to ensure its dispersal across the state. The impact of the "poison squad of whispering women" that Vivian Wheatcraft claimed as the invisible weapon of Indiana politics was profound. Women's poison squads could spread stories to every corner of the state within twenty-four hours. Even when the story in its entirety was known to be false, doubts lingered, as a woman in central Indiana attested: "Many of the rumors possibly had a degree of truth in them so you could not deny it all but it was not the truth as it was told."[56]

In its political efforts, the WKKK relied on the patterns of daily activities of Indiana women. Women visiting friends and relatives or stopping to chat with acquaintances at shops or schools and over the proverbial back fence passed information about who *owned* what and who *sympathized* with what. Women needed not identify their own sentiments to pass on information; the assumption that women's conversation was personal, not political, shielded women from accusations and attacks by anti-Klan forces. Some women heard the information and dismissed it as inconsequential. To receptive ears, however, the implications for action were clear.

Few rumors seemed too farfetched. In 1923 North Manchester was swept by a rumor that Negroes were coming north in great numbers, a rumor purportedly based on sighting one local man traveling in the South. Another rumor spread by the women's Klan in North Manchester proved embarrassing to the organization after it was made public. The incredible nature of this tale indicates not only the Klan's striking ability to disseminate rumors but also the immediacy of fears about a papal assault on Indiana:

> Some Klan leader said that the Pope was coming to take over the country, and he said he might be on the next train that went through North Manchester. You know, just trying to make it specific. So, about a thousand people went out to the train station and stopped the train. It only had one passenger train and one passenger on it. They took him off, and he finally convinced them that he wasn't the Pope. He was a carpet salesman. And so they put him on the next train and he went on to Chicago.[57]

The organized gossip of Klanswomen spread poison about Jews, Catholics, and others opposed to the crusade of militant Protestantism. Tales about the personal life, merchandise, and political allegiances of the town's outsiders destroyed the Klan's enemies without a trace. Since gossip left no visible traces on the participants, it created no trail for those opposed to or victimized by the Klan. Indeed, the political power of gossip lay precisely in its apolitical character. There were no reports to seize, no meetings to invade, no publications to refute. One might guess at its existence from its consequences, but even those were hard to measure on the local level. Did a department store go out of business because of an invisible boycott or because of poor management or shoddy goods? Did a Jewish family leave town because of actual economic pressure or because of its exaggerated fear of such pressure? Did stores and businesses go bankrupt, or did they simply move to areas of greater financial potential? Only in retrospect did the pattern of business closures and out-migration by Jewish owners across Indiana communities become clear. Only in retrospect, and by looking closely at the lives of women, can we reveal the political character and the economic power of these networks of gossip.

The nonchalance with which many Indiana residents regarded economic boycotts is astonishing. Virtually everyone I interviewed gave specific information about Jewish- or Catholic-owned stores that were driven into bankruptcy by the Klan. But in the memories of those who were in the Klan and who benefited from its economic power, boycotts of outsiders or non-Klansmembers were unremarkable.

[Before the Klan began] we were not a big printing plant at all. And, it so happens, we were the only Protestant printing plant anywhere around. And, that . . . we didn't even think too much about because I'm very . . . Dad was, of course, a member of the Klan, as I know. And, all that printing came to us.[58]

No one I interviewed saw the economic power of the Klan as a political act. None saw it as an act of violence. For the most part, they dismissed boycotts as simple harassment. One informant assured me that the Jewish family in her town suffered no repercussions from the Klan even while she acknowledged that Klansmembers, in this town with a sizable Klan population, refused to patronize the Jewish merchant's store. "Now, the one Jew in [small town] he became a part of the community. He went to church dinners and everything. I don't think anybody ever thought about doing anything to him. Maybe he was harassed in other ways. People didn't go to his store."[59] Commonly, informants would acknowledge the financial effect of the Klan's boycott but reassure themselves that Catholics and Jews (naturally "clannish" groups, according to the Klan) found compensating patrons among their own people. Stories of Catholic and Jewish business owners joining together in exclusive financial agreements were legendary through Indiana.

> [Klan members] affected business in the county because there was enough of them, that they would ostracize a Catholic. . . . For instance Kelly had a grocery store. Well, it hurt their business terribly because people wouldn't go in there, because the Klan would tell you not to. . . . If you had a empty house in [small town], why you were told not to rent it to a Catholic. As far as I know, the Catholics didn't bother anybody except they did kind of . . . they were clannish. And, if you were a Catholic groceryman why, at least your customers would be other Catholics.[60]

To victims, the Klan's power and tactics were confusing as well as destructive. Catholics and Jews who had been at least partially integrated into the social, cultural, and commercial life of the community now found themselves inexplicably labeled as outsiders and enemies. One woman gave an account of the Klan's boycott of her (Catholic) family's grocery store, made more ironic by the fact that the men's and women's Klans met in a room above the grocery.

> I blame the Klan indirectly for my father's death. . . . It just broke his heart to have people shun him, pass right in front of our door, our grocery store door and go upstairs and not look at him. Not look in our store, and he was never able to take that and he used to say, what did I do, and nothing

changed on his part, he was the same person. . . . I don't think he minded losing the customers so badly . . . but the fact that he lost friends and he just was never able to accept that.[61]

Although rumors and gossip were the most effective weapons, the Klan employed more visible mechanisms to direct the power of purchasing. The *Fiery Cross* published a "who's who" roster of Catholic businessmen, complete with names and addresses of their business establishments. No loyal Klanswoman need wonder what actions the list encouraged.[62]

Klan members developed an organizational policy of "vocational klannishness" in which Klan members pledged to conduct "trading, dealing with, and patronizing Klansmen in preference to all others." The Klan planned to publish a National Service Directory that would list all businesses in the United States owned by Klansmembers who took out a $35 membership in the National Service Corporation. This project was never completed, but local klaverns issued their own directories and the Indiana Klan compiled a listing that covered all cities in the state. Shopkeepers supplemented these directories with advertising that broadcast the owner's political sympathies. Shopkeepers who joined the KKK or WKKK received placards for their store windows that read TWK—Trade With a Klansman. Those who belonged to the National Service Corporation received a round red, white, and blue sign to display in their businesses.[63]

Klan papers as well as local non-Klan papers carried numerous ads openly proclaiming the klannish sympathies of local business owners. Rarely were these ads subtle. The *Franklin Evening Star* ran one such advertisement:

> Every person in Johnson County is invited
> to join the KKK Keystone Kleaning Kompany
> "keep klothes klean" campaign[64]

The Klan's claim to represent 100 percent Americans provided merchants with another advertising ploy. Evans's American Cafe in Kokomo promised the "best 100% 25-cent meals in state," Indianapolis barber shops declared their employees to be 100 percent American, underwriters in Logansport promised insurance that was 100 percent safe, a Haughville company guaranteed 100 percent service in delivering ice, coal, and wood, and an Indianapolis jeweler urged Klan couples to examine its 100 percent workmanship before purchasing a wedding ring, adding that it would give a 10 percent discount to any

100 percent American. The *Fiery Cross* even published its own business directory in every issue, with ads for Klan-owned companies, professional services, and evangelical preachers. The issue for June 1,
1923, for example, contained notices for hotels, furniture stores, real-
tors, seed stores, and many other businesses:

> Columbus, Indiana, Hunter Repair Shop—Everything for a Ford, 100%
> shop operated by 100% man with 100% workmen. We want 100% Amer-
> ican business.
>
> Marion, Indiana, Chiropractor—Dr. O. G. McKeever, for 100% service.[65]

The tactic of vocational klannishness affected workers as well as
merchants and professionals. Employers sympathetic to the Klan, or
fearing Klan reprisals, advertised for 100 percent American employees
and refused to hire Catholics, Jews, blacks, new immigrants, or people
of "poor character." For its own members, the Klan served as a quasi-
employment service. The state headquarters sent directives to all field
officers of the KKK and WKKK in Indiana, indicating employment situations for 100 percent women and men. The *Fiery Cross*, like commercial newspapers, listed notices of "Situation Wanted" or "Employees Wanted" separately for women and men.[66]

Workers who were Catholic, Jewish, or suspected of anti-Klan leanings often discovered vocational klannishness by being suddenly fired
from their jobs. A county extension agent who refused to join the Klan
found himself out of work. The treasurer of Marion County, who
owed his position to the Klan, received a threatening letter forbidding
him to hire Catholics. The *Muncie Post-Democrat* maintained that the
courthouse matron in Muncie was fired when it was discovered that
her daughter attended parochial school, even though she denied that
her family was Catholic.[67]

The Klan even used its economic power to try to drive anti-Klan
newspapers out of business. The most famous episode involved the
South Bend Tribune, which the WKKK and KKK klaverns in South
Bend identified as adverse to the interests of the Klan. A Klansman
later provided insights into the boycotting methods of the Indiana
Klan when he testified that Klanswomen and Klansmen decided to
"use all their influence possible . . . call up the *South Bend Tribune* by
'phone and not take their paper, and also to talk it over the streets . . .
refuse to buy any articles advertised in the *South Bend Tribune* . . . refuse to buy of those merchants who advertised in that paper."[68] The
South Bend WKKK provided leadership for this campaign.

The Klan in Indiana exerted its power through physical violence and terrorism, actions more often practiced by Klansmen than Klanswomen, and through threats and intimidation, actions of both men and women. But in Indiana and most other places incidents of physical violence by the 1920s Klan were scattered and sporadic. Although the 1920s Klan practiced kidnapping, beating, and even lynching, these were not the typical practice of WKKK klaverns or the daily practice of KKK chapters.[69] Rather, the more subtle destructive fury of the 1920s Klan lay in its use of rumor, gossip, and demonstrations of political strength. In these tactics—political tactics typically overlooked in scholarship on the Klan movement—Klanswomen were key actors.

CHAPTER VI

100% Cooperation

Political Culture in the Klan

Commitment to the Klan or other extremist right-wing movements is often depicted as aberrant behavior, radically disconnected from normal daily life. Extremist political values are viewed as fundamentally different from those of the larger society. Such a sense—of a political movement's separation and isolation from its social context—appears in many histories of the Klan: "When a man joins the KKK, a sensation seems to come over him as definite as falling in love. He simply drops out of society and enters a new world."[1]

This picture is not borne out in the Indiana Klan. There, continuity as much as divergence characterized the relations between Klan and alien society. The Klan was able to enlist such a high percentage of Indiana's eligible women and men precisely because it fit the life and values of many white Protestants. The Klan did not create sentiments of racism, anti-Semitism, or anti-Catholicism; these did not end with the demise of the 1920s Klan. Rather, the Klan nested within the institutions and assumptions of ordinary life of many in the majority population of Indiana.

Historians argue that the Klan gave voice to anti-Semitic, anti-Catholic, and antiblack sentiments that were deeply embedded in white Protestant society. It did so. The Klan's racism and xenophobia fit particularly well into the culture of white Protestants in the Midwest, a culture of religious and racial homogeneity and distrust of others. Ultimately, however, the Klan did more than simply mirror the bigotry of the majority population. It provided an organizational means to transform fears and resentments into political action.[2]

Klannish culture was key to the Klan's ability to transform social hatreds into a political movement. The Klan infused the culture of daily life with political content, forging a "political culture" based on belief in white Protestant supremacy. They did so in two ways. First, the cultural traditions and social life of the Klan became the core of a new Klan society, as yet in embryonic form. Klannish political culture offered a way of life, a sense of purpose, and a worldview that drew on the ordinary racism and intolerance of white Protestant society and gave these a political mission of white Protestant supremacy, at the same time that it helped Klansmembers resist the immorality of alien society. Second, klannish culture served as a powerful weapon against Klan enemies. Through it, the Klan socialized new members and youngsters into the values and political agendas of the Klan. The Klan used it to reinforce social hatred and to perpetuate its political agenda across generations. We should not dismiss the parties, weddings, and parades that made up much of Klan life in the 1920s as frivolous or apolitical. Indeed, klannish culture was intensely, and deliberately, political. And Klanswomen were central figures in the Klan's political culture.[3]

ORDINARY RACISM

Political culture in the Indiana Klan was shaped from the racism common to everyday life in white Protestant Indiana. Racist attitudes, as much as anti-Catholicism and anti-Semitism, pulled many women and men into the Invisible Empire. For some, it was fear that their racially homogeneous life was threatened. For others who had rarely seen blacks and had no reason to fear competition from them, the fear was more amorphous.[4]

Many of those I interviewed in Indiana described feeling strange when they encountered a nonwhite person on the street or in a store. One woman discussed her memories of visiting the metropolis of Indianapolis for the first time after growing up in a nearby, but socially distant, small town:

> I know the first time I went to Indianapolis, living in [town]. And I went into the . . . one of the stores on the circle that had just opened up and I went upstairs and the colored woman come to wait on me and I left. You

know, it was so shocking, somehow. I don't know as I was prejudiced against it, but it seemed so strange. And, then all at once in the drugstore they used to serve food. I never liked to go . . . I didn't have anything against them. It's just that I wasn't accustomed to it, I guess. Wasn't brought up thinking that way.[5]

Another woman sympathized with the Klan's racist sentiments but insisted that she was not racially prejudiced, since her response was based on a physical aversion, not on a conscious judgment: "I myself had to overcome some physical thing with working with [black] women. Not objective or intellectual. No objections to that. But, actually, being friends and caring about them. It's some physical thing."[6]

It would be misleading to imply that the racism, anti-Catholicism, or anti-Semitism of most women (or men) who joined the Klan in Indiana was even as direct or as conscious as these women's reactions. In fact, racism and intolerance lurked as often in what was *not* said, in the silences rather than the utterances of daily speech.[7] The Indiana Klan drew from assumptions deep within the culture of the state's native-born white Protestant population that white Protestants were the standard of human existence. As a man in central Indiana commented, "The colored people were hard to get along with. The Klan [that is,] the white people, got along with everybody."[8] In contrast to the universality of white Protestantism, blacks, Jews, Catholics, and immigrants were the other. To those in the universal category, others were completely invisible: as an informant from central Indiana commented, "never thought about."

We didn't have many people to hate because we didn't hate the niggers. We had the Wills family that lived right here in [this] township. And they were like pet coons to us. I went to school with them. And, went all through [school] and I never thought about them being black, colored as we called it then. I never even thought about it.[9]

Even when pushed to discuss specific discriminations against blacks, Catholics, or Jews, many informants found it impossible to step outside the universal experience of whiteness. Asked about the practice of serving blacks in the back rooms of restaurants, an informant answered in terms of the effect of segregation on local *white* people who were willing to make limited accommodations for known, but not visiting, black people: "I don't think anything . . . or anybody would have thought anything about it. I certainly wouldn't have of our local Negroes. But, not a strange Negro. You get several of them together and they become niggers. Individually they're fine people."[10]

Black people's lives were recognized only when they impinged on the lives of whites. A "black problem" existed when blacks made demands on whites—thus a problem blacks caused and could be blamed for. One woman in northern Indiana and one in west-central Indiana commented:

> There wasn't a black problem until . . . I never was aware of any black problem until the '30s.

> We always in this town, always had a very, very high class of black people in [this town] and they have stayed primarily to themselves and the police had no trouble. They have taken care of their own problems and there have been times when there would be agitators would come in from Indianapolis and tell these people, you ought to do this and you ought to do that, you've got the rights, take advantage of them and they'd take them to the edge of town and say, now back to Indianapolis and don't let us see you in [this town] again, that was the way they took care of their problems.[11]

THE POLITICAL CULTURE OF KLANNISHNESS

Deep-seated racism among Indiana's white Protestants did not automatically translate into Klan membership. Rather, the Klan's ability to consolidate racist and xenophobic attitudes into an organized political force in Indiana rested in part on its creation of alternative forms of leisure, culture, and social life. They allowed the Klan's political agenda to fit with the family, friendship, and community commitments of Klanswomen and Klansmen. Through the Klan, individuals could enact many of the activities and ceremonies of daily life in the company of like, and like-minded, persons.

One element in the Klan's alternative culture was auxiliaries for children and teenagers patterned after the children's orders of patriotic societies. These introduced klannish values to children during their formative years and gave the Klan a supply of new members as well as access to their parents. Klan children were recruited from families of Klan members, as well as through public announcement. Klanswomen and Klansmen visited Protestant churches to broadcast the formation of new children's chapters, stressing the Klan's ability to help children retain Protestant values.[12]

An organization for teenage boys, the Junior Ku Klux Klan, was the first children's auxiliary. Plans for the junior order were considered at a 1923 meeting of Grand Dragons of the Ku Klux Klan. Within a few months the adult Klan wrote a tentative constitution, a set of bylaws, and a ritual for the boys' order and established an office in Atlanta to oversee the new organization. A magazine designed for the new order, *The Junior Klansmen Weekly,* was published by Milton Elrod, editor of the *Fiery Cross.*[13]

Boys in the Junior KKK elected their own officers but a KKK or WKKK chapter supervised and directed each local. Adult kleagles even prepared a boys' ritual modeled after the men's ritual but dropped it when KKK officers complained that the phraseology was so complicated that boys would not understand it and would find it boring.

As adult Klan officers found in the Junior Klan a chance to expand their influence and power, they swept the boys' order into the controversies and power plays of the men's order. A midwestern KKK kleagle, for example, formed large junior orders in Indiana and Ohio and subsequently in West Virginia, New Jersey, and Michigan. He appointed Fred Poock from the adult KKK as national director for the order, ordered robes for the boys, and declared Indianapolis headquarters of the Junior KKK. Soon thereafter, the kleagle who appointed Poock was banished from the KKK, leaving the juniors in danger of becoming an illegitimate auxiliary. At the last minute Hiram Evans intervened and granted retroactive official status to the juniors but placed them under the direct supervision of the adult kloncilium and moved the office to Atlanta.[14]

By 1924 fifteen states, mostly in the Midwest, had chapters of the new junior order established by invitation of KKK grand dragons. Membership was open to all native-born white Protestant boys between the ages of twelve and eighteen who could demonstrate "an understanding of the meaning of the Constitution" and who would pay the three-dollar membership fee. Like the adult orders, the juniors were organized along a military chain of command.[15]

About the same time a separate junior order for girls (the Tri-K Klub) was organized under the direction of the WKKK. The Tri-K Klub had its own set of robes, hierarchy of officers, and ritual modeled after the ritual of the adult women of the Klan. Girls pledged themselves to the seven sacred symbols of the Invisible Empire: the fiery cross, water, mask, robe, Bible, sword, and flag. They recited the Klan katechism of loyalty, obedience, selflessness, and Christian patriotism. As the girls were formally dedicated into the sisterhood of the Klan, a quartet stood behind the kneeling candidates and sang, to the tune of "Auld Lang Syne,"

We pledge to you our friendship true
Through happiness and tears
The tie that binds our hearts to you
Will hold throughout the years.

Beneath this flag that waves above
This cross that lights our way
You'll always find a sister's love
In the heart of each TRI-K.[16]

Following their induction into the order, initiates and their Tri-K Klub sisters were addressed by an adult Klanswoman who shifted emphasis from sorority to the politics of the Klan, informing the girls of the "great principles, ideals, and the true reason and necessity" of the Klan.[17]

Only scattered records remain to indicate the size or the actual workings of the Tri-K Klub and the Junior KKK. According to the Exalted Cyclops of the Indiana Klan, the juniors in South Bend enrolled 200 boys in a chapter with 4,500 men and an unreported number of women. The Kokomo, Indiana, chapter counted 400 boys in its junior order, in a city with 2,500 WKKK and 7,500 KKK members.[18]

The main activity of the teen orders was social and familial. The KKK and the WKKK sponsored play parties for their juvenile orders. Juniors arranged competitive sporting events, sponsored Klan father and son nights, picnics for the entire family, and joint meetings of the juniors and KKK. In 1924 the Indiana Klan sponsored a statewide Junior Klan basketball tournament. The boys' order also ran summer camps under the sponsorship of the men's groups and formed a boys' drum corps. Both the boys' and the girls' groups participated in Klan demonstrations, sometimes with their own floats, and attended adult Klan rallies as pages and flag bearers. They had robes, masks, a set of passwords, and even a burial ritual unique to the teen order. The girls' order also sponsored all-girls bands and drum corps that performed at Klan rallies and parades, making it, in the words of an informant, "like the Girl Scouts."[19]

The family-based aspect of the teen orders was especially appealing to Klan parents. The Junior KKK and the Tri-K Klubs of South Bend were so active, according to the *Fellowship Forum*, because "parents of the young people are happy to be able to have whole families of 100 percenters interested."[20] Informants who were members of the Indiana children's orders remember vividly the sense of excitement of

being a part of Klan familial culture, where "you were junior Klan
members and that was big stuff." A member of the Tri-K Klub in
northern Indiana recalled the activities:

> [The Klan] started up the youth group and we had little uniforms, and we
> marched in parades and one time we had the largest group of children in
> the parade. It was really something. You know, we didn't know what it
> was all about. I remember we were taught the chants, or yells. And, one of
> them was: "Second Timothy, Five Twenty-two, tells you exactly what to
> do. Study to show yourself a Klu."[21]

The Klan also sought to solidify its tie to youth with the formation
of a Klan university to educate Klan girls and boys. As early as 1921
the Klan presented Lanier University in Atlanta with a substantial endowment, citing its full agreement with the principles of the university.
Although not exclusively Klan-run, Lanier University advertised itself
as an institution dedicated to the teaching of "pure Americanism" and
proclaimed that its doors were open to the sons and daughters of all
real Americans. Two years later, the Ku Klux Klan tried to purchase
Valparaiso University in northern Indiana to become a Klan university
but failed.[22]

Ideas about gender roles in the WKKK and KKK carried over into
the aspirations of the Klan for its teenage counterparts. The junior order for girls proclaimed itself the "future Klanswomen of America." It
promised to make certain that young women "receive the training
which will make them capable of assuming the responsibilities of the
future mothers of the race." In fact, the Klan portrayed the Tri-K Klub
as key to its continuing success, noting that "this young girls' organization is the most important of all, as it is from our mothers that we
receive our guidance." At a speech in 1925 symbolically delivered on
Mother's Day, Major Kleagle Leah H. Bell, the New Jersey state su-
pervisor of the Tri-K Klub, declared that many of the problems of
present-day morality could be solved through education of the young.
"Moral education is the need of America today," Bell insisted, "and
that is the reason for the Tri-K Klub. It is our purpose to bring the
young women of today who will become the mothers of tomorrow
into a sense of responsibility of their duties. These are the vital things
that they should know if the womanhood of America is to be kept
clean."[23]

Klan girls were not to embark on the serious program of character
building proposed by the boys' order. Indeed, the establishment of a

boys' order seemed to absolve teenage girls from most efforts at self-improvement for, in the eyes of the Klan, helping boys to be better would ultimately help girls as well. In the Tri-K Klub, teenage Klan girls were to learn the skills of motherhood and, not incidentally, serve as ornaments for Klan events. The female contingent at Klan parades often featured floats labeled "Miss 100 percent America" with young attractive girls waving to the crowds.[24]

The Klan had a very different agenda for its teenage male charges: learning to curb the natural excesses of boyish youth and develop into responsible Klansmen. According to one Klan propagandist, the junior Klan ensured that every mother knew where her child was at night, especially boys in the transition between boyhood and manhood, "the most dangerous period of a young man's life." The junior order, the Klan hoped, would "inculcate into the members a desire to live clean and wholesome lives, keep the laws of our land, and honor the flag." Men in the adult KKK argued that the junior order was necessary because female-dominated homes threatened to allow the "leaders of tomorrow" to be led into delinquency or idleness. The Junior KKK provided a substitute for the experience of direct male role modeling that was absent in a feminine domestic sphere. In the Klan, boys would learn self-reliance, usefulness, the value of work, and the importance of God. So important was this task that the Klan even proposed a minimal tuition correspondence high school and a program of college scholarships for boys from low-income families.[25]

The Junior Klan, like the Tri-K Klub, was a preparation for the responsibilities of adult klannishness. While girls were learning the virtues and tasks of motherhood and moral education of the young, boys were learning the secret agenda of the Klan itself. An address to parents of junior Klansmen at the state meeting of the Junior Ku Klux Klan of Michigan addressed the need to train future Klansmen at an early age and also suggested tension within the adult Klans over the lack of preparation of some of its own members.

> The average Klansman and Klanswoman joined the Klan without a great deal of knowledge as to what it was all about. They simply knew that America was sick and needed help. They believed the Klan furnished the vehicle to accomplish the cure and hence as good Americans they enlisted for the battle. . . . Those of us interested in the junior Klan desire to train your boys so that when they become members of the senior organization they will not have to go through the preparatory stage that each of you had to go through.[26]

The Klan stated that its teenage orders were "to cooperate with every father and mother in their effort to bring happiness and sunshine into the American home" and instructed teens that the Klan vows of secrecy did not apply between child and parent. But in reality things were more complex. The Klan wanted to prepare future Klanswomen and Klansmen and also to recruit the mothers and fathers of these teenagers. It felt that boys and girls whose parents were not Klan members should attempt to "interest" them in the work of the order. The loyalty of teens then was divided. On the one hand, Klan teens were to serve the Klan, to be "at all times the eyes and ears of the great [adult] Klan." On the other hand, the Klan stressed, teens were to be dutiful and loyal to their parents—even non-Klan parents.[27]

Indirectly, the Klan addressed this problem of loyalty in a *Kloran* issued for its younger members. The document encouraged Klan teens to role-play a situation in which a boy is taught by his father and mother to disbelieve "what you have said about the Constitution, and the Protestant Christian religion, and the public schools." It expected teens to respond that they would not tell the boy directly that his parents were wrong—since that would be encouraging disobedience to parents—but would only "smile and say to them kindly that each person is entitled to his own beliefs" and wait until the boy grew more distant from his parents, until "in the air of freedom they will think things out for themselves."[28]

In the continual quest for new members—and new revenue—the WKKK organized a cradle roll to enlist youngsters from birth through age twelve in the Klan's crusade. Parents made little Klan costumes for their youngsters, complete with hoods and masks (see photograph 13). A former member of the beginners unit recalls her time in the cradle roll: "It was just something to do and somewhere to go and nice little cookies and tea or cookies and Kool-Aid or something, and that was all it meant to us, you know . . . [but] you knew very much it was a secret. . . . It was fun. [Laughing] Can you imagine how much fun that would be for a five- or six-year old?"[29]

Like many Klan projects, the girls' and boys' orders eventually became ensnared in internecine Klan politics. The Tri-K Klub battled with the WKKK over which organization could enlist, and collect initiation fees and dues from, girls between the ages of sixteen and eighteen. The junior boys and the KKK became tangled in a dispute over whether to raise or lower the age eligibility, to what extent the junior boys should operate as an adjunct of the adult KKK, and to which organization dues of the juniors should go.[30]

Another aspect of its political culture was the Klan's rites of passage. These served two purposes. First, private rites solidified a sense of the totality of the Klan world. Within the Klan, members could be married, celebrate the birth of children, and mourn the departed. The Klan's culture replicated—and elaborated upon—the symbols of life passage traditionally commemorated in religious rites. Second, public rites contributed to the spectacle of the Klan. The 1924 state convention of the Pennsylvania WKKK, for example, drew a mammoth crowd to witness a day of baby dedications, mixed with the usual Klan fare of athletic contests, benedictions, military drills, parades, and musical performances. Likewise, the promise of Klan weddings and baby christenings lured an estimated crowd of ten thousand to a Klan condemnation of Smith's presidential bid.[31]

Weddings were one of the Klan's most effective public displays. The typical Klan wedding featured a Klanswoman and a Klansman exchanging vows before crowds of well-wishing robed Klansmembers. More spectacular weddings were held at night with Klan members arrayed before a burning cross to form a backdrop for the exchange of wedding vows. The Klan magazine, *Watcher on the Tower,* reported on a Klan wedding in the state of Washington:

> The bride was very charmingly attierd [*sic*] in a handsome satin gown bedecked with a wreath of beautiful flowers displaying the Klan colors. The groom was dressed in conventional black cloth with the usual Klan emblems. Honorable David Leppert, mayor of Kent, Washington, Exalted Cyclops, was the officiating clergyman.[32]

Large-scale public Klan weddings in Indiana brought additional recruits but also public mockery from anti-Klan forces. As the Klan reveled in the attraction created by a public wedding of fifty Klan couples in Muncie, for example, the *Muncie Post-Democrat* noted that the event proved that "marriage [is] a joke" to the Invisible Empire.[33]

A second rite of passage was birth observances (see photograph 11). WKKK klaverns sponsored both public and private christening ceremonies for infants born to sister Klanswomen. Open-air baptisms of groups of babies and small children performed by Klan ministers drew attention, and recruits, to the Klan. Secret Klan baptisms inducted newborns into the fellowship of the Klan. The *Fellowship Forum* reported on a typical Klan christening in South Bend, Indiana, where

"Klan no. 10 recently dedicated three very small babies at a regular meeting [of the WKKK]. Each baby was presented with a Holy Bible by a Klanswoman."[34]

An elaborate ceremony commemorated the final rite of passage for Klansmembers (see photograph 12). WKKK funerals featured Klanswomen in full regalia serving as pallbearers, eulogists, and bodyguards for their departed Klan sister and conducting services of Klan ritual at the graveside. There was even a guide to proper Klan funerals, with intricate instructions for the procession, the graveside hymn, the Exalted Cyclops's sermon, the kludd's readings, the placement of Klan regalia on the casket, and the presentation of floral offerings and sealed communications to the family. Some state Klan orders staged mammoth "lodges of sorrow" to memorialize all Klan members who died in that year. In Indiana, public funerals were commonplace for the women's and men's Klans.[35] The *Plainfield Messenger* described the elaborate graveside ceremonies performed by thirty members of the WKKK for the funeral of a local Klanswoman.

> They formed a procession and marched to the grave, headed by their organizer in royal purple and bearing an open Bible. Following was the flag bearer with the American colors at half mast. When the procession had formed about the grave the flag was raised to full mast for silent tribute. No word was spoken during the entire service. Following the rites by the officers each member cast rose petals on the casket and again formed a procession, leaving the cemetery in the order in which they came.[36]

Most Klan lodges also maintained "sick committees" whose purpose it was to visit and assist ailing members. With its rites for funerals, christenings, and marriages, lodges of the WKKK and KKK in Indiana provided an automatic circle of friendship to its members, a support system especially valuable to Klan members without families in the area.[37]

The political culture of klannishness was reinforced not only by rites of passage but also through Klan social events. WKKK chapters planned numerous socials for women only. The Marion County WKKK, for example, sponsored chautauqua events (outdoor lectures and entertainment) and movies and even produced their own movie using local Klanswomen as actresses. Virtually every WKKK klavern sponsored weekly cultural activities that ranged from readings and lectures to sewing circles and cooking demonstrations.[38]

Group sing-alongs were a favorite pastime. Many Indiana WKKK klaverns sponsored performing groups who were in high demand to enliven klonklaves and other Klan gatherings. Setting klannish verses to various familiar tunes resulted in such songs as "Yes, the Klan Has No Catholics" (to the tune of "Yes, We Have No Bananas"), "The Happy Klansmen," "Onward Christian Klansmen," and "Klansmen Keep the Cross A-burning." The Women's Quartet of Garrett, a popular feature at many WKKK initiations and rallies around northwestern Indiana, was famous for its rendition of "Onward, Ku Klux Klan." Other favorite groups included the Golden Queens, a WKKK quartet from Indianapolis that specialized in patriotic selections and "parodies of the better class," and the Ladies All-American Orchestra, also from Indianapolis.[39]

Not all social activities of Klanswomen were restricted to women members. Some were planned jointly with KKK chapters and included husbands or entire Klan families. The range of these family-based activities mirrored popular culture but with a political twist. Several WKKK chapters wrote and performed plays and skits that emphasized Klan beliefs and celebrated the superior status of white Protestants. One informant, for example, remembers his part in a Klan play as a child named "Ima White."[40]

The family-centered character of many WKKK activities encouraged busy married women to participate and integrated their Klan life into daily life in alien society. Klanswomen's activities were often indistinguishable from those of other middle-class white Protestant women—as, for example, when Indiana WKKK locals chartered trains to take their families to Mammoth Cave, Kentucky.[41] In Portland, Indiana, the WKKK and KKK chapters met in open-air meetings during the summer and early fall to which all members of Klan families were welcome: "Klan members had their fun, marched, sang songs and initiated new members. Both men, women and children were admitted. It was a common thing to hear the 'Old Rugged Cross' being sung. Also they sang 'Hail, Hail the Gang's All Here,' 'There'll Be a Hot Time in the Old Town Tonight,' and others."[42]

THE TOTALITY OF KLAN CULTURE

The Klan's rites of passage and carefully staged events created unprecedented spectacles in Indiana's small towns and cities. With its carnival-like ceremonies the Klan attracted thousands of onlookers. Local newspapers routinely reported that the crowd at a Klan rally or parade surpassed any ever assembled in the county. A woman in southern Indiana remembers vividly "two parades by this KKK, masked men (possibly some women) with the leader beating on drum an eerie strum-strum-strum-um-um-um."[43]

Little was left to chance in planning Klan spectacles. Local leaders of the women's and men's Klans received elaborate messages from state and national headquarters on how to stage a rally or klonklave. Instructions detailed the timelines for planning, how to form organizing committees, and how to use fireworks and other props.[44]

The success of the Klan's rallies was phenomenal. In Martin County, a rural south-central Indiana county with five hundred WKKK and five hundred KKK members, the Klan organized two thousand Klansmembers to march through the county in 1924. Every detail was carefully considered to maximize the march's effectiveness. As marchers reached a town, for example, street lights were turned off to highlight burning and electrically lit crosses and an airplane soared overhead dropping paper bombs that exploded to disgorge American flags suspended by tiny parachutes.[45] A man in a small town near Indianapolis recalled the Klan's skill at producing memorable events.

> Really there was a good deal of talent in the Klan. Their speakers were generally people that could do it, could cut it. The musicians were generally people who could cut it. The band director was one of the best anywhere in the country. He'd been well known in the circus for many years, and so on. And, that was the setup they had. . . . The parades were kind of a spectacular thing. They just had a lot of punch to them. A lot of theatrical stuff.[46]

Klan chapters vied with one another for the most original Klan event. In Lawrence County the Klan sponsored a charity performance of "kute girls, katchy songs, and kunning costumes." The Valparaiso klavern staged an "old-time frontier fete," complete with cowboys and mustangs, followed by twenty brass bands, five national WKKK speakers, and a trip to the Lake Michigan sand dunes to entertain— and impress—delegations of Klan sisters from five other WKKK chapters. In Sullivan, a small county seat in southwestern Indiana, a WKKK parade featured floats, decorated automobiles, lady horseback riders, and legions of white masked and hooded women. Here, as at many Klan events, spectacle mingled with ordinariness, the local newspaper noting "mothers with sleeping babies in their arms marching with the others." At a park in downtown Sullivan, a burning cross cast light over the women speakers and the men's quartet as a crowd of from three to five thousand observed the WKKK ritual.[47]

Spectacle was not restricted to parades and marches. Living fiery crosses, created by formations of Klanswomen holding burning torches aloft, and enormous wooden crosses wrapped in burlap, doused in coal oil, and set on fire, were common. Klan balloonists soared overhead in huge decorated balloons. Most informants describe the heyday of the Klan as a time of fun and spectacle. Asked to recall the feeling of being present at a cross burning, a woman from northern Indiana responded, "Oh, it was fun. And, the way they wrapped it in gunny sacks and soaked it in oil and then those guys went up and lit it, and it was just a fun thing to do."[48] Other informants remember Klan parades as an exciting break from daily life activities:

> Chautauqua was important but it was small-time as far as the time was concerned, to this. County fair would get a lot of people, but several thousand men walking around in white sheets and riding horses . . . that was exciting.

> Seven to ten thousand people marching in the streets, big electric sign in 1922. And, that was a fantastic thing even at that time, to have an electric sign [a cross] on an automobile.[49]

In many communities in Indiana, Klan events were difficult to distinguish—except for their excitement—from those of Protestant congregations. Protestant preachers flocked to the Klan, legitimating Klan membership and providing easy entrée for the Klan into their congregations. In turn, the women's and men's Klans celebrated the superiority of Protestantism and promised to restore Protestant unity and militancy.[50]

The ties between the women's Klan and Protestant denominations ranged from subtle gestures to major displays. In Greenfield, Indiana, the Presbyterian Ladies Aid Society served refreshments at a public initiation of one hundred Klansmembers to indicate their support for the Klan's cause. The WKKK of Marion County (Indianapolis) joined forces with the Colonial Dames to stage a two-day "pageant of Protestantism" that featured Klanswomen dressed as Columbia, Uncle Sam, liberty, and justice; it included a popularity contest. Another Indianapolis WKKK chapter met at a local Congregational church where illuminated fiery crosses and background music from a women's orchestra framed "fiery talks [in favor of] ending immigration, strengthening prohibition and standing for 'pure Americanism.' "[51]

The political culture and the activities of Indiana's WKKK, KKK, and children's auxiliaries closely paralleled the daily lives of many white Protestants in Indiana, creating an oft-stated sense among the majority population that "everyone was in the Klan." Klaverns met in lodge halls, church vestries, club rooms, YMCAs, and YWCAs; Klan lecturers spoke to schools and in school auditoriums. In many communities, including very small towns and rural commercial centers, the Klan was so large that it rented or purchased its own buildings for a meeting hall. Commonly, the men's Klan would purchase or rent space directly and the women's would sublet meeting space from the men.[52]

In most communities of Indiana the Klan was granted an astonishing amount of legitimacy. Local newspapers publicized routes for Klan marches and fostered excitement with Klan-supplied lists of expected delegations and featured entertainment. Town mayors issued parade permits and city police and county sheriffs' departments sent officers to assist robed Klanswomen and Klansmen with traffic and parking problems. Newspapers publicized the details of impending Klan events in the town, often doing little more than reprinting publicity mailed out by the Klan itself, as in this report in the *Kokomo Daily Tribune:*

> Nathan Hall Klan No. 11 and Kourt No. 2 of the Women of the Ku Klux Klan, the two local Klan organizations, are preparing for a big local celebration to be held in this city October 11 afternoon and evening. The plans contemplate a huge open air meeting at Foster Park and a big parade at night. State speakers of both the men's and women's organizations will be present. The local drum corps will be in action, and out-of-town bands will probably be there.[53]

Local newspapers covered Klan events—including public speeches, parades, and social events—as they would any other gathering in town. The *Kokomo Daily Tribune* announced upcoming events of the women's and men's orders, along with other planned events in town, in the daily front page column, "What's Doing in Kokomo." The *News Journal* of North Manchester made only one comment on a cross burning by the local Klan: it expressed the hope that future cross-lightings would not be marred by excessive wind. Both Kokomo newspapers characterized as "eloquent" a Klan speech that denounced black population growth, called for an end to Catholic education, and deplored Jewish control over the motion picture industry. Local city directories (which preceded phone books) listed Klan chapters under the heading "lodges and churches" or "miscellaneous societies" and gave information about local Klan headquarters, meeting places, and meeting times.[54]

Despite its trappings of secrecy, the Klan was commonplace, an accepted part of life in native-born white Protestant families. People *knew* but pretended not to know. A woman from northern Indiana summed up the feeling this way: "Even though you knew someone was a member of the Klan, cause you had been to the meetings, you didn't talk about it outside. Even to them, you didn't mention it outside."[55]

The world of the Klan overlapped with the minutia of everyday life. After the massive Klan celebration in Kokomo on July 4, 1923, children on the streets of Kokomo joined in the fun of adults by "playing Ku Klux." Klan rallies included picnic suppers or "basket dinners" in their agenda, to accommodate the schedules of Klan families. Kokomo Klans brought the ever-popular Rodgers and Harris circus for a five-day local engagement in 1925, tucking a Klan parade amidst the pageantry of the circus's "old fiddlers contest" and baby contest. The Klan even purchased public spaces, including Melfalfa Park in Kokomo, which had a lodge and a swimming pool and hosted some of Indiana's largest Klan events.[56]

The political culture of the Klan not only imitated but also operated within the dominant culture of Indiana. A spectator at an immense Klan demonstration in Valparaiso, Indiana, in 1923 noted that "a casual visitor might have mistaken this solemn occasion for a political rally, a county fair, a Fourth of July festival, or a circus." The *Fiery Cross* urged its klannish readers to support Miss Mary Edith Turch, "a 100% American Christian girl" in the popularity contest being run by the *Indianapolis News*. Music stores featured Klan records such as "The Kluxing of the Ku Klux Klan" in their advertisements.[57]

The apparent normalcy of the Klan in Indiana created odd sights and alliances. A Jewish man in Muncie recalled that his father took him as a child to Klan parades to enjoy the spectacle. The Klan organized a unit for foreign-born Protestants who were barred from full Klan membership (the American Krusaders). Even more strangely, the Klan tried to organize an order of black Protestants, a Klan "colored division" in Indiana and other states. Despite promises that the new order would have "all the rights of membership" of the white Klan, much preparation went into ensuring that the values of white supremacy would be preserved as the Klan expanded its racial base. The group was to wear red robes, white capes, and blue masks and was prohibited from being seen in public with white Klansmen or handling any membership funds.[58]

The situation in Johnson County, an agricultural county just south of Indianapolis, exemplifies the Klan's acknowledged place in the fabric of daily life in Indiana. The 1923 Johnson County fair reserved Monday and Tuesday for agricultural shows and designated Wednesday as Klan Day at the request of the Johnson County KKK and WKKK. Advertisements for the county fair headlined Wednesday's special events (including a balloon ascension and two speakers from state headquarters to address both women and men of the Klan) as well as typical county fair events such as baby shows, racing, and livestock judging. Arrangements for Klan Day involved nearly everyone in the county. Businessmen arranged to transport children and the elderly to the fair; musicians agreed to play music and housewives to bring food to the event. On Klan Day all stores, offices, banks, shops, and businesses in Franklin (the largest community) were ordered to close at noon "in order that 100 percent cooperation can be given to the fair." With such backing, it is little wonder that Klan Day broke all records for attendance at the fair. The exuberance of the crowd carried over into the evening as a large group of women and men gathered to hear a Christian pastor from Indianapolis speak on Protestant supremacy.[59]

Perhaps the clearest indication of the fusion of the Klan with its environment is the casualness with which Klan members in some areas protected their identities. Many Klansmembers adhered carefully to strict policies about klannish secrecy and privacy, fearful that discovery of their membership would cost them friendships, customers, or political support. Others, and even entire Klan locals in Indiana, were lax about secrecy. Women and men of the Klan commonly marched through the towns of Indiana in robes and hoods but with face visors up. Klan members felt little fear of the consequences of being publicly identified with the Invisible Empire. A woman in northeastern Indiana and a man in southwestern Indiana have similar recollections of the Klan's lack of fear of reprisals:

> I remember a big parade we had in [town] where we had to stand for so long before we could start marching because there were so many units to make it up. And, they had this great big flag they carried and people threw money in the flag and the flag was almost as wide as the street. And, I remember at first there was a mask down, but after a while they put the masks up . . . and they still marched.

> See, you had the hood, the pointed hood, and then the robe that went around. And this mask or face thing just dropped down over your face.

You could see through it. Incidentally, those things were really hell to try and play a horn when you were walking with one of those, so the result was that the band was practically all robed and hooded but not masked.[60]

Organized resistance to the Klan occurred in areas of Indiana, but it was sporadic and largely ineffectual. The enormity of the Klan in many communities made an open assault on the Invisible Empire difficult to mount, although there were notable exceptions. The American Unity League in Chicago and in Marion County, Indiana, attempted to break the secrecy of the Klan organization by publishing names of reputed Klansmembers. Some local Indiana officials passed municipal antimask ordinances or refused to issue parade permits to the Klan. Stories about other anti-Klan actions circulated throughout Indiana, providing hope and encouragement to those opposed to the Klan. One Indiana mayor was said to have strategically dispatched fire engines to false alarms during Klan parades in order to disrupt the gatherings. From other communities came word of those who physically blocked Klan parades and of violent confrontations between Klansmembers and organized anti-Klan groups.[61]

As a consequence of the absorption of the Klan into daily life, Klan members often found it difficult to comprehend negative reactions to the organization. An oral history of Muncie included a story about a housekeeper in a Jewish family who not only joined the Klan but expected the family to share in her pride at being a Klanswoman. This sense of normalcy continued to inform retrospective opinions of the Klan long after its demise. Few people expressed regrets about their participation in the Klan; most "just forgot about it." Others told the story of their participation in terms that made joining seem inevitable or disavowed the Klan as an organization but not the Klan's beliefs:

> When there were so many people leaning on me, I had little choice. Today, it's pretty easy for somebody to say, "Well, I sure wouldn't have done it." [Laughing] But, I joined up and . . . and as teachers do, I had an offer of a two-room school the following year and I went to that school. And, had about the same experience. The trustee was a Klansman. And, I attended one Klan meeting with him.

> White supremacy. No intermarriage of races, which I think I [still] agree with. I believe this causes a lot of unhappiness for the children of such . . . the byproducts of them.[62]

In the Indiana of the 1920s respectability lay in being a Klan member. As a Brown County Klanswoman explained, "it was considered the thing to do to join the Klan in the 1920s." In background, values, ideologies, and even politics, Klanswomen and Klansmen did not differ significantly from their racial and religious counterparts in Indiana. Far from the popular media image of people with weaknesses of character or temperament or intellect as the Klan's only adherents, the Klanswomen and Klansmen of the 1920s were more often—and perhaps more frighteningly—normal. They were women and men who loved their families, acted kindly and sympathetically to many other people, and even held progressive views on a number of issues.[63]

To say that Indiana Klanswomen and Klansmen were normal does not mean that the Klan was not racist, xenophobic, violent, intolerant, and bigoted. In public, speakers for the Klan commonly denied that the Klan was "anti-anything or anti-anybody," veiling their message in calls for "a stronger America" or a revitalized Christianity. Yet claims by contemporaries that the Klan was little more than a Protestant advocacy group are disingenuous. In the private halls of Klan meetings and rallies, the true purpose of the Klan was clear and well received by its adherents. In Whitley County the crowd applauded wildly as a Klan speaker harangued, "I want to put all the Catholics, Jews, and Negroes on a raft in the middle of the ocean and then sink the raft."[64] In Fort Wayne, Hiram Evans addressed five thousand assembled Klansmembers with a very clear message:

> The negroes of the South and the inferior immigrant population of New York and New England are largely responsible for much of the political prostitution that is now a curse to our country. We have our Hester Streets and our box car flats and shacks in every industrial center . . . unsanitary, unwholesome, uninspirational, the national habitation and breeding place of the moron, nomad, and criminal.[65]

The Klan's private agenda was well known throughout white Protestant Indiana. When D. C. Stephenson told Fort Wayne Klanswomen to "whisper" the proper message into the ears of their political leaders, "everybody" (as Klansmembers referred to themselves) knew the message. State Klan officials counseled speakers that "you can't make it too strong against the Jew and the Catholic in a closed meeting—give them hell." Klan speakers obliged, warning audiences that Jews, Catholics, and blacks were secretly organizing to destroy white Protestantism. Women and men in the Klan denounced Jews as "Christ-killers" and hinted of Jews amassing vast fortunes through the exploitation of Christian labor. The Klan argued that blacks were inherently stupid, socially inferior, and should be returned to Africa, and emphasized the point by showing *Birth of a Nation* at Klan rallies. Klan speakers charged that the Catholics controlled New York City, New York state, Chicago, and other cities; that most criminals were Catholics; and that 50 percent of the teachers in public schools were practicing Catholics.[66]

Klan leaders stopped at nothing to attack their enemies. In several cities in Indiana, Klan organizers and officers were arrested for arson of school buildings, for fires they set and attempted to blame on foreigners, Jews, or blacks. Though the arrest of a Klan organizer was a rare enough event in a state where law enforcement officers often owed their positions to the Klan or to Klan politicians, conviction was even rarer. Juries of Klan sympathizers, or of individuals afraid of Klan retribution, rarely convicted Klansmembers.[67]

Such attitudes and actions of racism, intolerance, and xenophobia found a fertile home in Indiana and in many other states in the 1920s. Even without laws mandating racial segregation, cities and towns practiced strict segregation of social life, schooling, and housing. Newspapers ran separate columns or pages for news for and about local blacks, reserving the newspaper as a whole for what was considered universal—the white experience.[68] Considerable social distance also existed between Catholics and Protestants and between Christians and Jews, exacerbated by stories of Jewish-Catholic plots to destroy the Protestant faith. In such an atmosphere the Klan movement of the 1920s was eerily unremarkable for many white native-born Protestants.

Epilogue

The second Klan collapsed rapidly. By 1928 membership declined to several hundred thousand. Two years later fewer than fifty thousand women and men still belonged to the Invisible Empire. Battles between contending leadership factions, disclosure of rampant corruption, and public exposure of Klan atrocities marred the image of the Klan and allowed public authorities to intervene against Klan violence.

Changing social conditions also lessened the appeal of the Klan to many white Protestants. The number of foreign-born residents in the United States declined drastically as new immigration laws took effect. Nationalist fervor from World War I decreased over time until revived in the 1940s. Moreover, the economic depression of the 1930s altered the political landscape of the nation. Although racism, anti-Semitism, and anti-Catholicism certainly did not disappear in the late 1920s, most white Protestants no longer perceived the Klan as the vehicle for expressing intolerance and racial hatred. From its heyday in the mid-1920s, the Klan fell into public disgrace and marginality.[1]

Between 1930 and the end of World War II the Ku Klux Klan was small and based primarily in the South. Women played no visible part in this Klan, which was noted for terroristic actions against organized labor, federal New Deal programs, Communist party organizers, and Southern blacks. Like the first Klan, this KKK relied on images of white women's and children's vulnerability to justify its virulent anti-bolshevik, anti-Semitic, and antiblack propaganda and actions.[2]

The third major Ku Klux Klan emerged in the 1950s in an effort to combat racial desegregation in the South. Klansmembers (largely Klansmen) bombed schools and homes, led riots, and embarked on a wave of lynchings and physical violence against blacks and those whites who supported integrationist efforts. Although this Klan found support among some white Southerners, the strength of the black civil rights movement, local anti-Klan organizing, and changing racial attitudes among many whites eventually provoked a backlash. Federal investigations and arrests, together with state and local ordinances against its parades or charters and public opposition forced the KKK into decline in the 1970s.

The fourth and current Klan movement dates to the early 1980s and is again largely based in the South, with a growing presence in the Far West and Midwest. Its main targets now are blacks, with Jews, Mexican-Americans, gay men and lesbians, Communists, and Southeast Asian immigrants also victimized. Although numerically small— perhaps as few as ten thousand members—the modern Klan has augmented its strength through alliances with other extralegal terrorist and paramilitary groups. Recently, a number of Klansmembers joined with self-proclaimed Nazis and right-wing survivalists and tax evaders in a secret network known as the Aryan Nations. Violently anti-Semitic and racist, the Aryan Nations has spawned a terrorist adjunct, The Order, whose members are linked through a computer bulletin board. The Order has vowed to assassinate anyone who interferes with its goal of world supremacy.

Women belong to the Klan and Aryan Nations (though perhaps not The Order) as members, but with few exceptions women play mostly supporting roles in the fourth Klan. Indeed, women's rights are antithetical to the agenda of the modern Klan, which affirms traditional gender roles as the only correct ones for God-fearing Christians and denounces affirmative action programs on the grounds that these curb the rights of white men.[3]

Unfortunately, the Klan's secret membership makes it impossible to trace the political activities of 1920s Klanswomen after the collapse of the second Klan, beyond the few for whom I present biographical accounts in chapter 4. Most likely, the majority of Klanswomen, like their male counterparts, simply dropped out of politics after the collapse of the Klan. Among those who remained politically active, some continued in nationalistic and patriotic politics, others worked for women's equality, and some even supported programs for economic justice.

Most women who participated in extremist right-wing movements after the collapse of the 1920s Klan entered political organizations that had less complicated views of women's proper place in society than did the 1920s Klan. The women's auxiliaries of the pro-Nazi German-American Bund and the women's patriotic societies of the 1930s and 1940s made little attempt to challenge traditional gender roles. Often, they framed their opposition to socialism and communism in terms of a threat to existing gender norms. Women accepted largely subordinate roles in these organizations.[4]

The politics of gender in the 1920s Klan are more difficult to categorize than those of most modern right-wing movements. The WKKK's promotion of women's rights resembled the nativist strand of women's suffrage when it excluded nonwhite and non-Protestant women from the struggle for full citizenship for women. But the Klan used its agenda of women's rights to justify—even to require—vicious and brutal actions against blacks, Catholics, Jews, immigrants, and others. Many women brought a women's rights politics into the 1920s Klan from earlier suffrage, temperance, or moral reform movements but reshaped and recontextualized that politics in the service of racism and nativism.

In the early twentieth century the contours of the American political order were still in flux. They did not find after World War I the firm alliances of social class and party that would emerge after World War II. Under the conditions of the 1920s, political movements fused odd, even contradictory, ideologies and political agendas. Currents within temperance endorsed female suffrage, many social reformers strove to discipline unruly immigrants, and a segment of women's rights advocates subscribed to nativism and racism. In this fluctuating political climate, it was possible for the WKKK to create a gender ideology that was neither fundamentally reactionary nor progressive. Rather, the women's Klan was contradictory: a reactionary, hate-based movement with progressive moments.

The impact of the women's Klan on early twentieth-century society was profound. Through its women's order, the second Klan brought an agenda of bigotry and intolerance into the marrow of white Protestant communities—into schools, leisure activities, and homes. Beyond political corruption and vigilante violence, the poison of the Klan seeped into the fabric of everyday life—into rituals of celebration and sorrow, networks of family and friendship, and the work of shopping and childcare.

The inclusion of women (and children) in the second Klan extended the order's influence in another way. Klanswomen, Klan teens, and Klan babies contributed to the normalization of the Klan. Seemingly innocuous family events strengthened the Klan's claim that it was just "a way to get together and enjoy." The perfunctory manner in which former Klansmembers (like the Indiana woman in the introduction) discuss their participation underscores the Klan's success in becoming a part of ordinary white Protestant life. The racist, nativist venom of Klan politics percolated easily, unremarkably, through this world.

It is clear that scholarship is beginning to unravel the complexities of women's role in political movements like those of the women's Klan. Over the past twenty years feminist scholars have challenged the assumption of female political insignificance and uncovered a rich legacy of women's involvement in progressive and egalitarian political movements. Using insights gained in research on women in progressive politics, we can now turn to the disturbing, but important, question of women's involvement in racist, reactionary, and fascist movements. Unencumbered by traditional assumptions that women are "naturally" drawn to right-wing politics, feminist scholars can take a new look at the ideology, motivations, and actions of women on the right.

The history of the WKKK also compels us to rethink our models of political ideology. The commonplace assumption that women in reactionary movements support an antifeminist agenda blinds us to complicated relations that exist among attitudes toward gender, race, economics, and nationalism. Clearly, these attitudes are not unrelated, but neither are they historically consistent. Support for gender equality, in particular, bears an uneasy relation to other progressive political beliefs.

A number of political movements of the late twentieth century exhibit similar contradictory interactions of gender politics with the politics of race, religion, and class. For example, women took significant roles in the black civil rights, anti–Vietnam War, and new left movements of the 1950s to the 1970s. But assertions of women's common interests *as women* often met bemusement or hostility from male leaders and participants. In the feminist movement of the 1970s and 1980s, by contrast, the commonality of women's experiences shaped the political agenda. Yet an assumption that women's awareness of their gender interests would lead them to progressive politics on race and social class proved empty. A concern for women's rights and gender equality led many, maybe most, feminists to a critical examination of national inequities of social class and race, but concerns for women's equality also created efforts to increase women's access to the ranks of the economic and political elite. Too, feminist political symbols of independent, autonomous, self-directed women led many working-class, poor, and minority women to view support for women's rights as embedded within the experiences of white middle-class women.

Many women, although disaffected with modern organized feminist politics, strongly support gender equality and women's rights issues in the home, workplace, and electoral arena. A minority, however—particularly those who identify themselves as homemakers, mothers, and wives rather than as wage earners—see their common interests as women in the support of openly antifeminist causes like antiabortion and anti-ERA movements. In this sense, the feminist movement's difficulty in promoting women's individuality without implicitly denigrating women's role in the family and home helped pave the way for women to enter the new right in great numbers in the 1970s and 1980s. Just as the second Klan used images of white masculine supremacy and pure white womanhood to chart a political effort to restore lost privileges, so, too, the new right wields a rhetoric of morality and nuclear families to create a momentum of support for the existing social order against threats to change it, by feminists or by political progressives.

Yet the seemingly consistent ideology of antifeminism and conservative economic and racial politics in the modern new right is rife with contradictions. The new right proclaims the centrality of home and family life to women, yet it produces spokeswomen like Phyllis Schlafly whose life is defined by public activities of employment and politics. Moreover, as in the 1920s Klan, the modern new-right movement has been hampered by the problems of mobilizing a political agenda around issues of morality. Under the political symbol of morality, the new right enlisted thousands of women and men to confront school boards, politicians, feminist activists, and the courts. But the scandals that later erupted among the leaders of these morality crusades—particularly around religious fundamentalist preachers—

then threatened the new right's efforts on a broad range of political issues.

Both the 1920s Klan and the modern new-right and antifeminist movements demonstrate that the politics of sexuality and gender are complex. Morality, sexuality, and women's roles are convenient symbols for political movements seeking to justify antiegalitarian or reactionary policies. But if gender and sex are powerful vehicles for political mobilizing, they also create expectations and political agendas that are difficult to sustain over time. The second Klan collapsed almost overnight, the victim in part of the contradictions of political moralism. With the Klan's disintegration, the ideological merger of women's rights with racism and nativism, too, nearly disappeared from the political landscape.

The short life of the 1920s KKK and WKKK demonstrates the fragility of mass movements of extremist racism and nativism. Yet it also suggests the potency and multifaceted appeal of reactionary politics. Certainly, women who joined one of the most vicious political campaigns in U.S. history shared the Klan's aspirations for white supremacy. It is important to note, however, that the Klan's appeal to women of the 1920s also lay outside the realm of traditional nativism and racism: in its purported quest for women's rights and in its offer of collective support, friendship, and sociability among like-minded women.

Notes

INTRODUCTION

1. Author's interview with anonymous informant, Aug. 24, 1987.

2. The most comprehensive histories of the 1920s Klan movement are the following: John Moffatt Mecklin, *The Ku Klux Klan: A Study of the American Mind* (Harcourt, Brace, 1924); David M. Chalmers, *Hooded Americanism* (Duke University Press, 1987); Wyn Craig Wade, *The Fiery Cross* (Simon and Schuster, 1987); Kenneth Jackson, *The Ku Klux Klan in the City, 1915–1930* (Oxford University Press, 1967); and Arnold Rice, *The Ku Klux Klan in American Politics* (Haskell, 1972). Important regional and local accounts include Charles Alexander, *The Ku Klux Klan in the Southwest* (University Press of Kentucky, 1965); Larry R. Gerlach, *Blazing Crosses in Zion: The Ku Klux Klan in Utah* (Utah State University Press, 1982); Frank Cates, "The Ku Klux Klan in Indiana Politics, 1920–1925" (Ph.D. diss., Indiana University, 1970); Norman F. Weaver, "The Knights of the Ku Klux Klan in Wisconsin, Indiana, Ohio, and Michigan" (Ph.D. diss., University of Wisconsin, 1954); Christopher Nicklas Cocoltchos, "The Invisible Government and the Visible Community: The Ku Klux Klan in Orange County, California, during the 1920s" (Ph.D. diss., University of California, Los Angeles, 1979); Robert Alan Goldberg, *Hooded Empire* (University of Illinois Press, 1981); William Jenkins, "The Ku Klux Klan in Youngstown, Ohio," *The Historian* 41 (November 1978): 76–93; Robert K. Hux, "The Ku Klux Klan in Macon, 1919–1925," *Georgia Historical Quarterly* 62 (1978): 155–68; Emerson Hunsberger Loucks, *The Ku Klux Klan in Pennsylvania* (Telegraph, 1936); David M. Chalmers, "The Ku Klux Klan in the Sunshine State," *Florida Historical Quarterly* 42 (January, 1964): 209–15; Frank Granger, "Reaction to Change: The Ku Klux Klan in Shreveport, 1920–1929," *North Louisiana Historical Association Journal* 9 (1978): 219–27; Bernard Howson, "The Ku Klux Klan

in Ohio after World War I" (Master's thesis, Ohio State University, 1951); Philip Racine, "The Ku Klux Klan, Anti-Catholicism, and Atlanta's Board of Education," *Georgia Historical Quarterly* 57 (Spring 1973): 63–75; William R. Snell, "Fiery Crosses in the Roaring Twenties: Activities of the Revised Klan in Alabama, 1915–1930," *Alabama Review* 23 (October 1970): 256–76; and Lila Lee Jones, "The Ku Klux Klan in Eastern Kansas during the 1920s," *Emporia State Research Studies* 23 (Winter 1975): 5–41.

3. For examples of how traditional Klan histories treat the role of women in the Klan, see Chalmers, *Hooded Americanism*, 240–41, 289; or Rice, *Ku Klux Klan*, 132 n2. Recent scholarship on women in Nazi Germany, however, is exploring contradictions of women's role in right-wing movements. See Claudia Koonz, *Mothers in the Fatherland* (St. Martin's Press, 1987); Renate Bridenthal, Atina Grossman, and Marion Kaplan, eds., *When Biology Became Destiny: Women in Weimar and Nazi Germany* (Monthly Review Press, 1984); Ann Taylor Allen, "Mothers of the New Generation: Adele Schreiber, Helene Stocker, and the Evolution of a German Ideal of Motherhood," *Signs* 20 (Spring 1985); Tim Mason, "Women in Germany, 1925–1940," *History Workshop* 1, 2 (Summer, Autumn 1976): 74–113, 5–32; and Jost Hermand, "All Power to the Women: Nazi Concepts of Matriarchy," *Journal of Contemporary History* 19 (October 1984).

4. This observation draws on a feminist argument that to use men's experience as the sole category of analysis distorts the experiences of both women and men. See Joan Kelly, "The Doubled Vision of Feminist Theory," in *Sex and Class in Women's History*, ed. Judith L. Newton, Mary P. Ryan, and Judith R. Walkowitz (Routledge and Kegan Paul, 1983), 259–70; and Joan Wallach Scott, *Gender and the Politics of History* (Columbia University Press, 1988).

5. Such traditional political categories persist despite extensive scholarship on the lack of support for women's rights within movements with progressive racial or social class politics. See Sara Evans, *Personal Politics* (Vintage, 1980); Alice Kessler-Harris, "Problems of Coalition-Building: Women and Trade Unions in the 1920s," in *Women, Work, and Protest*, ed. Ruth Milkman (Routledge and Kegan Paul, 1985); Patricia Cooper, *Once a Cigar Maker* (University of Illinois Press, 1987); Nancy Gabin, " 'They Have Placed a Penalty on Womanhood': The Protest Actions of Women Auto Workers in Detroit-area UAW Locals, 1945–1947," *Feminist Studies* 8 (Summer 1982): 373–98.

6. My analysis is based on Anne Firor Scott, "On Seeing and Not Seeing: A Case of Historical Invisibility," *Journal of American History* 71 (June 1984): 7–21. On "essential" aspects of femininity from which a case for female pacifism can be made, see Sara Ruddick, "Maternal Thinking," *Feminist Studies* 6 (Summer 1980): 342–67; and Mary O'Brien, *The Politics of Reproduction* (Routledge and Kegan Paul, 1981). Standard works on women and politics include Virginia Shapiro, *The Political Integration of Women: Roles, Socialization, and Politics* (University of Illinois Press, 1984), 1–35, 143–69;

and Sandra Baxter and Marjorie Lansing, *Women and Politics: The Invisible Majority* (University of Michigan Press, 1980); both use fairly conventional definitions of politics. Other important works include Vicky Randall, *Women and Politics* (St. Martin's Press, 1982), esp. 35–68; Louise Tilly, "Paths of Proletarianization: Organization of Production, Sexual Division of Labor, and Women's Collective Action," *Signs* 7 (Spring 1981): 400–417; Dana Frank, "Housewives, Socialists, and the Politics of Food: The 1917 New York Cost-of-Living Protests," *Feminist Studies* 11 (Spring 1985): 255–85; Karen Sacks, *Caring by the Hour* (University of Illinois Press, 1988); and Rudolf M. Dekker, "Women in Revolt," *Theory and Society* 16 (May 1987): 337–62. Studies of right-wing women include Kristin Luker, *Abortion and the Politics of Motherhood* (University of California Press, 1984); Rebecca E. Klatch, *Women of the New Right* (Temple University Press, 1987); Rosalyn Pollack Petchesky, "Antiabortion, Antifeminism, and the Rise of the New Right," *Feminist Studies* 7 (Summer 1981): 206–46; Susan E. Marshall, "Ladies Against Women: Mobilization Dilemmas of Antifeminist Movements," *Social Problems* 32 (April 1985): 348–62; Susan E. Marshall, "In Defense of Separate Spheres: Class and Status Politics in the Antisuffrage Movement," *Social Forces* 65 (December 1986): 327–51; Janet Saltzman Chafetz and Anthony Gary Dworkin, "In the Face of Threat: Organized Antifeminism in Comparative Perspective," *Gender and Society* 1 (March 1987): 33–60; and Pamela J. Conover and Virginia Gray, *Feminism and the New Right: Conflict Over the American Family* (Praeger, 1984). On the political consequences of the primacy of family life for working-class and lower-middle-class women, see Ruth M. Alexander, " 'We Are Engaged as a Band of Sisters': Class and Domesticity in the Washingtonian Temperance Movement, 1840–1850," *Journal of American History* 75 (December 1988): 763–85. On gender consciousness, see Temma Kaplan, "Female Consciousness and Collective Action: The Case of Barcelona," *Signs* 7 (Spring 1982): 545–66; Karen J. Blair, *The Clubwoman as Feminist: True Womanhood Redefined, 1868–1914* (Holmes and Meier, 1980); and Estelle B. Freedman, "Separatism as Strategy: Female Institution-Building and American Feminism, 1870–1930," *Feminist Studies* 5 (1979): 512–29. An interesting discussion of racial vs. gender-based ideologies is found in Gisela Bock, "Racism and Sexism in Nazi Germany: Motherhood, Compulsory Sterilization, and the State," *Signs* 8 (Spring 1983): 400–421. A number of these points are discussed in Paula Baker, "The Domestication of Politics: Women and American Political Society, 1780–1920," *American Historical Review* 89 (June 1984): 620–47; Jacquelyn Dowd Hall, "Disorderly Women: Gender and Labor Militancy in the Appalachian South," *Journal of American History* 73 (September 1986): 354–82; Malcolm I. Thomis and Jennifer Grimmett, *Women in Protest, 1800–1850* (St. Martin's, 1982), esp. 28–64; Sara Evans, *Personal Politics;* Judith R. Walkowitz, *Prostitution and Victorian Society* (Cambridge University Press, 1982); and Rosalind Pollack Petchesky, *Abortion and Woman's Choice* (Northeastern University Press, 1984).

CHAPTER ONE

1. Walter L. Fleming, "The Prescript of the Ku Klux Klan," *Southern Historical Association* 7 (September 1903): 327–48; David Annan, "The Ku Klux Klan," in *Secret Societies,* ed. Norman MacKenzie (Holt, Rinehart and Winston, 1967); Mecklin, *The Ku Klux Klan.*
2. Joint Select Committee on the Condition of Affairs in the Late Insurrectionary States, *Affairs in the Late Insurrectionary States,* 42d Cong., 2d sess., 1872 (reprint, Arno Press, 1969); Seymour Martin Lipset, "An Anatomy of the Klan," *Commentary* 40 (October 1965): 74–83; Frank Tannenbaum, "The Ku Klux Klan: Its Social Origin in the South," *Century Magazine* 105 (April 1923): 873–83; Wade, *The Fiery Cross,* pp. 31–80.
3. Jacquelyn Dowd Hall, " 'The Mind that Burns in Each Body': Women, Rape, and Racial Violence," in *Powers of Desire: The Politics of Sexuality,* ed. Ann Snitow, Christine Stansell, and Sharon Thompson (Monthly Review Press, 1983); Wade, *The Fiery Cross,* 54–79; Frank Tannenbaum, *Darker Phases of the South* (Negro Universities Press, 1924), 33–34. The Klan's unintended advertisement of sex parallels that of the social purity movement of the late nineteenth and early twentieth centuries, as described by David Pivar, *Purity Crusade* (Greenwood Press, 1973), and also the moral reform movement of the midnineteenth century, analyzed by Carroll Smith-Rosenberg, *Disorderly Conduct: Visions of Gender in Victorian America* (Oxford University Press, 1986), 109–28.
4. Despite the common stereotype of the first Klan as composed primarily of lower-class Southern whites, men in the professions and business were active also (Wade, *The Fiery Cross,* 31–80; David Bennett, *The Party of Fear: From Nativist Movements to The New Right in American History* [University of North Carolina Press, 1988]).
5. Jacquelyn Dowd Hall, *Revolt Against Chivalry: Jesse Daniel Ames and the Women's Campaign Against Lynching* (Columbia University Press, 1979); Jacquelyn Dowd Hall, " 'A Truly Subversive Affair': Women Against Lynching in the Twentieth-Century South," in *Women of America: A History,* ed. Carol Berkin and Mary Beth Norton (Houghton Mifflin, 1979); Elizabeth Fox-Genovese, *Within the Plantation Household: Black and White Women of the Old South* (University of North Carolina Press, 1988), esp. 37–70; see also Laurence Alan Baughman, *Southern Rape Complex: A Hundred-Year Psychosis* (Pendulum, 1966), 176–77.
6. Annan, "Ku Klux Klan."
7. Fleming, "Prescript," 10; see also Winfield Jones, *Knights of the Ku Klux Klan* (Tocsin, 1941), 98. Annie Cooper Burton, president of a chapter of the United Daughters of the Confederacy, wrote *The Ku Klux Klan* (Warren T. Potter, 1916) with thanks to the Klan and included an interview with Captain H. W. Head, former Klan Grand Cyclops of Nashville. Peter Stearns suggests that the nineteenth-century creation of an ideology of white female vulnerability was in part a response to the changing image of manhood in an industrial society (*Be a Man!* [Holmes and Meier, 1979]).

8. Baughman, *Southern Rape Complex*, 176–77; Chalmers, *Hooded Americanism*, 21.

9. S. E. F. Rose, *The Ku Klux Klan or the Invisible Empire* (L. Graham, 1914), 17.

10. Wade, *The Fiery Cross*, 20.

11. Catherine A. MacKinnon, "Feminism, Marxism, Method, and State," *Signs* 6 (March 1983): 30.

12. Fox-Genovese, *Plantation Household*, esp. 37–99.

13. This analysis assumes that collective frustration and structural positions cannot explain the development of social movements, in the absence of shared resources and a common worldview. See Sara Evans, *Personal Politics;* and Charles Tilly, *From Mobilization to Revolution* (Addison-Wesley, 1973).

14. Hall, " 'The Mind' "; see also Tannenbaum, *Darker Phases*, 31–33.

15. *Affairs in the Late Insurrectionary States;* Fleming, "Prescript"; Annan, "Ku Klux Klan."

16. Many social historians interpret the second Ku Klux Klan as a reaction to rapid social changes. Among the most significant are Gerlach, *Blazing Crosses in Zion;* Lipset, "An Anatomy"; Guy B. Johnson, "A Sociological Interpretation of the New Ku Klux Klan Movement," *Journal of Social Forces* 1 (May 1923): 440–45; Paul L. Murphy, "Normalcy, Intolerance, and the American Character," *Virginia Quarterly Review* 40 (Summer 1964): 444–59; James H. Shideler, " 'Flappers and Philosophers,' and Farmers: Rural-Urban Tensions of the Twenties," *Agricultural History* 47 (October 1973): 283–99. Other interpretations of the rebirth of the Klan in the 1920s occur in Tannenbaum, "Ku Klux Klan"; and in Richard Schaefer, "The Ku Klux Klan: Continuity and Change," *Phylon* 32 (Summer 1971): 143–57. For analyses of the political climate of the 1920s and the decline of the progressive movement, see James H. Shideler, "The Disintegration of the Progressive Party Movement of 1924," *The Historian* 13 (1950): 189–201; and William E. Leuchtenberg, *The Perils of Prosperity, 1914–1932* (University of Chicago Press, 1958). Several thoughtful studies give an overview of women's lives in the 1920s, esp. Nancy Cott, *The Grounding of Modern Feminism* (Yale University Press, 1987); and Dorothy M. Brown, *Setting a Course: American Women in the 1920s* (Twayne, 1987).

17. See, for example, the case study of Muncie, Indiana, by Robert S. Lynd and Helen Merrell Lynd, *Middletown: A Study in American Culture* (Harcourt, Brace, 1929).

18. Not all scholars connect membership in the 1920s Ku Klux Klan to participation in a fundamentalist religion. In an analysis of Klan membership data from southern California, Cocoltchos ("The Invisible Government") finds that Klansmen were not significantly more likely to belong to an evangelical or fundamentalist denomination than were non-Klansmen. Robert Moats Miller's overview of the national Klan movement of the 1920s ("The Ku Klux Klan," in *Change and Continuity in 20th-Century America: The 1920s,* ed. John Braeman, Robert Bremner, and David Brody [Ohio State University Press, 1968], 223), however, expresses a more typical conclusion of students

of the KKK: "Though not all Fundamentalists were Klansmen, virtually all Klansmen—aside from the obvious charlatans—were Fundamentalists." Miller concludes in another work ("A Note on the Relationship between the Protestant Churches and the Revived Ku Klux Klan," *Journal of Southern History* 22 [August 1956]: 368) that the "fundamentalist crusade and the Ku Klux Klan were parallel but independent currents in American history." See also Henry F. May, "Shifting Perspectives on the 1920's," *Mississippi Valley Historical Review* 43 (December 1956): 405–27; and Ward Greene, "Notes for a History of the Klan," *The American Mercury* 5 (June 1925): 240–43. For an excellent analysis of contemporary fundamentalist politics, see Dwight Billings and Robert Goldman on Southern book burning, "Comment on the Kanawha County Textbook Controversy," *Social Forces* 57 (June 1979): 1393–98.

19. William C. Bagley, "The Army Tests and Pro-Nordic Propaganda," *Educational Review* 67 (April 1924): 179–87; Arthur Mann, "Gompers and the Irony of Racism," *Antioch Review* 13 (June 1953): 203–14; John D. Hicks, "Research Opportunities in the 1920's," *The Historian* 25 (November 1962): 1–13; May, "Shifting Perspectives"; Devere Allen, "Substitutes for Brotherhood," *The World Tomorrow* 7 (March 1924): 74–76; Robert DeC. Ward, "Our New Immigration Policy," *Foreign Affairs* (1924): 99–111; Leuchtenburg, *The Perils*, 204–24; Willard S. Gatewood, Jr., ed., *Controversy in the Twenties* (Vanderbilt University Press, 1969); Murphy, "Normalcy, Intolerance"; Robert D. Warth, "The Palmer Raids," *South Atlantic Quarterly* 48 (January 1949): 1–23. Valuable discussions of the impact of the 1920s political backlash on women occur in Joan Jensen, "All Pink Sisters: The War Department and the Feminist Movement in the 1920s," in *Decades of Discontent: The Women's Movement, 1920–1940*, ed. Lois Scharf and Joan Jensen (Greenwood Press, 1983); and in Rayna Rapp and Ellen Ross, "The 1920s: Feminism, Consumerism, and Political Backlash in the United States," in *Women in Culture and Politics: A Century of Change*, ed. Judith Friedlander, Blanche Weisen Cook, Alice Kessler-Harris, and Carroll Smith-Rosenberg (Indiana University Press, 1986).

20. Knights of the Ku Klux Klan, *Ideals of the Ku Klux Klan* (KKK, n.d.) specifies the racial ideals of the Klan as white supremacy and preservation of the United States as a white man's country. See also Charles O. Jackson, "William J. Simmons: A Career in Ku Kluxism," *Georgia Historical Quarterly* 50 (December 1966): 351–65; William Joseph Simmons, *America's Menace, or the Enemy Within* (Bureau of Patriotic Books, 1926), 14–16; William J. Shepard, "How I Put One Over on the Klan," *Collier's*, July 14, 1928, 5–7, 32–34.

21. William Joseph Simmons, *Imperial Proclamation of the Imperial Wizard, Emperor of the Invisible Empire, Knights of the Ku Klux Klan* (KKK, 1917); William Joseph Simmons, *The Ku Klux Klan: Yesterday, Today, and Forever* (KKK, ca. 1916); Edgar I. Fuller, *Nigger in the Woodpile* (privately published, 1967).

22. Shepard, "How I Put." Simmons's comments on his loss of power in the Klan illustrate his theologically tinged megalomania: "I was in Gethse-

mane, and the gloom of its dense darkness entombed me; the cup which I drank surpassed bitterest gall" (cited in Charles W. Ferguson, *The Confusion of Tongues, A Review of Modern Isms* [Doubleday, Doran, 1928], 264). See also the interview with Simmons in William J. Shepard, "The Fiery Double-Cross," *Collier's,* July 28, 1928, 8–9; and Simmons, *America's Menace,* 66–67, 79 (emphasis in original).

23. Knights of the Ku Klux Klan, *The Practice of Klannishness* (KKK, n.d.); also Knights of the Ku Klux Klan, *The A B C of the Knights of the Ku Klux Klan* (KKK, 1917). Mary Ann Clawson's *Constructing Brotherhood* (Princeton University Press, 1989) is an incisive study of the masculinist emphasis of fraternal associations.

24. Simmons, *America's Menace,* 117–32; Ferguson, *Confusion of Tongues;* Edgar I. Fuller, *The Visible of the Invisible Empire: 'The Maelstrom'* (Maelstrom Publishing, 1925), 24; Robert Duffus, "Salesmen of Hate: The Ku Klux Klan," *The World's Work* (May 1923): 31–38.

25. Marion Monteval, *The Klan Inside Out* (1924; reprint, Negro Universities Press, 1970). Tyler also used the name Elizabeth Tyler Grow. Her volunteer work may have introduced her to nativist politics, as the early twentieth-century hygienics movement combined public health concerns with racism and belief in white Anglo-Saxon superiority. See Christopher Lasch, *Haven in a Heartless World: The Family Besieged* (Basic, 1979); and Barbara Ehrenreich and Deidre English, *For Her Own Good* (Anchor, 1979).

26. Duffus, "Salesmen of Hate," 31–38; Charles O. Jackson, "William J. Simmons"; Bennett, *The Party of Fear,* 209.

27. Duffus, "Salesmen of Hate," 35–38.

28. Benjamin Herzl Avin, "The Ku Klux Klan, 1915–1925: A Study in Religious Intolerance" (Ph.D. diss., Georgetown University, 1952).

29. Chalmers, *Hooded Americanism,* 34; Avin, "Ku Klux Klan."

30. Tyler later sued the *New York World* for $1 million for libel in its coverage of the Klan. See *New York Times,* Sept. 12, 1921, 15; Sept. 11, 1921, 22; Duffus, "Salesmen of Hate"; Bennett, *The Party of Fear;* Clement Charlton Moseley, "The Political Influence of the Ku Klux Klan in Georgia, 1915–1925," *Georgia Historical Quarterly* 57 (Summer 1973): 235–55.

31. Duffus, "Salesmen of Hate," 38. Winfield Jones states emphatically, if implausibly, that "Mrs Tyler has no connection with the KKK, as women are not admitted to membership" (*The Story of the Ku Klux Klan* [American Newspaper Syndicate, 1921], 81).

32. House Committee on Rules, *Hearings on the Ku Klux Klan,* 67th Cong., 1st sess., 1921 (reprint, Arno Press, 1969); Winfield Jones, *Story;* Charles Sweeney, "The Great Bigotry Merger," *The Nation,* July 5, 1922, 8.

33. Fuller, *Nigger,* 76.

34. Anonymous, *Ku Klux Klan: Secrets Exposed, Attitudes Toward Jews, Catholics, Foreigners, and Masons. Fraudulent Methods Used, Atrocities Committed in Name of Order* (Ezra Cook, 1921), 81; *New York Times,* Sept. 11, 1921, 22; Sept. 13, 1921, 5.

35. Clarke later returned to the United States to organize a rival to the Klan, an organization known as the Mystic Kingdom, which sought to "unite

Protestant white people for the furtherance of the Protestant faith and the preservation of racial integrity." The Mystic Kingdom enlisted several thousand members in the Midwest, but its grandiose plans were largely unrealized (*New York Times,* Dec. 2, 1922, 14; July 16, 1924, 6; see also Monteval, *The Klan Inside Out;* Charles O. Jackson, "William J. Simmons"; Duffus, "Salesmen of Hate").

36. *Papers Read at the Meeting of Grand Dragons, Knights of the Ku Klux Klan at Their First Annual Meeting Held at Asheville, North Carolina, July 1923, Together with Other Articles of Interest to Klansmen* (KKK, 1923), 3–6.

37. This argument from biology occurs in a number of publications by Hiram Evans, including *The Klan of Tomorrow* (KKK, 1924); "The Klan's Fight for Americanism," *North American Review* 223 (1926): 33–63; "The Klan: Defender of Americanism," *The Forum* 74 (December 1925): 801–14; "The Ballots Behind the Ku Klux Klan," *The World's Work* 15 (January 1928): 246; *Menace of Modern Immigration* (KKK, 1923); "The Klan," in Loren Baitz, ed., *Culture of the Twenties* (Bobbs-Merrill, 1970). See Ku Klux Klan publications, *Klan Building* (KKK, ca. 1923); *Constitution and Laws* (KKK, 1926); and *Creed of the Klansmen* (KKK, 1924). Also see George S. Clason, *Catholic, Jew, Ku Klux Klan: What They Believe, Where They Conflict* (Nutshell Publishing, 1924); *Roanoke* (Virginia) *Times,* May 31, 1931, 1; and Kenneth Jackson, *The Ku Klux Klan.*

38. Avin, "Ku Klux Klan," 137.

39. At its peak, the Klan published or influenced over 150 periodicals (Wade, *The Fiery Cross,* 175). A list of twenty-four Klan weekly papers is in the May 9, 1923, edition of the *Imperial Night-Hawk* (7). The Klan press was always embroiled in the power plays of Klan leaders. Evans wanted to destroy all Klan papers except his *Fellowship Forum.* At one time, Evans tried to establish a KKK Bureau of Education and Publication in Washington, D.C., which would publish the *Fiery Cross* (then controlled by Stephenson); he was not successful. These conflicts caused constant turmoil in the Klan press, with smaller publications forced out, state editions of the *Fiery Cross* promoted, then discontinued, and the names of the publications constantly changing. Details of this struggle are in Edgar Allen Booth, *The Mad Mullah of America* (Boyd Ellison Publications, 1927).

40. *Fiery Cross,* Dec. 8, 1922, 1; Feb. 2, 1923, 3.

41. Companionate marriage, based on a partnership of respect and mutuality between husband and wife, was replacing the hierarchical and formal marriage of the Victorian era as the ideal marital form in the 1920s (Rayna Rapp and Ellen Ross, "The Twenties' Backlash: Compulsory Heterosexuality, the Consumer Family, and the Waning of Feminism," in *Class, Race, and Sex: The Dynamics of Control,* ed. Ann Swerdlow and Hanna Lessinger [G. K. Hall, 1983]). Yet the norms of companionate marriage reflected a wide range of views about women's and men's place in this union. See J. G. Morawski, "Not Quite New Worlds: Psychologists' Conceptions of the Ideal Family in the Twenties," in *In the Shadow of the Past: Psychology Portrays the Sexes: A Social and Intellectual History,* ed. Miriam Lewin (Columbia University Press,

1984), 97–125; and Elaine Showalter, ed., *These Modern Women: Autobiographical Essays from the Twenties* (Feminist Press, 1978), 3–29. Clawson (*Constructing Brotherhood*, 207–8) makes a similar point about fraternal associations.

42. *Fiery Cross,* Feb. 2, 1923, 3.

43. *Fellowship Forum,* Jan. 13, 1923, 5; Apr. 14, 1923, 5.

44. *Fellowship Forum,* Oct. 13, 1922, 12; *New York Times,* Nov. 23, 1922, 23.

45. *Fiery Cross,* Feb. 23, 1923, 1; advertisement in *Dawn,* June 2, 1923, 13; *Fellowship Forum,* Aug. 18, 1922, 2; Nov. 25, 1922, 6; Dec. 9, 1922. Although for women the Grand League was a likely conduit to the Klan, its national organization refused to adopt the oath of the WKKK at a meeting called by the Klan to merge several women's organizations into the Klan (*Tolerance,* Aug. 5, 1923, 6).

46. Norman Hapgood, "The New Threat of the Ku Klux Klan," *Hearst's International,* February 1923, 58–61, 110. Other similar organizations in this region include the Order of American Women in Texas and the Order of Protestant Women in Texas and Oklahoma. See *New York Times,* Nov. 23, 1922, 23.

47. Hapgood, "The New Threat," citing an article in the *Searchlight; New York Times,* Oct. 1, 1922, 23.

48. *New York Times,* Jan. 7, 1923, 20.

49. *New York Times,* Nov. 30, 1922, 21; *Imperial Night-Hawk,* Apr. 25, 1923, 5.

50. *Fellowship Forum,* Mar. 31, 1923, 3; Charles O. Jackson, "William J. Simmons"; *New York Times,* Oct. 2, 1923, 6.

51. *Arkansas Gazette,* June 6, 1923, 1; June 8, 1923, 1, 7. *Fellowship Forum,* Apr. 21, 1923, 2; *New York Times,* Apr. 1, 1923, sect. 1, pt. 2, 5; Kenneth Jackson, *The Ku Klux Klan; The Truth about the Women of the Ku Klux Klan* (ca. 1923); *Fiery Cross,* Mar. 30, 1923; Mar. 16, 1923, 8; *Imperial Night-Hawk,* May 2, 1923, 1. The *Fiery Cross* (Mar. 2, 1923, 6) warned women "against impostors and colorful imitations of the one real organization," as did the *Fellowship Forum* (Apr. 28, 1923, 7).

52. Stephenson, a failed "wet" (anti-Prohibition) Democratic candidate for the U.S. House of Representatives in 1922, traded party and politics to reemerge as a "dry" Republican leader the following year. He subsequently took control of the midwestern Klan movement, building a legendary power base in the Klan. See Joseph White, "The Ku Klux Klan in Indiana in the 1920s as viewed by the *Indiana Catholic and Record*" (Master's thesis, Butler University, 1974); *Dawn,* Apr. 21, 1923, 15; Booth, *Mad Mullah.* Other regional Klan leaders also tried to organize their own women's Klans, although none was ultimately successful; see Goldberg (*Hooded Empire,* 106) on attempts in Colorado and Wyoming.

53. Booth, *Mad Mullah;* Lem A. Dever, *Masks Off! Confessions of an Imperial Klansman* (n.p., 1925), 9–10. Simmons unsuccessfully attempted to start a rival order, the Knights of the Flaming Sword, and later affiliated with the racialist White Band. He died in 1945 without further affiliation with the

KKK. See Charles O. Jackson, "William J. Simmons"; and *New York Times*, Nov. 6, 1923, 5; Feb. 13, 1924, 5. For details of the intricate legal proceedings between Simmons and Evans, see Ku Klux Klan, *Minutes of the Imperial Kloncilium* (KKK, 1923).

54. *Arkansas Gazette*, June 10, 1923, 1.

55. WKKK, *Constitution and Laws* (WKKK, 1927).

56. *Fellowship Forum*, Feb. 23, 1924, 6; Nov. 17, 1923, 6; *Imperial Night-Hawk*, Oct. 31, 1923, 1; Aug. 1, 1923, 8.

57. *Arkansas Gazette*, Aug. 30, 1925, 1; June 3, 1923, 1; *Imperial Night-Hawk*, June 13, 1923, 5; June 20, 1923, 8; WKKK, *The Truth about the Women of the Ku Klux Klan* (n.p., ca. 1923); *Fellowship Forum*, June 2, 1923, 8; *Fiery Cross*, June 29, 1923, 8; *Dawn*, June 23, 1923, 4; Charles Alexander, "Crusade for Conformity: The Ku Klux Klan in Texas, 1920–1930," *Texas Gulf Coast Historical Association* 6 (1962): 38.

58. *Woman's Who's Who of America: A Biographical Dictionary of Contemporary Women of the United States and Canada, 1914–1915* (Gale Research Company), 540; *Who's Who in Little Rock: An Accurate Biographical Record of Men and Women of Little Rock, Arkansas, Prominent in Various Lines of Civic Activity* (Little Rock, 1921), 96.

59. *The Truth*; also, *Fiery Cross*, July 13, 1923, 1; Sue Wilson Abbey ("The Ku Klux Klan in Arizona, 1921–25," *Journal of Arizona History* 14 [Spring 1973]: 10–30) discusses how Tom Akers was sent to organize the Phoenix, Arizona, chapter of the WKKK in 1923; Loucks, *The Ku Klux Klan in Pennsylvania*, 150–56; *Arkansas Gazette*, June 10, 1925, 1.

60. *Arkansas Gazette*, Oct. 7, 1923, 12; see also *Imperial Night-Hawk*, Oct. 31, 1923, 1; *New York Times*, Nov. 7, 1923, 15; Kenneth Jackson, *The Ku Klux Klan*; William M. Likins, *The Ku Klux Klan, Its Rise and Fall; Patriotism Capitalized or Religion Turned into Gold* (Privately published, 1925).

61. See Kenneth Jackson, *The Ku Klux Klan; Fellowship Forum*, 1924–1928.

62. WKKK, *Constitution and Laws*.

63. In an address to the 1926 Klonvokation, Evans claimed a Klan membership of 5 million men and 1.5 million women (*Washington* [D.C.] *Evening Star*, Aug. 14, 1926, 1; also Aug. 13, 1926, 1, 5; *Imperial Night-Hawk*, Aug. 1, 1923, 8; *St. Louis Post-Dispatch*, Jan. 16, 1927, 22; *Indianapolis News*, Aug. 5, 1927, 23; *Indianapolis Star*, Aug. 4, 1927, 5; *Fiery Cross*, Feb. 23, 1928, 12).

64. *Imperial Night-Hawk*, June 13, 1923, 5; Aug. 8, 1923, 6.

65. *Fiery Cross*, Mar. 2, 1923, 4; *Fellowship Forum*, June 2, 1923, 8.

66. *Fiery Cross*, June 29, 1923, 4; *Dawn*, June 16, 1923, 9.

67. *Fiery Cross*, Mar. 9, 1923, 8; also June 29, 1923, 4.

68. *Arkansas Gazette*, Oct. 7, 1923, 12.

69. *Dawn*, Jan. 26, 1924, 12.

70. *Watcher on the Tower*, Sept. 15, 1923, 12.

71. *Imperial Night-Hawk*, June 20, 1923, 8.

72. WKKK, *Ideals of the Women of the Ku Klux Klan* (WKKK, 1923), 2–3, 4–5; WKKK, *Women of America!*, 6–7, 9–10, 13–14 (WKKK, ca. 1923); WKKK, *Kreed* (WKKK, ca. 1924).

73. WKKK, *Women of America!;* WKKK, *Constitution and Laws,* 6–7; WKKK, *Kreed;* WKKK, *Ideals,* 2–3, 4–5; *Imperial Night-Hawk,* June 20, 1923, 8; May 14, 1924, 7; advertisement in *Dawn,* Aug. 11, 1923, 2.

74. WKKK, *Constitution and Laws.* From statement by Victoria Rogers, Major Kleagle for the Realm of Illinois, in *Dawn,* Feb. 2, 1924, 12.

75. WKKK, *Women of America!*

76. WKKK, *Catalogue of Official Robes and Banners* (WKKK, ca. 1923); WKKK, *Kloran or Ritual of the WKKK* (WKKK, 1923).

77. WKKK, *Constitution and Laws.*

78. WKKK, *Kloran or Ritual of the WKKK.* The *New York Times* (Aug. 19, 1923, 2) has detailed coverage of a naturalization ceremony involving seven hundred members of the women's Klan in Allenwood, New Jersey.

79. WKKK, *Second Degree Obligation of the Women of the Ku Klux Klan* (WKKK, n.d.); see also WKKK, *Installation Ceremonies of the Women of the Ku Klux Klan* (WKKK, n.d.).

80. Hiram Evans, *The Menace* and *The Attitude of the Knights of the Ku Klux Klan toward the Roman Catholic Hierarchy* (KKK, ca. 1923).

81. WKKK, *Flag Book* (WKKK, 1923); Ku Klux Klan record collection (hereafter cited as KKK), Indiana State Library (hereafter ISL); WKKK, *U.S. Constitution* (WKKK, n.d.); *Fiery Cross,* Oct. 10, 1924, 5; *Fellowship Forum,* July 5, 1924, 6–7.

82. *Fellowship Forum,* Sept. 19, 1925, 6; July 5, 1924; Mar. 3, 1926, 6. The anonymous speaker is identified only as a "Klan female speaker." January 1925 issues of the *Fellowship Forum* have other examples of such self-promotion, as does that of May 1, 1926, 7; see also Chalmers, *Hooded Americanism.*

83. *Imperial Night-Hawk,* May 9, 1923, 2; see also *New York Times,* July 11, 1926, 7.

84. *Arkansas Gazette,* Sept. 8, 1925, 1; *Fiery Cross,* Mar. 30, 1923, 5; *Fellowship Forum,* Jan. 24, 1925, 6; *New York Times,* Sept. 9, 1925, 1; Sept. 19, 1925, 20; Sept. 11, 1925, 5.

85. *New York Times,* June 3, 1923, sect. 1, pt. 2, 8; *Fellowship Forum,* Jan. 24, 1925, 6; *New York Times,* Mar. 21, 1922, 6; Dec. 8, 1922, 9; *Imperial Night-Hawk,* May 9, 1923, 3; *Fiery Cross,* Oct. 10, 1924, 5; *Fellowship Forum,* Jan. 17, 1925, 6; July 5, 1924, 6. For a detailed analysis of the conflict over the Klan during the 1924 election, especially during the Democratic party convention, see Lee Allen, "The McAdoo Campaign for the Presidential Nomination of 1924," *Journal of Southern History* 29 (1963): 211–18; "The Klan and the Democrats," *Literary Digest,* June 14, 1924, 12–13; Rice, *Ku Klux Klan;* Chalmers, *Hooded Americanism,* 282–90.

86. *Fiery Cross,* July 18, 1924, 6. In an odd twist—"because of their affiliation with the KKK"—two women were excluded from the will of a third woman with whom they had lived for sixteen years (will of Alice Reid, filed in surrogate's court in Brooklyn in 1928 and reported in the *New York Times,* Oct. 10, 1928, 16).

87. Testimony of Mamie H. Bittner in U.S. District Court for the Western District of Pennsylvania, *Knights of the Ku Klux Klan, Plaintiff, v. Rev. John F. Strayer et al., Defendants,* 1928 (Equity 1897 in National Archives–

Philadelphia Branch [hereafter cited as Equity 1897]); William M. Likins, *The Trail of the Serpent* (n.p., 1928), 64–67.

CHAPTER TWO

1. Hiram Evans, *Attitude toward the Roman Catholic Hierarchy.*

2. I am indebted to George L. Mosse's insightful analysis in *Nationalism and Sexuality* (University of Wisconsin Press, 1985), esp. 23–47, 133–52.

3. Wade, *The Fiery Cross,* 172–75; Blaine Mast, *K.K.K. Friend or Foe: Which?* (Privately published, 1924), 64.

4. Knights of the Ku Klux Klan, *The Klansman's Manual* (n.p., 1924), 16–17; *Fiery Cross,* Feb. 9, 1923, 1, 5.

5. Grand Dragon of the Realm of Arkansas [James Comer], "A Tribute and a Challenge to American Women," in *Papers Read at First Annual Meeting, 1923,* 89; Official document issued from the office of the Grand Dragon, Realm of Indiana, Indianapolis, on May 6, 1925, to all exalted cyclops and kligrapps in the realm of Indiana, no. 40, box 1, folder 2, in Ku Klux Klan–Wayne County, Indiana Collection of Indiana Historical Society [hereafter KKK-WC, IHS]).

6. *Klansman's Manual,* 14–16; House Committee on Rules, *Hearings on the Klan,* 26, 114; Simmons, cited in Avin, "Ku Klux Klan," 227.

7. Grand Dragon of the Realm of Colorado, "Klansman's Obligation as a Patriot to His God, His Country, His Home, and His Fellowmen," in *Papers Read at First Annual Meeting, 1923,* 59–63; reissued by Knights of the Ku Klux Klan, in *Articles on the Klan and Elementary Klankraft* (1923, 1924, 1925) and distributed to local Klans for discussion. Also see Lois Carlson, "The Sanctity of the Home," *The Kourier Magazine,* June 1929, 46–47.

8. "Women of America," *Dawn,* Aug. 11, 1923, 8; Grand Dragon of the Realm of Arkansas [James Comer], "A Tribute and a Challenge to the Wonderful Womanhood of America," *Imperial Night-Hawk,* Oct. 3, 1923, 2; F. N. Graff, "A Tribute to the Women of the Ku Klux Klan," *Dawn,* Jan. 26, 1924, 7; Hiram Evans, "Preserving the American Home," *The Kourier Magazine,* March 1927, 9–11.

9. KKK, *Ku Klux Klan Song Book: Ten Stirring Songs for Americans* (KKK, ca. 1923).

10. Walter C. Wright, *Religious and Patriotic Ideals of the Ku Klux Klan* (Privately published, 1926); *New York Times,* Apr. 25, 1926, 16; Apr. 16, 1927, 32; *Dawn,* Oct. 21, 1922, 11–12; KKK, *Song Book.*

11. See, for example, "A Tribute to the Women of the Ku Klux Klan," *Dawn,* Jan. 26, 1924, 7; also *Dawn,* Oct. 21, 1922, 11; Wright, *Religious and Patriotic;* Avin, "Ku Klux Klan," 228.

12. The Klan patterned itself after other popular fraternal orders in a number of ways. Its ranks of membership mimicked those of chivalrous and fraternal orders, including Knights Kamelia (Primary Order of Knighthood), K-Uno (Probationary), K-Duo (Knights of the Great Forest), K-Trio (Order of American Chivalry), K-Quad (Knights of the Midnight Mystery). The Klan not only paralleled fraternal lodges, it recruited directly through local fraternal orders,

especially Masonic and Masonic-affiliated lodges. In 1922 a Klan lecturer claimed that 75 percent of Klansmen were Masons, a charge Masonic leaders denied. In the South the Klan tried to absorb entire chapters of the Order of Owls (*New York Times,* Dec. 30, 1922, 26; Nov. 25, 1922, 1). See also Eckard V. Toy, "The Ku Klux Klan in Tillamook, Oregon," *Pacific Northwest Quarterly* 53, April 1962): 60–64; Gerlach, *Blazing Crosses in Zion;* Fuller, *Visible of the Invisible,* 165–71; *Fellowship Forum,* 1925–1926; *Fiery Cross,* July 6, 1923, 3; Dana R. Skinner, "Is the Ku Klux Klan Katholik?" *The Independent* 111 (November 1923): 242–43; *Klansman's Manual; Inspirational Addresses Delivered at the Second Imperial Klonvokation held in Kansas City, Missouri, September 23, 24, 25, and 26, 1924* (KKK, 1924); Chalmers, *Hooded Americanism,* 2; Weaver, "The Knights," 70–71. See also Simmons's testimony in House Committee on Rules, *Hearings on the Klan.*

13. Oscar Haywood, cited in *New York Times,* Nov. 27, 1922, 1–2.

14. *Fiery Cross,* Aug. 1, 1924, 5; *Inspirational Addresses, Second Imperial Klonvokation.*

15. *Fiery Cross,* Dec. 14, 1923, 9; Aug. 15, 1924, 3; *Fellowship Forum,* Jan. 17, 1925, 6. The article on the passport is in *Fellowship Forum,* Dec. 27, 1924; "The American Women" page is in many issues of the *Fellowship Forum,* esp. in 1924.

16. *The K.K.K. Katechism: Pertinent Questions, Pointed Answers* (Patriot Publishing, 1924), 29–30, 48–49.

17. *Fellowship Forum,* Dec. 27, 1924, 6; Graff, "A Tribute"; also *Fellowship Forum* issues throughout 1925, esp. Mar. 21, 1925, 6.

18. Grand Dragon, "A Tribute"; "The Part that Woman Plays in the Destiny of America," *Imperial Night-Hawk,* Sept. 3, 1924, 6.

19. "The Part that Woman Plays."

20. Graff, "A Tribute."

21. Carlson, "The Sanctity," 46–47; Grand Dragon, "A Tribute and a Challenge to American Women," in *Papers Read at First Annual Meeting, 1923.*

22. *Fiery Cross,* July 6, 1923, 23; *Imperial Night-Hawk,* Sept. 3, 1924, 6.

23. *Christian Century,* May 21, 1925, 677–78.

24. *New York Times,* May 11, 1925, 19; *The Kourier Magazine,* April 1925, 19.

25. *Fiery Cross,* July 6, 1923, 23; Dorothy A. Squires, "History of the Ku Klux Klan in Wabash County, Indiana" (Unpublished paper, Ball State Teachers' College, ca. 1963), 17–18.

26. Robbie Gill, "American Women," address to KKK's second Imperial Klonvokation in Kansas City, printed in KKK, *Inspirational Addresses* (KKK, 1924).

27. Gill, "American Women."

28. Sara Alpern and Dale Baum, "Female Ballots: The Impact of the Nineteenth Amendment," *Journal of Interdisciplinary History* 15 (Summer 1985): 43–67. For other interpretations of women's voting patterns after suffrage, see Anne Firor Scott, "After Suffrage: Southern Women in the Twenties," *Journal of Southern History* 30 (August 1964): 298–318; and Paul Kleppner, "Were

Women to Blame? Female Suffrage and Voter Turnout," *Journal of Interdisciplinary History* 12 (1982): 621–43.

29. Robbie Gill Comer, address to KKK Klonvokation in Washington, D.C., September 14, 1926, in *The Kourier Magazine,* November 1926, 11–21.

30. Robbie Gill Comer, address to WKKK in *Proceedings of Fourth Imperial Klonvokation* [KKK], Chicago, Ill., July 17–19, 1928, 97–117 (emphasis in original).

31. There is an interesting feminist literature on deconstructing debates over women's equality and gender equity. See Joan Wallach Scott, "Deconstructing Equality-versus-Difference, Or, the Uses of Poststructuralist Theory for Feminism," *Feminist Studies* 14 (Spring 1988): 33–49. Conflicts over equality vs. special privileges for women in the workplace have been common themes in the women's trade union movement. See Nancy Schrom Dye, *As Equals and As Sisters: Feminism, Unionism, and the Women's Trade Union League of New York* (University of Missouri Press, 1980); and Cott, *Grounding of Modern Feminism,* esp. 17–49.

32. Robbie Gill Comer, "Where the Credit Belongs," *The Kourier Magazine,* January 1929, 16–20.

33. "Address of the Imperial Commander, Women of the Ku Klux Klan at the Third Imperial Klonvokation [WKKK], June 29, 1931, Columbus, Ohio," *The Kourier Magazine,* August 1931, 3–19.

34. Klan rules and regulations, statement of responsibility, 1923 Klan constitution (box 1, folder 4, KKK-WC, IHS).

35. The Klan Management: Standard Plan for the Organization and Operation of Klans in Indiana. Adopted by Grand Dragon and Great Titans in Official Meeting, Apr. 12, 1925 (KKK, ISL); letter from the office of the Grand Dragon, Invisible Empire, Knights of the Ku Klux Klan, Realm of Indiana, Indianapolis to all Excellent Commanders, Realm of Indiana (box 1, folder 1, KKK-WC, IHS).

36. Box 208, KKK, ISL.

37. Deposition of James R. Ramsey, Marion County Circuit Court, *State of Indiana, Plaintiff, v. Knights of the Ku Klux Klan et al., Defendants,* May 25, 1928 (pp. 3, 8, Marion 41769, KKK, ISL).

38. Deposition of Hugh F. Emmons (ibid., pp. 336, 342).

39. Affidavit of William M. Likins in Equity 1897; Alexander, *Ku Klux Klan in the Southwest;* Charles Alexander, "Defeat, Decline, Disintegration: The Ku Klux Klan in Arkansas, 1924 and After," *Arkansas Historical Quarterly* 23 (Winter 1963): 311–31. See, for example, the interview with James Comer on the eve of the WKKK national klonvokation in 1927 in Indianapolis (*Indianapolis News,* Aug. 5, 1927, 23) or his presence, together with Hiram Evans and Charles Orbison (also an attorney for the WKKK) at the head of the WKKK parade through the streets of Indianapolis (*Indianapolis News,* Aug. 8, 1927, 28).

40. *Arkansas Gazette,* Aug. 30, 1925, 1.

41. *Arkansas Gazette,* Sept. 1, 1925, 1; Sept. 7, 1925, 12; Sept. 16, 1925, 1; Alexander, *Ku Klux Klan in the Southwest.*

42. *Arkansas Gazette,* Jan. 31, 1926, 1; Aug. 18, 1926, 9; Oct. 4, 1926,

28; Oct. 8, 1926, 7, and subsequent issues; Alexander, *Ku Klux Klan in the Southwest,* 323; Alexander, "Defeat, Decline, Disintegration," 324.

43. Deposition of Robbie Gill Comer in Equity 1897.

44. Others denied the association between the women's and men's orders: see, for example, the deposition of Joseph R. Shoemaker, a klokard and kleagle in the Pittsburgh KKK who denied any connection with the women's Klan in Pennsylvania (Equity 1897).

45. Deposition of Likins in Equity 1897.

46. *New York Times,* July 11, 1926, 7; testimony of Cora V. Brubaker (treasurer of Klan Haven Association) in Equity 1897.

47. Affidavit of Likins, deposition of Gill Comer, and affidavit of Mary E. King in Equity 1897.

48. *New York Times,* Mar. 13, 1926, 13.

49. Affidavits of Cecelia V. Sacrey and Mary E. King in Equity 1897. For an elaboration of the WKKK's position as a militant organization, see the address by Victoria B. Rogers, Major Kleagle and presiding officer of the WKKK, Realm of Illinois, cited in *Dawn,* Feb. 2, 1923, 12.

50. Based on interview with Pearl Cantey in Loucks, *The Ku Klux Klan in Pennsylvania,* 156, 161, 170; see also affidavit of Pearl Cantey in Equity 1897.

51. Dever, *Masks Off!,* 46; Lawrence J. Saalfeld, *Forces of Prejudice in Oregon, 1920–1925* (Portland, Oregon Archdiocesan Historical Commission, 1984), 44–49.

52. Dever, *Masks Off!,* 47–48.

53. Dever, *Masks Off!,* 48; Saalfeld, *Forces of Prejudice,* 46.

54. *Arkansas Gazette,* Nov. 6, 1925, 1; Nov. 8, 1925, 1; Nov. 11, 1925, 1; Feb. 19, 1926, 8; Alexander, *Ku Klux Klan in the Southwest;* testimony of Clayton C. Gilliand in *Gilliand v. Symwa Club et al* as reported in *Detroit News,* Jan. 22, 1930, 1; also discussed in Weaver, "The Knights."

55. *Muncie Post-Democrat,* Aug. 29, 1923, 1; other anti-Klan propaganda portrayed the Klan as a cover for the sexual activities of adulterous Klan husbands (*New York Times,* July 14, 1928, 5) or the Klan as using violence to coerce women to marry KKK officials (*New York Times,* Jan. 8, 1925, 12).

56. Lynd and Lynd, *Middletown,* 122; *New York Times,* Mar. 27, 1927, 19.

57. See the contrasting views in Steven R. Caldemeyer, "The Legal Problems of a Liberal in Middletown during the 1920s" (Master's thesis, Ball State University, 1970), 12–16; and in Robert A. Warrner, "George Dale versus Delaware Klan No. 4" (Master's thesis, Ball State University, 1972).

58. *Muncie Post-Democrat,* June 8, 1923.

59. Jill Suzanne Nevel, "Fiery Crosses and Tempers: The Ku Klux Klan in South Bend, Indiana, 1923–1926" (Senior thesis, Princeton University, 1977); Lawrence A. Giel, "George R. Dale—Crusader for Free Speech and a Free Press" (Ph.D. diss., Ball State University, 1967), 17–51, 77–79; Carrolyle M. Frank, "Politics in Middletown: A Reconsideration of Municipal Government and Community Power in Muncie, Indiana, 1925–1935" (Ph.D. diss., Ball State University, 1974); *Muncie Post-Democrat,* Jan. 2, 1924.

60. *Muncie Post-Democrat,* May 23, 1924.

61. Ibid., Aug. 1, 1924, 2.
62. Ibid., May 16, 1924; Aug. 1, 1924, 10.
63. Chalmers, *Hooded Americanism*, 127–34; Goldberg, *Hooded Empire*, 80–82.
64. Ben B. Lindsey, "My Fight with the Ku Klux Klan," *Survey*, June 1, 1925, 271–74, 319–20; Ben B. Lindsey, "The Beast in a New Form," *New Republic*, Dec. 24, 1924, 121.

CHAPTER THREE

1. Many Klan historians point to morality as a motivating force for the 1920s Klan; a good example is Gerlach (*Blazing Crosses in Zion*), who explores the role of traditional morality in the Utah Klan movement.
2. Paul J. Gillette and Eugene Tillinger, *Inside the Ku Klux Klan* (Pyramid Books, 1965), chap. 4; Skinner, "Is the Ku Klux Klan Katholik?", 242–43; Stanley L. Swart, "A Memo on Cross-Burning—and Its Implications," *Northwest Ohio Quarterly* 43 (Fall 1971): 70–74; Robert A. Garson, "Political Fundamentalism and Popular Democracy in the 1920s," *South Atlantic Quarterly* 76 (Spring 1977): 219–33; Leuchtenburg, *The Perils*, 120–39, 204–24; Ferguson, *Confusion of Tongues*; Weaver, "The Knights," 73–76.
3. *Dawn*, June 30, 1923, 5; Alexander, "Crusade for Conformity," 10; Hux, "The Ku Klux Klan," 165–66.
4. Alma White, *Musings of the Past* (Pillar of Fire Press, 1927); "Alma White," in *Notable American Women*, ed. Edward James and Janet James (Harvard University Press, 1971), 581–83; Alma White, *The Story of My Life*, vol. 1 (Pillar of Fire Press, 1919); Alma White, *Looking Back from Beulah* (Pillar of Fire Press, 1902).
5. White, *Looking Back*, 96, 221; "Faithful Trek of Zarephath Zion," *Literary Digest*, September 5, 1936, 30–31; Alma White, *The Story of My Life and the Pillar of Fire* (Pillar of Fire Press, 1935), 2:70.
6. James and James, *Notable American Women*, 582; White, *The Story of My Life*, vol. 2; "Evolution," in Alma White, *Short Sermons* (Pillar of Fire Press, 1932); Elmer Clark, *Small Sects in America* (Cokesbury Press, 1937), 100–103; Alma White, *The Story of My Life* (Pillar of Fire Press, 1936), 4:234; Alma White, *Klansmen: Guardians of Liberty* (Pillar of Fire Press, 1926).
7. Arthur White, *Some White Family History* (Pillar of Fire Press, 1948); White, *Looking Back;* "Faithful Trek," 30–31; *New York Times*, Nov. 1, 1923; *The American Magazine* 123 (May 1937); "Alma White," *The National Cyclopedia of American Biography* (James T. White, 1949), 35, 150–52; Clark, *Small Sects*.
8. Alma White, *My Heart and My Husband* (Pillar of Fire Press, 1923); Arthur White, *Some White Family;* White, *The Story of My Life*, 4:144–46.
9. White, *My Heart*, 7, 23, 31.
10. White, *The Story of My Life* (Pillar of Fire Press, 1936), 3:237.
11. Alma White, *Woman's Chains* (Pillar of Fire Press, 1943), 30–36; White, *Klansmen*.

12. White, *The Story of My Life*, 3:293; see the sermons, "Whipping Children," "Flowing Tears Made a Blessing," "The Unity of the Spirit," and "Evolution," in White, *Short Sermons;* and "Woman's Ministry" and "Woman's Place in Church and State," in White, *Woman's Chains.*

13. *New York Times*, Nov. 1, 1923, 18; Alma White, *Ku Klux Klan in Prophecy* (The Good Citizen Press, 1925); Alma White, *Heroes of the Fiery Cross* (The Good Citizen Press, 1928), 3, 9; White, *Klansmen;* Ferguson, *Confusion of Tongues*, 271–76.

14. White, *Klansmen;* White, *Heroes*, 102–3, 171–76.

15. White, *Ku Klux Klan*, 53–54; also White, *Heroes*, 33–34, 36, and the essay, "Tyranny of Woman's Fashions—Man's Responsibility," in White, *Woman's Chains*, 49–59.

16. White, *Heroes*, 55, 138–44.

17. Wade, *The Fiery Cross*, 181.

18. Irving Leibowitz, *My Indiana* (Prentice-Hall, 1964), 190–211.

19. Author's interviews with three anonymous informants in central and northern Indiana, May 24, 1987; Aug. 25, 1987; Aug. 28, 1987.

20. Emma Lou Thornbrough, "The Race Issue in Indiana Politics During the Civil War," *Indiana Magazine of History* 47 (June 1951): 165–88; Emma Lou Thornbrough, *Since Emancipation: A Short History of Indiana Negroes, 1863–1963* (n.p., n.d.); Emma Lou Thornbrough, "Race Relations in Indiana: A Summary View," in *Readings in Indiana History*, ed. Ralph Gray (William B. Eerdmans, 1980), 2:362–66; James H. Madison, *Indiana Through Tradition and Change* (Indiana Historical Society, 1982), 1–19; author's interview with anonymous informant, August 26, 1987.

21. Cyril J. Conen, "Politico-Religious Disturbances in Indiana, 1922–1928" (Ph.D. diss., Catholic University, 1938); Thomas M. Conroy, "The Ku Klux Klan and the American Clergy," *Ecclesiastical Review* (June 1924): 47–58; John A. Davis, "The Ku Klux Klan in Indiana, 1920–1930" (Ph.D. diss., Northwestern University, 1960), 1–15; Robert Duffus, "Ancestry and End of the Ku Klux Klan," *The World's Work* (September 1923): 275–84, 527–36; letter to author from an anonymous informant, May 3, 1987.

22. Author's interview with an anonymous informant, Aug. 20, 1987.

23. Edward A. Leary, "White Cap Gangs Punished Victims by Own Decree (n.p., n.d.); Ray Mathis, "Brown County History" (Unpublished paper, 1936). In *Trial by Mob* (Redland Press, 1957), Robert E. Cunningham discusses a men's whitecapper organization in Oklahoma and a women's whitecapper organization in Nebraska, both of which whipped offenders against community morality.

24. Patience Northerner, "Morgantown," in *Morgantown* (Indiana) *Scrapbook*, vol. 1 (n.p., n.d.).

25. Davis, "The Ku Klux Klan," 120–21; Conen, "Politico-Religious Disturbances"; Dorothy Alice Stroud, *My Legacy for Mitchell, Indiana* (Privately published, 1985).

26. *Indianapolis News*, June 27, 1922; author's interview with anonymous informant, Aug. 26, 1987.

27. Lila Lee Jones, "The Ku Klux Klan," 30; Davis, "The Ku Klux Klan"; also reported in Abbey, "The Ku Klux Klan."

28. *Fiery Cross,* Feb. 2, 1923, 5. See the numerous articles on disorderly houses in the *Muncie* (Indiana) *Evening Press* during February and March 1914 for a typical example of the early twentieth-century debate over vice in Indiana's small cities and towns; the intensity of concern set the stage for the Klan of the 1920s. On the variety of the Klan's attacks on prostitution and gambling in different regions of the country, see Snell, "Fiery Crosses" (Alabama); Abbey, "The Ku Klux Klan" (Arizona); Chalmers, "The Ku Klux Klan" (Florida); Granger, "Reaction to Change" (Louisiana); and Frank Mark Cates, "The Ku Klux Klan in Indiana Politics, 1920–1925" (Ph.D. diss., Indiana University, 1970). An interesting look at the situation in northern Indiana is in *Fiery Cross,* Feb. 2, 1923, 5. Two excellent studies of the social conditions of 1920s Indiana, both focused on Muncie, are Lynd and Lynd, *Middletown;* and Dwight Hoover, *Magic Middletown* (Indiana University Press, 1986).

29. The *Fort Wayne* (Indiana) *Journal-Gazette* (Aug. 2, 1977) reported on a 1923 incident in which the KKK twice burned a cross on the lawn of a local family accused of moonshining. Similar incidents are reported in Chalmers, "The Ku Klux Klan"; Snell, "Fiery Crosses"; Lila Lee Jones, "The Ku Klux Klan"; also in *Franklin Evening Star,* Aug. 20, 1923, 1; *Fiery Cross,* Feb. 2, 1923, 5; William E. Wilson, "The Long Hot Summer in Indiana," *American Heritage* 16 (August 1965): 57–64; Sweeney, "The Great Bigotry Merger," 8–10.

30. Hershel N. Denney, "The Ku Klux Klan in Henry County During the 1920s" (Ball State Teachers' College, 1963); *Fiery Cross,* Mar. 23, 1923; see also Davis, "The Ku Klux Klan," 65–66.

31. Jean Smethurst, "The Ku Klux Klan in Huntington County" (Ball State Teachers' College, 1963); see also Waldo Roberts, "The Ku-Kluxing of Oregon," *The Outlook,* Mar. 7, 1923, 490–91; Stanley Frost, "When the Klan Rules: Old Evils in a New Klan," *The Outlook,* Jan. 2, 1924, 20–25.

32. Smethurst, "The Ku Klux Klan." Chalmers ("The Ku Klux Klan," 214) cites the *Tampa Tribune's* assessment that the Klan targeted local undesirables. Snell ("Fiery Crosses") discusses the Klan's assault on loafers in Alabama. Lila Lee Jones ("The Ku Klux Klan") discusses Klan raids on "blind tigers." The *Fiery Cross* (Feb. 16, 1923, 8) reports on the expulsion of a Kentucky disorderly house operator by the Klan and Baptist church members. For Indiana, see James Guthrie, *A Quarter Century in Lawrence County, Indiana, 1917–1941* (Stone City Press, 1984); also the deposition of Roy F. Barclay (Marion 41769, KKK, ISL); and Howard Tucker, *History of Governor Walton's War on the Ku Klux Klan* (Southwest Publishing, 1923).

33. For example, the Klan flogged, tarred and feathered, or lynched men it accused of annoying or harassing women. See the deposition of W. H. Norris (Marion 41769, KKK, ISL); Abbey ("The Ku Klux Klan") recounts an incident in which Klansmen flogged a Phoenix high school principal accused of moral misconduct with a female student. Also see Stanley Frost, *The Challenge of the Klan* (Negro Universities Press, 1924), 207.

34. Letter dated Nov. 5, 1923, in George R. Dale collection, box 1, folder 3, Ball State University (hereafter BSU). The Indiana Klan was not alone in punishing adulterous husbands; see Lila Lee Jones, "The Ku Klux Klan," 29–32; Granger, "Reaction to Change," 219–27; Sweeney, "The Great Bigotry Merger," 8–10; *New York Times*, Jan. 19, 1927, 8; John Bartlow Martin, *Indiana: An Interpretation* (Books for Libraries, 1927), 192–93.

35. Field letter no. 56, dated Aug. 23, 1923 (box L-208, KKK, ISL); letter from Ella Hittle of Glenwood, dated Oct. 4, 1927 (box 1, folder 1, KKK-WC, IHS); Jerrell J. Brooks, "The Ku Klux Klan and Its Activities in Wayne County" (Master's thesis, Ball State Teachers' College, 1962).

36. Anonymous informant, Apr. 6, 1987; also Leuchtenburg, *The Perils*, 213; Smethurst, "The Ku Klux Klan"; and Lila Lee Jones, "The Ku Klux Klan," 30.

37. Miller, "The Ku Klux Klan," 230–31.

38. Author's interview with anonymous informant, Aug. 19, 1987; also Weaver, "The Knights"; Tucker, *History of Governor Walton's*, 56; Denney, "The Ku Klux Klan"; Avin, "The Ku Klux Klan," 227. The Wildwood, N.J., Klan flooded the city with little crosses bearing the inscription in red, "Wife beaters and wrong doers, watch your step. Vengeance is mine, said the Lord" (*New York Times*, Jan. 31, 1924, 30). In Gainesville, Florida, the Klan tarred and feathered a man accused of neglecting his wife (Chalmers, "The Ku Klux Klan," 214). The deposition of Harry E. A. MacNeel (Marion 41769, KKK, ISL) reports that orders to flog delinquent and offending husbands sometimes came from the Klan's leaders. See also Granger, "Reaction to Change."

39. Author's interview with anonymous informant, May 1, 1987.

40. Author's interview with anonymous informant, Aug. 21, 1987.

41. Author's interview with anonymous informant, Aug. 25, 1987; also Brooks, "The Ku Klux Klan," 14–15.

42. Madison, *Indiana Through Tradition and Change*, 47; also *Fiery Cross*, Dec. 7, 1923, 9. Married women could also come under the Klan's protective veil in this regard, as in the case of a Klan-posted reward for the arrest of twelve men accused of kidnapping a married woman in Oregon (*Fiery Cross*, Sept. 15, 1923, 11); see also Leroy A. Curry, *The Ku Klux Klan Under the Searchlight* (Western Baptist Publishing, 1924), 205.

43. Author's interview with anonymous informant, May 24, 1987.

44. Address by Imperial Wizard, no. 518 (KKK, ISL).

45. Leibowitz, *My Indiana*, p. 189; *Fiery Cross*, Mar. 30, 1923, 1; Feb. 23, 1923, 1.

46. An anonymous informant related the story of the KKK's burning down a dancing pavilion in Hartford City, Indiana (author's interview, Mar. 25, 1988); see also Hoover, *Magic Middletown;* Lila Lee Jones, "The Ku Klux Klan," 32; Avin, "Ku Klux Klan," 183.

47. *Fiery Cross*, Mar. 30, 1923, 1; also see Snell, "Fiery Crosses," 256–77; Conen, "Politico-Religious Disturbances," 46.

48. *Muncie Post-Democrat*, July 27, 1923, 1. Details about Klan reprisals against nonwhite men for dating white women can be found in the depositions of Clarence Wilson Ludlow and Roy F. Barclay (Marion 41769, KKK, ISL).

Other incidents are reported in *Fiery Cross,* Mar. 23, 1923, 4; Granger, "Reaction to Change"; Chalmers, "The Ku Klux Klan," 214; and Gillette and Tillinger, *Inside the Ku Klux Klan.*

49. *Fiery Cross,* Apr. 27, 1923, 4. Another editorial in *Fiery Cross* (Feb. 29, 1924, 4) denounced the casting of a black man opposite a white woman in "All God's Chillun Got Wings."

50. Allen Safianow, "Konklave in Kokomo Revisited," *The Historian* 50 (May 1988): 329–47; Dwight Hoover, "To Be a Jew in Middletown," *Indiana Magazine of History* 81 (June 1985): 131–58; Mast, *K.K.K.*

51. The Murderous Knights of Columbus Oath, Fourth Degree (box L-208, KKK, ISL). Among the most interesting, and obtainable, of these tracts are those by William Lloyd Clark: *Priest and Woman* (n.p., n.d.); *Hell at Midnight in Springfield or a Burning History of the Sin and Shame of the Capitol City of Illinois* (n.p., 1910); and *The Devil's Prayer Book or an Exposure of Auricular Confession as Practiced by the Roman Catholic Church, an Eye-Opener for Husbands, Fathers, and Brothers* (Rail Splitter Press, 1923); and one by Ford Hendrickson, *The 'Black Convent' Slave: The Climax of Nunnery Exposures* (Protestant Missionary Publishing, 1914); see also a later work by William Lloyd Clark, *The Story of My Battle with the Scarlet Beast* (Rail Splitter Press, 1932).

52. *Fiery Cross,* Apr. 18, 1924, 1; Mar. 27, 1924, 8; address of Robbie Gill Comer to KKK Klonvokation (KKK, 1927), 20; Elmer T. Clark, *Would You Take Sides with the Pope?* (Centenary Commission, ca. 1920).

53. *Fiery Cross,* Jan. 5, 1923, 1.

54. Lynd and Lynd, *Middletown,* 482.

55. Author's interviews with three anonymous informants, Aug. 21, 1987; Aug. 28, 1987; Aug. 26, 1987; *Fiery Cross,* Mar. 27, 1924, 5; Oct. 17, 1924, 8; Madison, *Indiana,* chap. 1; Roberts, "The Ku-Kluxing," 490–91.

56. Author's interview with anonymous informant, Mar. 25, 1988; also Saalfeld, "Forces of Prejudice," 4; Wade, *The Fiery Cross,* 180; Helen Robb, "The Ku Klux Klan in Blackford County, Indiana" (Master's thesis, Ball State Teachers' College, 1962); deposition of Bemenderfer (pp. 85–89, Marion 41769, KKK, ISL).

57. See Lynd and Lynd, *Middletown,* 482. A letter from W. Lee Smith, Chief of Staff of the KKK Realm of Indiana, to all Exalted Cyclops on Jan. 27, 1925, indicates that some local KKK chapters were dissatisfied with Jackson's appearances and found her message somehow not in accord with the Klan's program (folder 1, M407, KKK-WC, IHS). Ads for Jackson's autobiography appear in many issues of the *Fiery Cross* and *Dawn,* both Klan publications. See discussion in Carol Elrod, "A Descriptive Study of the Ku Klux Klan's Anti-Catholic Propaganda from 1922 to 1924 in Two of Its Publications Distributed in Indiana: The *Fiery Cross* and *Dawn*" (Master's thesis, Ball State University, 1979), 74–76; Helen Jackson, *Convent Cruelties* (Privately published, 1919).

58. King published and distributed a book on the horrible implications of the unmarried Catholic priesthood (Justin D. Fulton, *Why Priests Should Wed* [Published by L. J. King, 1911]).

59. *Fiery Cross,* Mar. 2, 1923, cited in Elrod, "A Descriptive Study," 67; also author's personal correspondence with an informant in Blackford County, May 30, 1987.

60. Author's interviews with anonymous informants (Mar. 25, 1988 and Mar. 26, 1988) and artifacts from a private collection, including a card advertising King's visit to the sales pavilion in Hartford City, Indiana. Frank E. Cline, "Activities of the Ku Klux Klan in Jay County" (Master's thesis, Ball State Teachers' College, 1964), describes an incident of local opposition to Helen Jackson's visit to Dunkirk, Indiana, in which the board of public safety issued a restraining order against her talk. Such opposition was unusual. Other local accounts of Jackson's visits are in Joan E. Morton, "The Ku Klux Klan in Blackford County" (Unpublished paper, Ball State Teachers' College, n.d.). See Lewis J. King, *The Scarlet Mother on the Tiber or Trials and Travels of Evangelist L. J. King,* vol. 2 (Converted Catholic Book House, 1922), especially "The Battle at Omaha"; "The Black Nunnery"; and "Auricular Confession: The Devil's Invention." Also L. F. Martique, *The Scarlet Mother on the Tiber or Trials and Travels of Evangelist L. J. King,* vol. 1 (Privately published, 1908), especially "Experience in St. Louis Nunneries"; and "A Few Pages from Rome's Diary."

61. Author's interview with anonymous informant, Aug. 21, 1987; also *Awful Disclosures by Maria Monk of the Hotel Dieu Convent of Montreal or, The Secrets of the Black Nunnery Revealed* (Jordan Books, 1891). A refutation of the Maria Monk story is in William L. Stone, *Maria Monk and the Nunnery of the Hotel Dieu, Being an Account of a Visit to the Convents of Montreal and Refutations of the "Awful Disclosures"* (Howe and Bates, 1936); see also Robb, "The Ku Klux Klan." Examples of King's assaults on convents are in L. J. King, *House of Death and Gate of Hell* (Protestant Book House, 1928), 12–13; 58–59.

62. The ad in *Fiery Cross* (Feb. 2, 1923, 2) for *The Devil's Prayer Book* by William Lloyd Clark, billed as reading for "real, red-blooded he-men," promotes the volume as "a great eye opener for husbands, fathers, and brothers" as it unveils the atrocities of auricular confessions where "no male relative is allowed to be in the confessional or to be so located that he can hear the questions asked his wife, sister, or sweetheart during the ordeal of confession"; also discussed in Elrod, "A Descriptive Study." See also L. J. King, *Secret Confession to a Roman Priest Exposed,* 5th ed. (Protestant Book House, 1943), 7–51.

63. *The Converted Catholic and Protestant Missionary Annual* (Published by Ex-Romanist L. J. King, 1922), 12:16, 134, 147.

64. Author's interview with anonymous informant, Aug. 28, 1987; also King, *Converted Catholic,* 12:55.

65. *Fiery Cross,* June 27, 1924, 1; Feb. 22, 1924, 6; Elrod, "A Descriptive Study," 68–70.

66. Frost, "When the Klan Rules: The Business of 'Kluxing,'" *The Outlook,* Jan. 23, 1924, 144–47. Catholic responses to the Klan's charges, some written specifically for Klan members, include Martin J. Scott, "The Ku Klux Klan," *North American Review* 223 (1926): 268–81; and "The Ku-Klux

Klan," *The Catholic World* 116 (January 1923): 433–43. See also *KKK Katechism.*

67. Elrod, "A Descriptive Study"; Bertrand M. Tipple, *Alien Rome* (The Protestant Guards, 1924) (KKK, ISL); also Lowell Mellet, "Klan and Church," *Atlantic Monthly,* November, 1923, 586–92.

68. Elrod, "A Descriptive Study"; *New York Times,* Nov. 7, 1925, 1; Madison, *Indiana,* 46; M. Paul Holsinger, "The Oregon School Bill Controversy, 1922–1925," *Pacific Historical Review* 37 (August 1968): 327–41. For the WKKK's position on Catholicism, see WKKK, *Out of Their Own Mouths Shall They Be Condemned* (WKKK, n.d.).

69. Lynd and Lynd, *Middletown,* 482.

70. The Murderous Knights (box L-208, KKK, ISL); Elrod, "A Descriptive Study."

71. Author's interview with anonymous informant, Aug. 20, 1987; also Safianow, "Konklave"; and Mellet, "Klan and Church."

72. *Chicago Tribune,* Mar. 15, 1936; Alva W. Taylor, "What the Klan Did in Indiana," *The New Republic,* Nov. 16, 1927, 330–32; Cates, "The Ku Klux Klan"; Jackson, *Ku Klux Klan;* Leibowitz, *My Indiana; Indianapolis Times,* May 27, 1956, 27; depositions of Orion Norcross and Thomas W. Swift and testimony of Clyde A. Walb, Willis B. Dye, and Arthur P. Bruner (Marion 41769, KKK, ISL); Joseph White, "The Ku Klux Klan in Indiana."

73. *Chicago Tribune,* Mar. 15, 1936. Some of Stephenson's orations survive as pamphlets in the Harold C. Feightner papers, KKK, ISL.

74. Stephenson alleged that Samuel Bemenderfer tried to trick him into kidnapping an Ohio woman (Stephenson deposition in Marion 41769, KKK, ISL); also Joseph White, "The Ku Klux Klan in Indiana."

75. *Reports of Cases Decided in the Supreme Court of the State of Indiana,* vol. 205, May term 1933 (State of Indiana, 1934), 141–248.

76. Martin, *Indiana,* 195; Robert A. Butler, *So They Framed Stephenson* (Privately published, 1940), 14.

77. Author's interview with anonymous informant, Aug. 26, 1987; Leibowitz, *My Indiana,* 194.

78. Author's interview with anonymous informant, Aug. 19, 1987.

79. Author's interview with anonymous informant, Mar. 24, 1988.

80. Taylor, "What the Klan"; Martin, *Indiana,* 198–99; Weaver, "The Knights." On the signature campaign for Stephenson's release, see *Parke County's Monthly Magazine* (May 1983). For an example of Stephenson's influence from prison, see D. C. Stephenson, *Science of Government* (Privately published, 1936) and Harry E. Hodsden, *Stephenson Was Framed in a Political Conspiracy,* 2d ed. (Privately published, 1936). An assessment of Stephenson's sentence is in William Billings, *Tales of a Hoosier Village* (Privately published, 1949); also see Leibowitz, *My Indiana,* 224–26; and Weaver, "The Knights."

81. Excellent discussions of the politics of sexuality are in Snitow, Stansell, and Thompson, eds., *Powers of Desire;* Jeffrey Weeks, *Sex, Politics and Society* (Cambridge University Press, 1981); and Judith R. Walkowitz, "Male Vice and Feminine Virtue," *History Workshop* 13 (Spring 1982): 79–93.

CHAPTER FOUR

1. Letter to the author from an anonymous woman in Green County, Indiana, May 20, 1987.

2. *Fellowship Forum*, Mar. 7, 1925, 10.

3. Ruth Bordin, *Woman and Temperance: The Quest for Power and Liberty, 1873–1900* (Temple University Press, 1981), 9; also Barbara Leslie Epstein, *The Politics of Domesticity: Women, Evangelism, and Temperance in Nineteenth-Century America* (Wesleyan University Press, 1981), 1–6, 115–46. In "Women Against Prohibition" (*American Quarterly* 28 [Fall 1976]: 465–82), David E. Kyvig argues that women framed their arguments around the family, whether they supported or opposed Prohibition.

4. Robert Moats Miller, "A Footnote to the Role of the Protestant Churches in the Election of 1928," *Church History* 25 (June 1956): 145–61; *New York Times*, Nov. 22, 1922, 1. The Indiana attorney general, an anti-Klan crusader, denounced the Indiana Anti-Saloon League as a "tyranny" (*New York Times*, July 22, 1927, 3). The head of the New York Anti-Saloon League, William Anderson, claimed that politicians allied with Tammany Hall conspired to link it to the Klan; he also defended the Klan against attacks from its enemies (*New York Times*, Sept. 9, 1923, sect. 2, 1); Leibowitz, *My Indiana*, 182–83; Louis Francis Budenz, "Scandals of 1927—Indiana," *Nation*, Oct. 5, 1927, 332–33; Washington Pezet, "The Temporal Power of Evangelism: The Methodists in National Politics," *The Forum* 76 (October 1926): 481–91.

5. Richard J. Jensen, "An Ethnocultural Analysis of Midwestern Politics" in *Readings in Indiana History*, ed. Ralph Gray (William B. Eerdmans, 1980), 2:39–46; also Davis, "The Ku Klux Klan," 292–93.

6. *Indiana Authors and Their Books*, vols. 1967–1980 and 1981 (Wabash College Press, 1981); Rolland Lewis Whitson, *Centennial History of Grant County, Indiana, 1812 to 1912* (Lewis Publishing, 1914), 2:830–31; Daisy Douglas Barr, "He Leadeth Me," in *Springs That Run Dry and Other Addresses* (Butler Printing House, n.d.), 17–28.

7. Women ministers were not uncommon in Indiana Friends' meetings of the early twentieth century. Barr followed in the footsteps of the celebrated evangelist Esther Frame, a Prohibition activist whose revival meetings in central Indiana were legendary. See Dwight Hoover, "Daisy Douglas Barr: From Friends' Memorial to the Ku Klux Klan" (Unpublished paper, Ball State University); *Indianapolis News*, Nov. 1, 1916, 2; William Heiss, ed., *Abstracts of the Records of the Society of Friends in Indiana* (Indiana Historical Society, 1970), 3:3, 378; 4:418; 6:250; Edgar M. Baldwin, *Making of a Township, Fairmount Township, Grant County, 1829–1917* (Privately published, 1917), 163; Barr, "He Leadeth Me"; Whitson, *Centennial History of Grant County*, 831; *Minutes of the Yearly Meetings of Friends, Held at Richmond, Indiana* (1938), 57.

8. Author's interview with anonymous informant, Aug. 26, 1987.

9. Whitson, *Centennial History*, 831.

10. Author's interview with anonymous informant, Aug. 26, 1987.

11. Hoover, "Daisy Douglas Barr."

12. Daisy Douglas Barr, "The Serpent's Sting," in *Springs That Run Dry* (Butler Printing House, n.d.); author's interview with anonymous informant, Aug. 26, 1987.

13. Daisy Douglas Barr, "Hope for the Fallen Woman" and "The Bloodless Battle," in *Springs That Run Dry* (Butler Printing House, n.d.).

14. Daisy Douglas Barr, "Return of an Unbeliever to Faith in Jesus," in *Springs That Run Dry* (Butler Printing House, n.d.).

15. Daisy Douglas Barr, "Women in the Ministry," *Indianapolis News,* Nov. 1, 1916, women's supplement, 2; see also Daisy Douglas Barr, "Tent Makers Story," in *Springs That Run Dry* (Butler Printing House, n.d.).

16. *Muncie Evening Press,* Jan. 12, 1914, 1, 3; Jan. 21, 1914, 10.

17. Daisy Douglas Barr, "Factory Meeting," in *Springs That Run Dry* (Butler Printing House, n.d.).

18. Notes on Daisy Douglas Barr in Biographical Card Index, ISL; Daisy Douglas Barr entry in *Indiana Biography,* vol. 17 (ISL); Hoover, "Daisy Douglas Barr."

19. Squires, "History of the Ku Klux Klan," 18. An article in the *Fiery Cross* (Feb. 27, 1923, 6) describes the Klan's visit to a Friends' meeting in Wabash, Indiana, where it gave the minister an electric fiery cross, to be placed on the pulpit and illuminated during the sermon. This was the first appearance of the Klan in Wabash. The service at the Friends' meeting included a prayer by a local Quaker minister, Ida Stauffer, and a sermon on "The Dangers and Defenses of America" delivered by another Quaker minister; the latter claimed that the greatest dangers facing society were "race problems," lack of political leadership, and widespread religious indifference.

20. Daisy Douglas Barr, "The New Patriotism," in *Springs That Run Dry* (Butler Printing House, n.d.).

21. See the pledge of loyalty for the Queens of the Golden Mask: field representatives pledged "lofty respect, whole-hearted loyalty and an unwavering devotion at all times . . . to the Empress of the Symbolic Realm" (i.e., Daisy Douglas Barr). A copy of the pledge signed on October 18, 1922, is in Harold C. Feightner papers, box L55, KKK, ISL.

22. Daisy Douglas Barr, "The Soul of America," in *Papers Read at the First Annual Meeting,* 135.

23. The WKKK in Indiana was officially constituted in 1924 (see the Certification of Incorporation, Women of the Ku Klux Klan, Dec. 31, 1924, in the Department of State, Indiana); official certifications through 1927 exist in the Indiana Secretary of State's office. Oddly, in 1969, two Indianapolis women presented themselves at this office, filed official papers as the current officers of the Indiana WKKK, and paid back organizational taxes from 1946 through 1968, claiming that the organization was continuing to meet in Indianapolis on an annual basis. An attached budget claimed that the group was paying $1.50 a month in Imperial Taxes, suggesting a continuing realm or national organization as well.

24. *Franklin Evening Star,* Feb. 27, 1923.

25. *Muncie Post-Democrat,* Dec. 7, 1923, 1; Jan. 4, 1924, 4.

26. The American War Mothers formed at a national convention in 1918. It published two magazines, *The Soldier* and *The Indianian,* which promoted patriotism and nationalism among mothers of servicemen and former servicemen. The Barr quote comes from Alice Moore French manuscript collection, box 1, scrapbook, IHS. See also *Richmond* (Indiana) *Daily Paladium,* Sept. 4, 1923, 2; *Muncie Evening Press,* Sept. 2, 1921, 3.

27. Alice Moore French manuscript collection, box 1, scrapbook and History, IHS.

28. *Muncie Post-Democrat,* Apr. 20, 1923; *Franklin Evening Star,* Mar. 28, 1923; *Muncie Star,* Mar. 27, 1923, 1; Alice Moore French manuscript collection, box 1, History, IHS.

29. Samuel Bemenderfer, a leader of the splinter group the Independent Klan of America (IKA), made this charge at an IKA convention in Muncie, quoted in *Franklin Evening Star,* Mar. 25, 1924, 1; also see *Muncie Post-Democrat,* Dec. 7, 1923, 1; *Indianapolis News,* June 3, 1924, 12; *Muncie Star,* June 3, 1924, 1; *Knightstown Banner,* June 6, 1924; *Franklin Evening Star,* Jan. 22, 1924; *Noblesville Daily Ledger,* Mar. 25, 1924, 1.

30. *Muncie Post-Democrat,* June 6, 1924, 1.

31. Hoover, "Daisy Douglas Barr."

32. *Indianapolis Star,* Nov. 4, 1925, 11; *Indianapolis Times,* June 4, 1926, 1; *Indianapolis News,* Nov. 6, 1944, pt. 2, 11; *Indianapolis Times,* Jan. 14, 1957, 11; Emma Lou Thornbrough, "Segregation in Indiana During the Klan Era of the 1920s," *Mississippi Valley Historical Review* 47 (March 1961): 594–618; Joseph White, "The Ku Klux Klan in Indiana"; Louis Francis Budenz, "There's Mud on Indiana's White Robes," *The Nation,* July 27, 1927, 81–82; Morton Harrison, "Gentleman from Indiana," *Atlantic Monthly,* May 1928, 676–86.

33. For example, see the speaker's program for the Richmond Women's Club in 1923 (printed in each issue of the *Richmond Daily Paladium*) or the listings for Ladies' Missionary Societies and women's Protestant church societies (*Fiery Cross,* Mar. 23, 1923, 4; Mar. 2, 1923, 2; Mar. 9, 1923, 6). See also Bennett, *The Party of Fear,* 183–98; *Rushville Daily Republican,* Apr. 4, 1923, 6. A general account of women's patriotic societies in the 1920s is found in Cott, *Grounding of Moden Feminism,* chap. 6.

34. *Who's Who and What's What in Indiana Politics* (James Perry, 1944), 755.

35. Jenkins, "The Ku Klux Klan in Youngstown, Ohio," 84.

36. *New York Times,* Jan. 8, 1924, 25.

37. Records of the Grant-Delaware County court; Hoover, "Daisy Douglas Barr"; *Muncie Star,* Jan. 3, 1924, 1; *Indianapolis News,* Jan. 3, 1924, 17; *Richmond Daily Paladium,* Jan. 3, 1924; *Franklin Evening Star,* Jan. 3, 1924; *Muncie Evening Post,* Nov. 14, 1924, 1; *Indianapolis News,* Jan. 3, 1924, 17.

38. *Indianapolis Star,* Jan. 3, 1954, 1; "Klansmen Crusade for Dewey," *New Masses* 53 (October 1944).

39. *Indianapolis News,* Apr. 4, 1924, 11; Mar. 28, 1925, 18; July 21, 1925, 1.

40. *Indianapolis News,* July 17, 1925, 1; July 21, 1925, 1; Mar. 1, 1926,

1; Nov. 28, 1925, 23; *Indianapolis Star,* July 18, 1925, 8; July 21, 1925, 1; July 30, 1925, 1; *Baltimore* (Maryland) *Sun,* Aug. 29, 1926, 1.

41. *Indianapolis Star,* Sept. 1, 1926, 1, 2; *Baltimore Sun,* Aug. 29, 1926, 1.

42. *New York Times,* July 15, 1927, 19; *Baltimore Sun,* Aug. 29, 1926, 1.

43. See Cott, *Grounding of Modern Feminism,* esp. 68–81; Anne Firor Scott, *The Southern Lady: From Pedestal to Politics, 1830–1930* (University of Chicago Press, 1970), 164–211; Bettina Aptheker, *Woman's Legacy: Essays on Race, Sex, and Class* (University of Massachusetts Press, 1982), 1–52; Paula Giddings, *When and Where I Enter: The Impact of Black Women on Race and Sex in America* (William Morrow, 1984), 159–70; Rosalyn Terborg-Penn, "Discrimination Against Afro-American Women in the Women's Movement, 1830–1920," in *The Afro-American Woman: Struggles and Images,* ed. Sharon Harley and Rosalyn Terborg-Penn (National University Publications, 1978).

44. These names are both pseudonyms to protect the anonymity of my informants.

45. *Indiana Biographical Clippings,* 56:17; *Indianapolis Star,* Mar. 26, 1960, 8; *Fiery Cross,* Dec. 8, 1922.

46. Author's interview with anonymous informant, Aug. 21, 1987.

47. Also pseudonyms.

48. Author's interview with anonymous informant, Aug. 28, 1987.

49. From author's interview with anonymous informant, Aug. 21, 1987; also *Morgantown* (Indiana) *Scrapbook,* vol. 1 (Privately published, n.d.).

50. Newspaper sources for obituaries are: Elwood *Call-Leader,* Jan. 14, Feb. 4, and Apr. 21, 1924; Princeton *Clarion-News,* Nov. 22, 1923; Anderson *Daily Bulletin,* Jan. 15, Apr. 21 and 24, 1924; Clinton *Daily Clintonian,* Mar. 24–25, 1924; Princeton *Daily Democrat,* Nov. 20–23, 1923; Sullivan *Daily Times,* Nov. 24, 1923; Tipton *Daily Tribune,* Oct. 8–9 and Nov. 5, 1923; Owen County *Democrat,* Jan. 10, 1924; Columbus *Evening Republican,* Nov. 13, 1923; Huntington *Herald,* Aug. 2, 1924; Indianapolis *News,* Nov. 6, 1944; Osgood *Journal,* Mar. 19, 1924; Lafayette *Journal and Courier,* Apr. 4, 1924; Spencer *Leader,* Jan. 9, 1924; Hartford City *News,* Jan. 21–24, 1924; Connersville *News-Examiner,* June 20, 1923 and Jan. 17 and 22, 1924; North Vernon *Plain-Dealer,* Jan. 7, 1924; Winamac *Pulaski County Democrat,* Jan. 10, 1924; Versailles *Republican,* Mar. 19, 1924; North Vernon *Sun,* Feb. 7, 1924; Terre Haute *Tribune,* Feb. 6, Mar. 25, and Sept. 28–29, 1924.

51. *Muncie Post-Democrat,* Apr. 25, 1924; *Fiery Cross,* Mar. 30, 1923, 5.

52. In September 1924 the Richmond, Indiana, KKK sent a mailing to every man who had ever belonged to the Indiana KKK; the bill for this mailing included a lengthy list of women and men who were each paid fifty cents per hour for their work on the mailing (Statement of Expenses, Wayne County (Indiana) KKK, box 1, folder 8, KKK-WC, IHS).

53. Many rural women whose occupations were not listed were probably wives of farm owners, a status that feminist scholars recognize as an occupational category. I do not include it here because I am interested in the extent of

women's economic independence from their husbands. Married farm women are not likely to receive separate pay for their work on the farm. See Carolyn E. Sacks, *The Invisible Farmers: Women in Agricultural Production* (Rowman and Allanheld, 1983). For an application of the theory of status politics to the 1920s KKK, see William V. Moore, "Status Politics in the Ku Klux Klan of the 1960's," in *Perspectives on the American South,* ed. Merle Black and John Shelton Reed (Breach Science Publishers, 1984), 237–49. This theory is prevalent in the popular mythology about the Klan; see, for example, ". . . Its Past Story," *Fort Wayne* (Indiana) *Journal-Gazette,* May 7, 1977.

54. Kenneth Jackson argues (*The Ku Klux Klan,* 108, 63) that in Chicago most of the estimated 40,000–80,000 Klan members were lower-class white-collar workers, small business owners, and semiskilled laborers, and that data from the Knoxville Klan indicate that 29 percent of its members were white-collar workers and 71 percent blue-collar workers; also see Cocoltchos ("Invisible Government," 392), who finds that in Orange County, California, Klansmen were slightly more prosperous than non-Klansmen.

CHAPTER FIVE

1. *Seymour Daily Tribune,* July 11, 1923, 8; June 30, 1923, 1.

2. Personal informant of Patricia P. Mahan, "The Ku Klux Klan in Anderson and the State of Indiana" (Master's thesis, Ball State Teachers' College, 1964); also see *Fiery Cross,* May 9, 1924, which describes a parade in Elwood that featured drum corps from Alexandria and Peru and bands from Elwood, Anderson, and Kokomo.

3. Kokomo estimate in Safianow, "Konklave"; also see James Glenn Hamilton, "The Klan in Kokomo, 1921–1936" (Honors paper, Ball State Teachers' College, 1973), based on information supplied by a local Grand Cyclops; Indianapolis estimate in Kenneth Jackson, *The Ku Klux Klan;* Hartford City estimate in Robb, "KKK in Blackford County"; and *Hartford City News-Times,* Nov. 6, 1976; Martin County estimate in Harry Q. Holt, *History of Martin County, Indiana* (Privately published, 1953), 193–95; Blackford County estimate in *A History of Blackford County, Indiana* (Blackford County Historical Society, 1986), 26.

4. See Safianow, "Konklave," on Couglan's estimates of Kokomo rally.

5. Interview in Mahan, "The Ku Klux Klan in Anderson"; also *Fiery Cross,* May 23, 1924.

6. *Fiery Cross,* Feb. 15 and May 23, 1924; also discussion about the degrees in the women's order by an informant in Robb, "KKK in Blackford County."

7. *Indianapolis News,* July 16, 1923, 3; *Kokomo Daily Dispatch,* July 15, 1924, 10; *Plainfield Messenger,* July 12, 1923, 1; July 19, 1923, 1; *Franklin Evening Star,* July 16, 1923, 1; *Fiery Cross,* July 13, 1923, 9; July 20, 1923; *Mooresville Times,* July 20, 1923, 1.

8. Anonymous informant, Green County, Indiana, May 20, 1987.

9. Described in Robb, "KKK in Blackford County." For example, the WKKK of Attica gave a big party for their departing organizer and gave her a

silk flag as a memento of her time in Attica (*Fiery Cross*, Jan. 4, 1924). The WKKK of Galveston reported that it was feted by the WKKK of Logansport (*Fiery Cross*, Apr. 11, 1924). The WKKK of Elnora had a busy social schedule, according to a report in the *Fiery Cross* of Apr. 18, 1924. The Terre Haute WKKK hosted a party for its organizer, according to the Mar. 21, 1924 issue of *Fiery Cross*, although the local group was then too large to be accommodated in any local hall. The situation in Hartford City was described to the author by an anonymous informant (Feb. 20, 1988). See also a receipt book from the Hartford City WKKK in the Blackford County Historical Society Museum.

10. *Muncie Post-Democrat*, Apr. 18, 1924.

11. Letter from Samuel Bemenderfer to Hiram Evans on July 30, 1925, in Bemenderfer deposition (Marion 41769, KKK, ISL); Booth, *Mad Mullah*, 72–74.

12. Based on an interview with a female informant in Mahan, "The Ku Klux Klan in Anderson."

13. *Franklin Evening Star*, Feb. 27, 1923, 1.

14. This was the "spiritual phase" of klankraft, as detailed by the Grand Dragon of the Realm of Oklahoma ("The Definition of Klankraft and How to Disseminate It," in *Papers Read at First Annual Meeting, 1923*, 45–51).

15. Quote is from *Franklin Evening Star*, Feb. 7, 1923, 1; also Feb. 19, 1923, 1; Feb. 27, 1923, 3; Jan. 31, 1923, 4; Feb. 6, 1923; Feb. 28, 1923, 4; Mar. 5, 1923, 1; Feb. 1, 1923, 1.

16. *Franklin Evening Star*, Mar. 9, 1923, 3; Mar. 1, 1923, 1. Other descriptions of this meeting are found in *Tolerance*, Apr. 15, 1923, 15; *Muncie Post-Democrat*, Apr. 20, 1923, 1.

17. *Franklin Evening Star*, Mar. 28, 1923, 1, 2; Mar. 9, 1923, 1.

18. Ibid., Apr. 1, 1924, 1; May 5, 1923, 1; Apr. 9, 1923, 1.

19. Ibid., May 19, 1923, 1; June 5, 1923, 1.

20. Ibid., Aug. 13, 1923, 1; July 31, 1923, 1; *Seymour Daily Tribune*, Aug. 11, 1923, 1; *Fiery Cross*, Aug. 17, 1923, 5.

21. *Kokomo Daily Tribune*, July 2, 1923, 1; July 3, 1923, 1; July 4, 1923, 1; July 5, 1923, 1; *Fiery Cross*, July 11 and 13, 1923; *Kokomo Daily Dispatch*, July 5, 1923, 1; John Lewis Niblack, *The Life and Times of a Hoosier Judge* (Privately published, n.d.), 194–95; Safianow, "Konklave."

22. *Kokomo Daily Dispatch*, July 15, 1923, 1; Safianow, "Konklave"; *Kokomo Daily Tribune*, July 6, 1923, 1.

23. *Kokomo Daily Tribune*, July 18, 1923, 1.

24. *Indianapolis News*, July 26, 1923, 8; *Fiery Cross*, July 20, 1923; *Kokomo Daily Tribune*, July 26, 1923, 1.

25. *Kokomo Daily Tribune*, July 28, 1923, 1.

26. *Fiery Cross*, Aug. 10, 1923, 1.

27. *Fiery Cross*, Sept. 26, Oct. 12, and Nov. 16, 1923; *Kokomo Daily Tribune*, Oct. 12, 1923, 2; Sept. 19, 1923, 2.

28. *Fiery Cross*, May 9, 1924, 1; *Kokomo Daily Tribune*, June 23, 1924, 2; Hamilton, "The Klan in Kokomo."

29. *Kokomo Daily Tribune*, Sept. 11, 1923, 3.

30. *Fiery Cross,* Dec. 7, 1923, 1; Jan. 4 and May 14, 1924; *Muncie Post-Democrat,* Dec. 7, 1923, 1; *Kokomo Daily Tribune,* Sept. 3, 1923, 10.

31. Anonymous informant, Greene County, Indiana, May 20, 1987.

32. Blackford County WKKK receipt book.

33. *Seymour Daily Tribune,* June 8, 1923, 1; also see Edwin J. Boley, *First Documented History of Jackson County* (Privately published, 1980), 499–500.

34. *Seymour Daily Tribune,* June 30, 1923, 1.

35. *Plainfield* (Indiana) *Messenger,* June 5, 1925, 1.

36. For example, note the Knoxville (Tenn.) Klan's drive to raise $200,000 for a home for Klan widows and children (*Dawn,* Sept. 29, 1923, 13), the gifts from the Roanoke (Indiana) WKKK to the Odd Fellows and Rebekah Lodge (*Fiery Cross,* July 4, 1924), or the Russellville WKKK's gift to the local American Legion post (*Fiery Cross,* July 4, 1924); the *Plainfield Messenger* reported on five cases within a two-month period in which the Plainfield WKKK gave "substantial aid" to widowed women who had been "left on their own resources" (Dec. 6, 1923, 1).

37. *Dawn,* Nov. 24, 1923, 13; *Fiery Cross,* Jan. 10, May 2, and Oct. 10, 1924; Errol W. Smith, "Activities of the Ku Klux Klan in Delaware County Indiana During the 1920s" (Unpublished paper, Ball State University, 1970).

38. Mahan ("The Ku Klux Klan in Anderson") discusses a gift of $200 from the Anderson WKKK to the Anderson YWCA; *Fiery Cross,* Jan. 5, 1923, 1 (Muncie); Jan. 11, 1924 (Lebanon, Martinsville); Jan. 4, 1924 (Elwood); see also issue of Oct. 5, 1923.

39. *Fiery Cross,* Dec. 14, 1923.

40. Robert Coughlan, "Konklave in Kokomo," in *The Aspirin Age,* ed. Isabel Leighton (Simon and Schuster, 1976); Safianow, "Konklave"; Hamilton, "Klan in Kokomo," 7–8; *Fiery Cross,* Aug. 24, 1923, 1.

41. *Fiery Cross* (Apr. 18, 1924) has a notice of the Anderson WKKK's Protestant hospital drive and campaign to put Bibles in Madison County schools. The *Bulletin of the Whitley County Historical Society* (October 1986) describes a donation by the Whitley County WKKK to the Riley Hospital Fund. See reports on WKKKs in *Fiery Cross,* Nov. 9, 1923 (Morgantown); Dec. 14, 1923 (Poseyville); Apr. 11, 1924 (Huntington); Jan. 11, 1924 (Greenwood and White River townships); Jan. 25, 1924 (Sheridan, Connersville, Walkerton, Bourbon); Feb. 1, 1924 (Culver); Feb. 15, 1924 (Chesterton, Kewanna); Mar. 21, 1924 (Warren County, Terre Haute, Noblesville); Apr. 27, 1923 (Burlington).

42. *Fiery Cross,* Mar. 21 and Apr. 11, 1924.

43. For example, see the Howard County (Kokomo) Klan's unfilled promise to raise $50,000 to build a Protestant hospital (*Kokomo Daily Tribune,* July 11, 1923, 1) or the similar one of the Anderson WKKK (Mahan, "KKK in Anderson").

44. *Fiery Cross,* issues from Feb. 15 through May 19, 1924, carried reports from Peru, Chesterton, Amo, Rockport, St. Paul, Winslow, Perryville, Frankfort, Petersburg, Terre Haute, Dugger, Columbus, and Homer, Indiana; Emmons's deposition (Marion 41769, KKK, ISL) describes minister-lecturers

who carried revolvers when they preached Klan sermons; also *Indianapolis Star,* Feb. 21, 1928, 1.

45. *New York Times,* Mar. 10, 1926, 4; Mar. 21, 1922, 6; Nov. 28, 1922, 23. The latter two references are to incidents involving the Ladies of the Invisible Empire, an early women's Klan group; see *Fiery Cross* (Oct. 12, 1923, 10) for a description of the situation in Jackson County, Indiana; also see its discussion of the campaign in Indianapolis (Apr. 18, 1924).

46. This tactic was by no means unique to the Indiana Klan. Racine reports on a campaign to get Catholic teachers fired in Atlanta ("The Ku Klux Klan and Atlanta"); based on personal interviews with informants in Mahan, "KKK in Anderson"; *Fiery Cross,* Apr. 18, 1924 (Indianapolis); Giel, "George R. Dale," 36 (Muncie); Conen, "Politico-Religious Disturbances," 41 (Jennings County); Safianow, "Konklave," notes that Coughlan, author of the famous description of Klan culture "Konklave in Kokomo," was the son of a Catholic teacher in Kokomo.

47. The Indiana Klan occasionally drafted its own candidates for office but more often endorsed major party candidates, usually Republicans. See *Franklin Evening Star,* Mar. 9, 1923, 3; Elrod, "A Descriptive Study"; William G. Carleton, "The Popish Plot of 1928," *Forum* 111–113 (1949–1950): 141–47; deposition of MacNeel (Marion 41769, KKK, ISL); *New York Times,* Nov. 7, 1923, 15; Oct. 16, 1924, 10; Weaver, "The Knights."

48. *Muncie Post-Democrat,* May 23, 1924.

49. Cates, "Ku Klux Klan"; letter from A. C. Terhune of Indianapolis (Mar. 24, 1924) and undated candidate questionnaire from Indiana Klan, both in KKK, ISL; Emmons's deposition (Marion 41769, KKK, ISL); *New York Times,* Dec. 10, 1922, sect. 9, 6; Smethurst, "The Ku Klux Klan."

50. *Indianapolis News,* Feb. 20, 1928, 1, 23; "The Klan in Parke County," *Parke Place: Parke County's Monthly Magazine,* May 1983); see letter of Mar. 13, 1925, signed by all Klan candidates for mayor of Indianapolis in KKK, ISL; Walter Myers, "Are Hiram W. Evans and His Ku Klux Klan Bigger than Either or Both Political Parties?" (n.p., 1928) (Harold C. Feightner papers, box L55, KKK, ISL); *New York Times,* Oct. 19, 1924, sect. 2, 1; Apr. 1, 1923, 5; Oct. 14, 1926, 3; Sept. 17, 1927, 3; May 13, 1924, 3, 23.

51. Depositions of Emmons, Norcross, and Walb, and exhibits (pp. 71–72, 99, 167–68, Marion 41769, KKK, ISL); also *Fiery Cross* (May 2, 1924) on the electoral work of the WKKK of Fort Wayne, Indiana; Gilliom memorandum (KKK, ISL); Weaver, "The Knights," 189–221.

52. *New York Times,* Nov. 10, 1925, 6; Nov. 4, 1925, 4; Weaver, "The Knights."

53. Even in 1927 after the D. C. Stephenson scandal, seventeen legislators attended the Klan's banquet to announce its legislative platform for Indiana, and thirty-one other legislators were reputed to be secret Klansmen (*Indianapolis Times,* Jan. 5, 1927, 9). A similar legislative campaign for Oregon is discussed in Holsinger, "The Oregon School Bill Controversy." Also see Niblack, *Life and Times,* 233–34; *New York Times,* May 14, 1924, 2; *Fort Wayne Journal-Gazette,* Apr. 3, 1925; *Indianapolis News,* May 13, 1924, 2; May 14, 1924, 2; Davis, "Ku Klux Klan," 196–219.

54. Emphasis in the original report of the speech, found in *Tolerance,* Apr. 8, 1923, 6.

55. Squires, "History of the Ku Klux Klan"; Morton, "Blackford County"; Conen, "Politico-Religious Disturbances"; Sweeney, "The Great Bigotry Merger"; testimony of MacNeel (Marion 41769, KKK, ISL); Harrison, "Gentleman from Indiana."

56. Author's interview with anonymous informant, Mar. 25, 1988; also Davis, "Ku Klux Klan"; Robert Hull, "Klan Aftermath in Indiana," *America,* Oct. 15, 1927, 8; Frost, "When the Klan Rules," 146; Leon Brandenburg, "The Klan Era in Indiana" (Unpublished paper, Ball State Teachers' College, 1962), 9. Likins discusses a similar system of local poison squads in the Pennsylvania Klan. As in Indiana, the purpose of these whispering campaigns was to circulate falsehoods about prominent members of the community who opposed the Klan, especially those whose opposition was public (William M. Likins, *KKK, or the Rise and Fall of the Invisible Empire* [KKK, 1927]). Patricia Meyer Spacks, *Gossip* (Alfred A. Knopf, 1985), provides a useful framework for deconstructing gossip.

57. *Manchester Herald,* June 4, 1923; author's interview with anonymous informant, Aug. 21, 1987; Brandenburg, "The Klan Era"; Coughlan, "Konklave"; Harrison, "Gentleman from Indiana."

58. Author's interview with anonymous informant, May 24, 1987.

59. Author's interview with anonymous informant, Aug. 21, 1987.

60. Author's interview with anonymous informant, Aug. 26, 1987; also Morton, "Blackford County."

61. Author's interview with anonymous informant, Feb. 25, 1988.

62. "Who's Who," *Fiery Cross,* May 11, 1923, 1; KKK, ISL, reel 199, exhibit 9 contains letters to and from companies on their attitude toward the Klan, lists of 100 percent companies, and advertisements soliciting such employees.

63. Schaefer, "The Ku Klux Klan"; Emmons deposition (pp. 260–82, 286, Marion 41769, KKK, ISL); Davis, "The Ku Klux Klan," 320–21; Wade, *The Fiery Cross,* 226.

64. *Franklin Evening Star,* Mar. 16, 1923, 4.

65. *Fiery Cross,* June 1, 1923, 3; examples abound throughout every issue of the *Fiery Cross* and many local newspapers. The advertisements cited are in issues of the *Fiery Cross* from May 18, 1923, 7, 8; Mar. 23, 1923, 7, 8; Apr. 27, 1923, 2; June 1, 1923, 3.

66. Field letter no. 59, August 27, 1923, from "State" (D. C. Stephenson) (box L-208, KKK, ISL). Many issues of the *Fiery Cross* carry the notices—see, for example, those of February 1923; also Neil Betten, "Nativism and the Klan in Town and City," *Studies in History and Society* 4 (Spring 1973): 9–10.

67. Author's anonymous informants, Aug. 20, 1987; Feb. 25, 1988; Mar. 24, 1988; also letter of Mar. 14, 1924 (KKK, ISL); *Muncie Post-Democrat,* Jan. 25, 1924, 2.

68. Emmons deposition (p. 121, Marion 41769, KKK, ISL).

69. As an example, see the coverage of the multiple cross-burning episodes by the WKKK of Burlington, reported in the *Fiery Cross* (Apr. 27, 1923, 8) or

the discussion in Mahan ("KKK in Anderson") of letters threatening a mayor whose child was in a Catholic hospital and a judge who was naturalizing Catholics. Klanswomen were accused of violence in a Klan riot in 1923 in Carnegie, Pennsylvania (John Strayer, "The Decline of the Ku Klux Klan in Pennsylvania" [Privately published, 1927]). Reputable reports of Klan violence can be found in Giel, "George R. Dale" (Muncie); Smethurst, "The Ku Klux Klan" (Huntington County); *Indianapolis Freeman*, Dec. 12, 1925 (box 1, folder 13, George Dale papers, BSU) (Indianapolis); *New York Times*, Sept. 29, 1927, 1 (Gary). Accusations of arson by the Klan were made in an anonymous interview (May 13, 1987) and in a letter from a Catholic priest in central Indiana (Mar. 13, 1987). On Klan violence in other states, see Robert Duffus, "How the Ku Klux Klan Sells Hate (part 2)," *The World's Work* (June 1923): 174–83 (Louisiana); and deposition of MacNeel in Marion 41769, KKK, ISL. James R. Ramsey testified that the Ohio Klan sponsored the Knight Riders of America, a semimilitary organization responsible for carrying out the Klan program of terror and violence, including whipping priests and burning churches (Marion 41769, KKK, ISL). On Tennessee, see R. A. Patton, "A Ku Klux Klan Reign of Terror," *Current History* 28 (April 1928): 51–55. Other reports are found in *New York Times*, Jan. 23, 1929, 3; Dec. 28, 1922, 7; and in Albert DeSilver, *The Ku Klux Klan* (American Civil Liberties Union, 1921).

CHAPTER SIX

1. Cited in Schaefer, "The Ku Klux Klan."
2. Weaver, "The Knights," 293–300; also Budenz, "There's Mud," 81; Betten, "Nativism and the Klan." See Detlev J. K. Peukert, *Inside Nazi Germany: Conformity, Opposition, and Racism in Everyday Life* (Yale University Press, 1987) for an excellent discussion of everyday fascism in Nazi Germany. A substantial scholarship explores the social-class basis of definitions of morality and leisure. Important examples are Frances G. Couvares, "The Triumph of Commerce: Class Culture and Mass Culture in Pittsburgh," in *Working-Class America: Essays on Labor, Community, and American Society,* ed. Michael H. Frisch and Daniel J. Walkowitz (University of Illinois Press, 1983); and Kathy Peiss, *Cheap Amusements* (Temple University Press, 1982).
3. Here I draw on the theoretical work on political culture and public spheres in Ronald Aminzade, *Class, Politics, and Early Industrial Capitalism* (State University of New York Press, 1981); Eberhard Knodler-Bunte, "The Proletarian Public Sphere and Political Organization: An Analysis of Oskar Negt and Alexander Kluge's *The Public Sphere and Experience,*" *New German Critique* 4 (Winter 1975): 51–75; and Kathleen Blee and Al Gedicks, "The Emergence of Socialist Political Culture Among Finnish Immigrants in Minnesota Mining Communities," in *Classes, Class Conflict, and the State,* ed. Maurice Zeitlin (Winthrop, 1980), 172–92.
4. Murphy, "Normalcy, Intolerance," 455. Also see letter from an anonymous informant, Mar. 13, 1987.
5. Author's interview with anonymous informant, May 1, 1987.

6. Author's interview with anonymous informant, Aug. 21, 1987.

7. See Rosalind Coward, *Patriarchal Precedents* (Routledge and Kegan Paul, 1983).

8. Author's interview with anonymous informant, Aug. 25, 1987.

9. Author's interview with anonymous informant, Aug. 26, 1987.

10. Author's interview with anonymous informant, Aug. 26, 1987.

11. Author's interviews with two anonymous informants, Aug. 21, 1987; Mar. 25, 1988.

12. One of these was the Protestant Juniors of America, a semisecret ritualist society for children from five to fifteen years sponsored by the Grand League of Protestant Women to teach Bible study and citizenship as an extension of Sunday school classes, discussed in *Fellowship Forum*, Sept. 8, 1923, 6; also see *Imperial Night-Hawk*, July 25, 1923, 1; Report of the National Director of the Junior Ku Klux Klan, in *Proceedings of the Second Imperial Klonvokation*, [KKK] *1924*, 213–17; *Fiery Cross*, Aug. 10, 1923, 1, 7.

13. *New York Times*, Apr. 20, 1925, 4; Avin, "Ku Klux Klan," 139.

14. Fuller, *Visible of the Invisible;* also Frank E. Cline, "Activities of the Ku Klux Klan in Jay County" (Master's thesis, Ball State University, 1964), on the junior Klan in Portland, Indiana.

15. *Fiery Cross*, Aug. 3, 1923; see also Report of the National Director of the Junior Ku Klux Klan; and Davis, "The Ku Klux Klan."

16. *Ritual of the Tri-K Klub* (Tri-K Klub of the Women of the Ku Klux Klan, 1925), 16.

17. Ibid.

18. Deposition of Hugh F. Emmons, cited in *Indianapolis News*, Feb. 20, 1928, 1, 23; Safianow, "Konklave"; Hamilton, "The Klan in Kokomo," 7–8.

19. Cates, "The Ku Klux Klan in Indiana"; author's interviews with two anonymous informants, Aug. 20, 1987; Aug. 28, 1987; also see *Kokomo Daily Tribune*, Sept. 10, 1923, 2; Oct. 12, 1923, 2; Avin, "Ku Klux Klan," 139; *Fiery Cross*, Aug. 17 and Sept. 28, 1923, July 25, 1924; *Richmond Daily Paladium*, Oct. 6, 1923, 9. On Shreveport see Granger, "Reaction to Change"; also see *Kloran*; Hamilton, "The Klan in Kokomo," 8.

20. *Fellowship Forum*, May 2, 1925, 6.

21. Author's interviews with two anonymous informants, Aug. 28, 1987 and May 24, 1987; the quote is likely a misremembered reference to the second letter of Paul to Timothy (2:22 in the New Testament, Standard Revised Bible): "So shun youthful passions and aim at righteousness, faith, love, and peace, along with those who call upon the Lord from a pure heart."

22. A clause in the original charter of Valparaiso University prevented the Klan from purchasing the school. In fact, the actual reason for the deal's collapse might have been Evans's refusal to commit funds to a purchase Stephenson instigated. Ironically, the Indiana American Legion's Americanization Committee investigated this same school after its president resigned amidst charges that the university was a "hotbed of Bolshevism" (*Fiery Cross*, Sept. 7, 1923; *New York Times*, Feb. 3, 1924, 15; Sept. 6, 1923, 19; July 28, 1923, 6; July 27, 1923, 15; Aug. 16, 1923, 17; Aug. 18, 1923, 4; Sept. 12, 1921, 15; *Fiery Cross*, Aug. 24, 1923; Booth, *Mad Mullah; Indianapolis News*, July 26,

1923, 5; *Muncie Evening Press,* Apr. 27, 1921, 3; Avin, "Ku Klux Klan," 231).

23. *Fellowship Forum,* July 25, 1925, 6; May 2, 1925; *New York Times,* May 11, 1925, 9; Leah H. Bell appeared earlier as WKKK Grand Councillor of Realm no. 3 (New Jersey) to address ten thousand people at a Klan rally in 1923 (*Fiery Cross,* Oct. 26, 1923, 3).

24. Grand Dragon of Oregon, "Responsibility of Klankraft to the American Boy," *Papers Read at First Annual Meeting, 1923,* 81–89; *Washington Evening Star,* Sept. 14, 1926, 2.

25. Curry, *Under the Searchlight,* 225; *Fiery Cross,* Aug. 17, 1923, cited in Davis, "Ku Klux Klan in Indiana," 135–36. For an elaboration of this theme from a psychoanalytic feminist perspective see Nancy Chodorow, *The Reproduction of Mothering* (University of California Press, 1978); Grand Dragon of Oregon, "Responsibility of Klankraft."

26. "Junior Klansmen," *The Kourier Magazine,* October 1925, 14 (box 2, folder 1, KKK-WC, IHS).

27. Grand Dragon of Oregon, "Responsibility of Klankraft," 85; Avin, "Ku Klux Klan," 138, citing Curry, *Under the Searchlight,* 224–25.

28. Junior Order of the Ku Klux Klan, *Kloran* (n.d.) (box 2, folder 1, KKK-WC, IHS).

29. "Discussion of Junior Klan and WKKK," *Proceedings of the Fourth Imperial Klonvokation,* 30–193; author's interview with anonymous informant, Aug. 28, 1987.

30. *Fellowship Forum,* Nov. 17, 1923, 6; *Fiery Cross,* Oct. 12, 1923; "Discussion of Junior Klan and WKKK."

31. *Fellowship Forum* (Aug. 23, 1925, 6) puts the attendance at the Pennsylvania rally at seventy thousand, no doubt a great exaggeration; also *New York Times,* Apr. 27, 1924, 2.

32. *Watcher on the Tower,* Oct. 20, 1923, 12; *Fellowship Forum* (July 21, 1923, 5) had a feature on a Klan wedding in New Jersey; the Dec. 27, 1924 issue featured a Blacksville, North Carolina, Klan wedding; also see Weaver, "The Knights," 108; Craig F. Swallow, "The Ku Klux Klan in Nevada During the 1920s," *Nevada Historical Society Quarterly* 24 (Spring 1981): 209.

33. *Muncie Post-Democrat,* Aug. 10, 1923, 1.

34. *New York Times,* July 15, 1924, 19; *Fellowship Forum,* May 2, 1925, 6. A WKKK event in Suffolk County, New York, featured a wedding and three Klan baby christenings, in addition to a meeting and initiation of one hundred Klanswomen (*New York Times,* Oct. 19, 1924, 31).

35. Ku Klux Klan, *In Memorium: Klorero of Sorrow* (n.d.); for example, see the description of a WKKK funeral in Quasqueton, Iowa, as reported in *Fellowship Forum* (June 13, 1925, 6) and the WKKK funeral in Roscoe, Pennsylvania, reported in *Fellowship Forum* (July 19, 1924, 8); Ku Klux Klan, *Funeral Services* (KKK, 1925) (box 1, folder 1, KKK-WC, IHS). See Snell, "Fiery Crosses," on Alabama; also Weaver, "The Knights," 108 n30; Niblack, *Life and Times.*

36. *Plainfield* (Indiana) *Messenger,* July 12, 1923, 1.

37. Avin, "Ku Klux Klan," 229–30.
38. *Fiery Cross*, Aug. 23, 1924; Charles Rambow, "The Ku Klux Klan in the 1920s: A Concentration on the Black Hills," *South Dakota History* 4 (Winter 1973): 63–80.
39. *Fiery Cross*, Sept. 21 and Nov. 23, 1923; Sept. 7, 1923, 9; Sept. 14, 1923, 7; Sept. 28, 1923, 9; Avin, "Ku Klux Klan," 204–5; songs by KKK in George R. Dale papers, BSU; also *Song Book*.
40. Author's interview with anonymous informant, Mar. 25, 1988; also *Fellowship Forum*, Dec. 27, 1924, 6, had news from several seasonal Klan parties.
41. *Fiery Cross*, Aug. 1, 1924.
42. Frank E. Cline, "Activities of the Ku Klux Klan in Jay County" (Master's thesis, Ball State Teachers' College, 1964); *Fiery Cross*, May 25, 1923, 6.
43. Boley, *First Documented History*, 496; *Indianapolis News* (July 16, 1923, 3) reports on a huge Klan meeting and parade in Evansville, Indiana, to which a special train was commissioned jointly by the women's and men's Klans of Terre Haute, Sullivan, Vincennes, and Princeton; anonymous letter to author from a woman in Grant County, Indiana, May 30, 1987.
44. *Catalogue of the Almor Fireworks Company* (box 2, folder 1, KKK-WC, IHS).
45. Holt, *Martin County*.
46. Author's interview with anonymous informant, May 24, 1987.
47. *Carlisle News*, Aug. 31, 1923, 1; *Fiery Cross*, Aug. 24 and Sept. 28, 1923; May 11, 1923, 7. Anonymous letter to author from an informant from Spencer County, May 15, 1987; James M. Guthrie, *A Quarter Century in Lawrence County, Indiana 1917–1941* (Stone City Press, 1984).
48. Author's interview with anonymous informant, Aug. 28, 1987; also letter to author from informant in Florida, June 3, 1987.
49. Author's interviews with two anonymous informants, Aug. 26, 1987; May 24, 1987.
50. Samuel Bemenderfer, a Klan officer from Delaware County, said that "every preacher in Delaware County was friendly" to the Klan and "practically all" were members (pp. 105–6, Marion 41769, KKK, ISL). The extreme integration of the Klan into the fabric of local communities was not unique to Indiana. In Wisconsin, "rare was the white Protestant man who did not receive one or two or a dozen invitations to join the klan" (Weaver, "The Knights," 95). See also Roberts, "The Ku-Kluxing," 490–91. Speech by Hiram Evans, quoted in *Roanoke* (Virginia) *Times*, May 31, 1931, 1; see Miller, "The Ku Klux Klan," 223. A similar interpretation, of the Marion County Ohio Klan, is in Frank Bohn, "The Ku Klux Klan Reinterpreted," *American Journal of Sociology* 30 (January 1925): 385–407.
51. *Fiery Cross*, Oct. 28, 1923, 2; July 27, 1923; July 25, 1924; July 11, 1924, 1.
52. Author's interviews with anonymous informants, Feb. 25, 1988; Aug. 21, 1987; also Avin, "Ku Klux Klan," 122; Boley, *First Documented History; Fiery Cross*, Sept. 28, 1923, Mar. 14, 1924; audit of books of Whitewater

Klan no. 40, July 31, 1925–Aug. 20, 1926 and July 1–Dec. 31, 1926; also Enoch P. Shrigley, "Sheeted Brethren Proudly Strutted," *Parke Place: Parke County's Monthly Magazine,* May 1983.

53. *Kokomo Daily Tribune,* Sept. 25, 1923, 2; for other examples, see *Rushville Daily Republican,* June 6, 1923, 1; *Richmond Daily Paladium,* Oct. 4, 1923, 16; *Fiery Cross,* Sept. 7, 1923. Letter to all Great Titans and Kligrapps in Indiana by Lee Smith, KKK Chief of Staff, Realm of Indiana, July 29, 1925, discusses the Klan publicity sent to state newspapers announcing the annual Klan Day celebration in Noblesville (box 1, folder 2, KKK-WC, ISH).

54. *News Journal* (North Manchester), Feb. 15, 1923; also Nov. 23, 1922, Mar. 15, May 21, Sept. 10, 1923; Safianow, "Konklave," 15. For example, see the Kokomo city directory for 1926, or the Seymour city directories for 1925–26 and 1927–28.

55. Author's interview with anonymous informant, Aug. 21, 1987.

56. *Kokomo Daily Tribune,* July 13, 1923, cited in Hamilton, "The Klan in Kokomo," 7–8; *Plainfield Messenger,* June 25, 1925, 1; Weaver, "The Knights," 156 n28; Safianow, "Konklave."

57. Duffus, "Ancestry and the End," 528; *Fiery Cross,* Mar. 30, 1923; advertisement, *Franklin Evening Star,* Aug. 22, 1923, 6.

58. Davis, "The Ku Klux Klan," 152–53. Also see transcribed interview of Sid Levine, conducted by Anita Wells, June 16, 1981, oral history program, Vigo County Public Library, Terre Haute. Davis and Weaver ("The Knights," 83–84) argue that these subsidiary organizations never enrolled more than a few thousand members in the midwestern states; also Giel, "George R. Dale," 51. At a large rally of Klanswomen in Suffolk County, New York, a Klan minister addressed the crowd on his plans to incorporate "Protestant Negroes" into the Klan (*New York Times,* Oct. 19, 1924, 31); on Ohio, see *New York Times,* Mar. 22, 1924, 12. Also see Exhibit 10 (Marion 41769, KKK, ISL) on the American Krusaders.

59. *Franklin Evening Star,* Aug. 20, 1923, 1; Aug. 21, 1923, 1; Aug. 22, 1923, 1, 6; Aug. 23, 1923, 1.

60. Author's interviews with anonymous informants, May 24, 1987; May 13, 1987; also *Fiery Cross* (June 1, 1923, 8) discusses a Klan parade in Columbus, Indiana, that included two hundred members of the women's organization and an unreported number of Klansmen parading without masks before a crowd estimated at two thousand. The *Indianapolis News* described an unmasked parade of several thousand Klanswomen in Indianapolis, as part of the fourth annual convention of the WKKK (Aug. 6, 1927, 1; Aug. 8, 1927, 28). Robert Duffus ("Ancestry and the End of the Ku Klux Klan," *The World's Work* [Sept. 1923]: 528) discusses a parade of unmasked Klansmembers in May 1923 in Valparaiso, Indiana.

61. *Indianapolis News,* Jan. 24, 1923; *New York Times,* Aug. 22, 1923, 16; Sept. 7, 1923, 17; Weaver, "The Knights," 109; *Richmond Daily Palladium,* Aug. 16, 1923, 1; *New York Times,* Dec. 19, 1923, 8; Nov. 12, 1922, sect. 2, 1; on Marion County see *Indianapolis News,* May 28, 1923.

62. Author's interviews with anonymous informants, May 13, 1987; Aug. 21, 1987; also Hoover, "To Be a Jew," 153–55.

63. Letter from an anonymous informant, Mar. 13, 1987; also letter from woman in Corbin, Kentucky, discussing her mother's participation in the Klan, July 20, 1988.

64. Egner Willadene, "Whitley County Survives the Ku Klux Klan," *The Bulletin of the Whitley County Historical Society* (October 1987): 3–17.

65. *New York Times*, Nov. 11, 1923, 18.

66. Emmons deposition (Marion 41769, KKK, ISL); *New York Times*, Nov. 11, 1923, 18; Indiana Grand Dragon W. Lee Smith, cited in Kenneth Jackson, *The Ku Klux Klan*, 147; *Rushville Daily Republican*, June 9, 1923, 1, 6; Shrigley, "The Klan in Parke County," *Parke Place; Parke County's Monthly Magazine*, May 1983; *Kokomo Daily Tribune*, Sept. 4, 1923, 1; *Rushville Daily Republican*, June 1, 1923, 1; *Richmond Daily Palladium*, May 23, 1923, 20.

67. Shrigley, "Sheeted Brethren," 17–18.

68. Safianow, "Konklave," 15–18. For example, see "News of Colored Folk in and about Muncie" in the *Muncie Evening Press* during the 1920s; *Fort Wayne Journal-Gazette*, Feb. 27, 1983.

EPILOGUE

1. Chalmers, *Hooded Americanism*, 305–19; Wade, *The Fiery Cross*, 248–54; *New York Times*, Feb. 21, 1926, sect. 8, 1.

2. See, for example, an article in a Klan magazine on alleged Communist plots to destroy the American family in *The Kourier Magazine*, March 3, 1934, 9; also see Wade, *The Fiery Cross*, 257–75. This sentiment continues in the contemporary Klan (David Lowe, *Ku Klux Klan: The Invisible Empire* [W. W. Norton, 1967], 51).

3. Chalmers, *Hooded Americanism*, 426; Betty Dobratz and Stephanie Shanks-Meile, "The Contemporary Ku Klux Klan and the American Nazi Party: A Comparison to American Populism at the Turn of the Century," *Humanity and Society* 12 (1988): 20–50. See also Arnold Forster and Benjamin Epstein, *Report on the Ku Klux Klan* (Anti-Defamation League of B'nai B'rith, n.d.); Annan, "Ku Klux Klan"; and John Turner, *The Ku Klux Klan: A History of Racism and Violence* (Klanwatch/Southern Poverty Law Center, 1982). Excellent coverage of the modern Klan and other white supremacist groups is in *The Monitor*, a publication of the Center for Democratic Renewal (P. O. Box 50469, Atlanta, Ga. 30302).

4. On women's participation in pro-Nazi activities in the U.S., see Senate Subcommittee on War Mobilization of the Committee on Military Affairs, *Nazi Party Membership Records*, submitted by War Dept., 79th Cong., 2d sess., 1946, pt. 2, pp. 2–19; House of Representatives Special Committee on Un-American Activities, *Nazi Activities*, Appendix *German-American Bund*, 78th Cong., 1st sess., H. Res. 282, 1943, esp. pts. 4, 7; House of Representatives Special Committee on Un-American Activities, *Testimony of Miss Helen Vooros*, 76th Cong., 1st sess., 1939, vol. 16; William Francis Hare, *The Brown Network: The Activities of Nazis in Foreign Countries* (Knight Publishers, 1936), 239–63. Information on women's patriotic and national de-

fense societies can be found in the files of the First Women's Patriotic Conference on National Defense, at the Arthur and Elizabeth Schlesinger Library of the History of Women in America; the Educational Committee of the American Coalition of Patriotic Societies; American Coalition; and the Women's Patriotic Conferences on National Defense, all available at the Library of Congress; and on rightist mothers' groups and women's patriotic groups in the 1940s and 1950s, at the Anti-Defamation League of B'nai B'rith, New York; also see Norman Hapgood, *Professional Patriots* (Albert and Charles Boni, 1929).

A Postscript on Sources

A particular challenge in researching the 1920s women's Klan is that information on the membership and activities of the organization is limited and fragmentary. The major archival collections of Klan materials from the early twentieth century contain very few documents from the women's Klan and no single collection is complete. Information on the women's Klan is scattered throughout a myriad of libraries, county and state historical societies, Klan and non-Klan newspapers, and private collections. Much Klan material that was deposited and catalogued in public libraries is now missing, no doubt a testimony to the profitability of selling Klan materials within the furtive yet extensive network of collectors of Klan memorabilia.

I uncovered information on the organization, public ideology, and private actions of the women's Klan in a variety of locations. For the national WKKK, libraries around the country possess a number of internal organizational documents, including charters, articles of incorporation, legal incorporation papers, and internal correspondence between leaders and members; substantial collections exist at the Arkansas History Commission, Ball State University Library, Cornell University's Olin Library, the Indiana State Library, the Indiana Historical Society, the New York Public Library, the Library of Congress, and in the archives of the Fort Wayne–South Bend Roman Catholic Archdiocese.

The Klan-owned or Klan-influenced press—including the *Fiery Cross, Watcher on the Tower, Imperial Night-Hawk, The Kourier Magazine, Fellowship Forum,* and *Dawn*—gave extensive coverage to the creation of the women's Klans and devoted special pages and issues to topics of interest to Klanswomen. Anti-Klan newspapers, particularly *Tolerance* (Chicago) and the *Muncie* (Indiana) *Post-Democrat,* had frequent articles about Klanswomen and the women's order. The *New York Times* covered Klan activities throughout the nation and the *Arkansas Gazette* had lengthy reports on the formation and subsequent legal wranglings of the WKKK.

Legal actions involving the Klan or Klan officials as plaintiff or defendant give an unusual glimpse into the inner workings of the secret order. A legal suit filed in 1928 in the U.S. District Court for western Pennsylvania, *Knights of the Ku Klux Klan, Plaintiff, v. Rev. John F. Strayer et al., Defendants* (Equity case 1897), contains informative affidavits and testimony by several Klanswomen, including Robbie Gill Comer. Two lawsuits in 1924 involved Daisy Douglas Barr, one for breach of contract filed in the Grant–Delaware Superior Court in Indiana and one for defamation of character filed in Muncie, Indiana, circuit court. Other important legal documents are D. C. Stephenson's trial and appellate record, stretching from 1925 to 1933 and a lawsuit to revoke the charter of the Klan in Indiana by the attorney general of Indiana, Arthur Gilliom; although dismissed by a subsequent attorney general, it resulted in an invaluable collection of depositions and documents (Marion 41769) housed at the Indiana State Library.

The best sources of information on the women's Klan in Indiana are those at the Indiana State Historical Society (IHS), the Indiana State Library (ISL), and the Ball State University Library (BSU). Their collections on the Indiana Klan include seized Klan documents, trial transcripts, publications, and writings of Klan and anti-Klan activists. The IHS has membership and organizational records and papers from the Wayne County and (Crown Point) Lake County Ku Klux Klans; its Alice Moore French collection offers information on Daisy Douglas Barr and the American War Mothers. In addition to extensive manuscript and microfilm collections on the 1920s Klan in Indiana, the Indiana State Library has a biographical card catalogue that makes it possible to trace otherwise obscure leaders of the Indiana WKKK. Incorporation documents of the WKKK are available from the Indiana Secretary of State, Corporate Division for scattered years from 1924 to 1969. Other important manuscript collections on the Indiana Klan are the Harold C. Feightner papers at the ISL and the George R. Dale papers at BSU.

Unfortunately, there is no central inventory of sources or repository of information on the women's Klan. To piece together the story of the WKKK I traveled across Indiana several times, visiting dozens of local public libraries and historical societies. A number of these possess interesting materials from or about the WKKK, including pamphlets and printed cards, records of social and political events, and declarations of principles. County histories and commemorative historical books prove a rich source of local Klan history.

Most Indiana newspapers covered local Klan activities and sent reporters to Klan rallies and events. Indeed, many Indiana newspapers sympathized with the Klan's political agenda and provided a public voice for Klan propaganda and publicity; these are important, if tedious, sources for information on the women's Klan. The most comprehensive accounts of Klan activity in Indiana are those in the *Indianapolis Star, News,* and *Times;* the *Kokomo Daily Tribune* and *Daily Dispatch;* the *Muncie Star* and *Evening News;* the *Franklin Evening Star;* and the *Richmond Palladium.*

A final, though now disappearing, source of information on the Indiana women's Klan was oral history. In addition to the interviews I conducted personally, there are accounts of local Indiana KKK and WKKK klaverns in oral histories conducted by students at Ball State Teachers' College (later Ball State University), in oral histories conducted by the Vigo County (Indiana) Historical Society, and in numerous locally published city and county histories.

Index

Alexander, Flora, 60
American Protective Association (APA), 78, 80
American Trust Company of Kokomo (Ind.), 136
American War Mothers (AWM), 109–10, 121–22
Anti-abortion movement, 179
Anti-ERA movement, 179
Anti-Klan forces: in Indiana, 171; attack on Klanswomen by, 65–68; attack on Stephenson by, 95; attack on Tyler by, 65
Anti-Saloon League (ASL), 20, 104
Anti–Vietnam War movement, 178
Arkansas: court actions between KKK and WKKK in, 60–61
Automobiles: Klan crusade against immoral use of, 85–86

Baltimore Sun, 115
Barr, Daisy Douglas, 27, 113–14, 125, 129, 133, 135, 139, 140, 143; anti-prostitution campaign of, 107–8; and Evans, 109–11; financial opportunism of, 108; as head of Queens of the Golden Mask, 108–9; ministerial career of, 103, 104–9; oratorical abilities of, 105; political career of, 106–8; as president of Indiana War Mothers, 109–10; and Stephenson, 108–9, 110; sued and indicted, 110–11; on suffrage, 106; in temper-

ance movement, 103–4, 105–6; in violent confrontation with Benadum, 113–14; as WKKK organizer, 109; xenophobia of, 108
Barr, Thomas, 105, 108, 114
Bell, Leah H., 160
Benadum, Clarence E., 113
Benadum, Mary, 110–11, 113–14
Betsy Ross Federation, 111
Birth of a Nation (film), 18, 173
Bittner, Mamie H., 41
Bordin, Ruth, 103
"Bright Fiery Cross" (hymn), 50
Brown, Mable, 135
Business and Professional Women's Club of Indiana, 112, 113

Cantey, Pearl, 63
Carroll, Ann (pseud.), 116
Catholic Church: supposed moral depravity of, 86–91, 97
Cavalier Motion Picture Corporation, 129, 138
Chalmers, David: *Hooded Americanism*, 14
Christenings, Klan, 163–64
Civic League, 121
Civil rights movement, 176, 178
Clarke, Edward, 20–23
Clarke, May, 21
Cloud, Alice, 60
Comer, James, 46, 60–61, 62, 64–65, 114

Compositor: Interactive Composition Corporation
Text: 10/13 Sabon
Display: Sabon
Printer: Edwards Brothers, Inc.
Binder: Edwards Brothers, Inc.